Ultimate AWS Certified Security Specialty (SCS-CO2) Exam Guide

Master AWS Cloud Security with Expert Guidance, Practical Scenarios, and Proven Strategies to Ace the Certified Security Specialty (SCS-C02) Exam

Ajit S. Inamdar

www.orangeava.com

First Published: November 2025

Published By: Orange Education Pvt Ltd, AVA®

Address: 9, Daryaganj, Delhi, 110002, India

275 New North Road Islington Suite 1314 London,
N1 7AA, United Kingdom

ISBN (PBK): 978-93-49888-23-4

ISBN (E-BOOK): 978-93-49888-58-6

Dedicated To

My Beloved Parents,

Sandesh Inamdar (late)

Meenal Inamdar

And

My Wife, Priyam, My Daughter, Jiza,

And My Brother, Omkar.

About the Author

Ajit S. Inamdar is a technology professional with a deep passion for innovation and building transformative solutions. His career spans multiple leadership and technical roles, including Senior Cloud Architect, Senior Manager, and Technology Lead, where he has gained extensive hands-on experience in cloud architecture, platform engineering, and bespoke application development. Throughout his career, he has consistently focused on leveraging technology to help businesses thrive, and solve complex challenges.

Currently serving as the **Chief Technology Officer at Ampity Infotech**, Ajit leads product application development, platform engineering, and cloud services. His work centres on creating secure, scalable, and efficient solutions that align with the evolving needs of modern enterprises. From **DevSecOps transformation** to **cloud infrastructure management**, he has built a reputation for helping organizations navigate their digital journeys with confidence and agility.

Ajit's contributions to the cloud ecosystem have been widely recognized. He has been honoured as an **AWS Ambassador (2021–2024)** for his thought leadership and impact within the AWS community, and as an **ET Great People Manager** for his commitment to fostering strong teams, and nurturing talent.

As the author of this book, Ajit brings together his professional expertise, and his dedication to continuous learning. This work reflects his commitment to guiding others in **mastering AWS security practices**, and **achieving success in the AWS Certified Security – Specialty Certification**. His goal is to empower readers not only to pass the exam, but also to apply these principles to real-world scenarios, thereby building secure, resilient, and future-ready cloud environments.

About the Technical Reviewers

Avinash Reddy Thipparthi is a seasoned Cloud and DevOps Engineer, AWS Community Builder, and Docker Captain with over a decade of experience in architecting scalable, secure, and resilient AWS solutions. Holding seven AWS certifications, he specializes in infrastructure automation, DevSecOps, container orchestration, and CI/CD pipelines using AWS CloudFormation and GitHub Actions. Avinash focuses on secure automation, cloud optimization, and modern DevOps integration across the software lifecycle. Recognized globally for his technical leadership, he actively contributes to the cloud-native ecosystem, and educates through his YouTube channel, AWS *with Avinash Reddy*, which has nearly 40,000 subscribers! A frequent speaker at AWS user groups and cloud conferences, he is known for delivering practical insights on AWS security, observability, and cost efficiency. Currently a Senior Specialist at LTIMindtree, Avinash continues to mentor professionals, and simplify cloud technologies through community-driven learning.

Akesh is a passionate cloud enthusiast and Principal Cloud Architect at Blazeclan Technologies. With expertise in Fullstack Development, Cloud Consulting, DevOps, and Infrastructure Automation, Akesh excels in creating innovative solutions. He has extensive experience in developing, deploying and replatforming applications on Amazon Web Services (AWS), as well as transforming traditional environments into virtualized systems using Java, Python, and various AWS services. Akesh is dedicated to empowering customers by designing and implementing secure, highly available, and cost-optimized AWS solutions, while harnessing the full potential of cloud infrastructure automation.

Acknowledgments

There are several people I would like to thank for their support, encouragement, and inspiration throughout the process of writing this book.

First and foremost, I am deeply grateful to my parents, whose values continue to shape me every day. To my late father, **Sandesh Inamdar**, and my mother, **Meenal Inamdar**, whose blessings and constant encouragement have been the foundation of everything I have achieved.

I thank my wife, **Priyam** and my daughter, **Jiza** for their love, patience, and unwavering support during this journey. They have been my strength and motivation throughout. I also want to thank my brother, **Omkar,** for always standing by me with encouragement and positivity.

I am also grateful to my colleagues, mentors, and the wider cloud community who have been instrumental in my learning journey. Their knowledge-sharing, collaboration, and inspiration have enriched my professional growth, and helped me put together the insights shared in this book.

Lastly, I extend my heartfelt gratitude to all the readers and learners - this book is written with you in mind! It is my hope that the knowledge and experiences shared here will support you in mastering AWS security, and applying it meaningfully in your respective careers.

Preface

Cloud computing has revolutionized how we build, scale, and secure digital systems. With this shift, security has become more critical than ever- ensuring that sensitive data, applications, and infrastructure remain protected against evolving threats. This book is written for professionals, learners, and practitioners who want to deepen their understanding of **AWS Security**, while also preparing for the **AWS Certified Security – Specialty Exam**.

Unlike traditional study guides that focus solely on theory, this book takes a **practical, hands-on approach**. Each chapter combines foundational concepts, AWS service deep-dives, best practices, and real-world examples. You will not only gain the knowledge needed to pass the exam, but also the skills to apply security principles effectively in enterprise environments.

The content is structured to build progressively:

Chapter 1 introduces cloud security fundamentals, AWS core services, and an overview of the exam format and objectives.

Chapter 2 explores Identity and Access Management (IAM), emphasizing secure access control, permission boundaries, and federation.

Chapter 3 covers data protection and encryption with AWS KMS, S3, RDS, and EBS, ensuring compliance with regulatory frameworks.

Chapter 4 focuses on network security, including VPC design, security groups, NACLs, AWS WAF, and Shield.

Chapter 5 addresses logging, monitoring, and incident response, using CloudTrail, CloudWatch, GuardDuty, and Security Hub.

Chapter 6 introduces DevSecOps and automation strategies to integrate security seamlessly into CI/CD pipelines.

Chapter 7 provides detailed exam preparation strategies, study plans, and time management techniques.

Chapter 8 offers a full-length practice test with explanations, and connects exam topics to real-world industry applications.

Chapter 9 concludes with advanced security topics such as serverless security, ML-driven threat detection, and compliance strategies.

Throughout the book, you will find **exam tips, case studies,** and **labs** designed to reinforce learning. Hence, whether you are a cloud architect, security engineer, DevOps practitioner, or IT professional seeking certification, this book will serve as both a **study guide and a practical reference** for securing AWS workloads.

By the end of this journey, you will not only be ready to succeed in the exam, but also be prepared to design, implement, and maintain **secure, scalable, and resilient AWS environments** in the real world.

Get a Free eBook

We hope you are enjoying your recently purchased book! Your feedback is incredibly valuable to us, and to all other readers looking for great books.

If you found this book helpful or enjoyable, we would truly appreciate it, if you could take a moment to leave a short review with a 5 star rating on Amazon. It helps us grow, and lets other readers discover our books.

As a thank you, we would love to send you a free digital copy of this book, and a **30%** discount code on your next cart value on our official websites:

www.orangeava.com

www.orangeava.in (For Indian Subcontinent)

☑ **Here's how:**

Leave a review for the book on Amazon.

Take a screenshot of your review, and send an email to **info@orangeava.com** (it can be just the confirmation screen).

Once, we receive your screenshot, we will send you the digital file, within 24 hours.

Thank you so much for your support – it means a lot to us!

Downloading the code bundles and colored images

Please follow the links or scan the QR codes to download the
Code Bundles and Images of the book:

https://github.com/ava-orange-education/Ultimate-AWS-Certified-Security-Specialty-SCS-CO2-Exam-Guide

The code bundles and images of the book are also hosted on
https://rebrand.ly/4c1e09

In case there's an update to the code, it will be updated on the existing GitHub repository.

Errata

We take immense pride in our work at **Orange Education Pvt Ltd,** and follow best practices to ensure the accuracy of our content to provide an indulging reading experience to our subscribers. Our readers are our mirrors, and we use their inputs to reflect and improve upon human errors, if any, that may have occurred during the publishing processes involved. To let us maintain the quality and help us reach out to any readers who might be having difficulties due to any unforeseen errors, please write to us at :

errata@orangeava.com

Your support, suggestions, and feedback are highly appreciated.

DID YOU KNOW

Did you know that Orange Education Pvt Ltd offers eBook versions of every book published, with PDF and ePub files available? You can upgrade to the eBook version at **www.orangeava.com** and as a print book customer, you are entitled to a discount on the eBook copy. Get in touch with us at: **info@orangeava.com** for more details.

At **www.orangeava.com**, you can also read a collection of free technical articles, sign up for a range of free newsletters, and receive exclusive discounts and offers on Print Books and eBooks.

PIRACY

If you come across any illegal copies of our works in any form on the internet, we would be grateful if you would provide us with the location address or website name. Please contact us at **info@orangcava.com** with a link to the material.

ARE YOU INTERESTED IN AUTHORING WITH US?

If there is a topic that you have expertise in, and you are interested in either writing or contributing to a book, please write to us at **business@orangeava.com**. We are on a journey to help developers and tech professionals to gain insights on the present technological advancements and innovations happening across the globe and build a community that believes Knowledge is best acquired by sharing and learning with others. Please reach out to us to learn what our audience demands and how you can be part of this educational reform. We also welcome ideas from tech experts and help them build learning and development content for their domains.

REVIEWS

Please leave a review. Once you have read and used this book, why not leave a review on the site that you purchased it from? Potential readers can then see and use your unbiased opinion to make purchase decisions. We at Orange Education would love to know what you think about our products, and our authors can learn from your feedback. Thank you!

For more information about Orange Education, please visit **www.orangeava.com**.

Table of Contents

Chapter 1
Cloud Security and AWS Overview

Introduction

Cloud computing has transformed how organizations manage data, applications, and infrastructure, but with this shift comes the critical responsibility of ensuring security. This chapter serves as your starting point to understand the fundamentals of cloud security and AWS. It highlights the importance of securing cloud environments, while leveraging AWS services, such as IAM, KMS, and S3 to create scalable, resilient, and secure solutions.

Before diving into technical details, we will also cover the AWS certification exam overview, breaking down its format, objectives, and the skills required to excel. By mastering these foundational concepts and aligning them with real-world use cases, you will be well-prepared to secure cloud environments and tackle complex architectural challenges. So, let us get started!

Structure

In this chapter, we will discuss the following topics:

- AWS Exam Overview and Objectives
    - Exam Format and Question Types
    - Scoring System and Duration
    - Recommended Experience and Skills
    - Exam Domains and Weightage
- How Can This Book Help You
    - Chapter Breakdown and Learning Flow
    - Practice Tests and Hands-on Labs
    - Study Strategies and Exam Tips

- The Importance of Cloud Security
    - Why Cloud Security Matters
    - Key Security Risks in Cloud Environments
    - Building Customer Trust through Security
- The AWS Shared Responsibility Model
    - AWS vs. Customer Security Responsibilities
    - Breakdown of Responsibilities across Layers
    - Security of the Cloud vs. Security in the Cloud
- Core AWS Security Services
    - IAM (Identity and Access Management)
    - KMS (Key Management Service)
    - AWS Security Hub
    - Amazon GuardDuty
    - AWS WAF and AWS Shield
    - AWS CloudTrail and AWS Config
- Common Cloud Security Challenges
    - Misconfiguration and Human Error
    - Compliance and Regulatory Risks
    - Insider Threats and Data Breaches
    - Visibility and Monitoring Challenges

AWS Exam Overview and Objectives

Securing an AWS Security Specialty certification is not for the faint-hearted and might seem intimidating at first. However, understanding the format of the AWS exam and its objectives will enable you to approach it confidently and create an effective study plan to tackle it.

The AWS exam consists of two types of questions:

- **Multiple Choice:** These are rather straightforward questions that have four options to choose from. You need to choose the correct one out of them after reading the question carefully.
- **Multiple Response:** These questions can be more challenging than MCQs as there might be more than one correct answer. Make sure that you are able to identify all the correct responses to obtain full points.

The AWS exam consists of 65 questions in all, out of which only 50 are counted to generate your final score. The remaining 15 are unscored pilot questions that AWS uses for its future exams. You will not know which questions are unscored, which is why you must attempt every question.

Note: *Do not leave any questions unanswered. Leaving a blank is same as getting a question wrong, so even if you are unsure, take an educated guess. The exam does not penalize you for incorrect answers. Hence, it is always better to try.*

Exam Duration

You will have 170 minutes (2 hours and 50 minutes) to complete the exam. This gives you a little over 2.5 minutes per question on average. While taking the exam, use your time wisely, flag questions you are unsure about, and revisit them later if time permits. Effective time management is the key to succeed in this exam, especially when navigating complex multiple-response questions.

Scoring System

The AWS Security Specialty exam allots you scores on a scale of 100 to 1000, with 750 being the passing marks. It is not a simple pass-or-fail test–AWS employs a scaled scoring system to measure your performance against other test takers.

While the exam includes multiple domains, such as Identity and Access Management, Infrastructure Security, and Data Protection, even if you underperform in one domain, you can make up for it by excelling in others.

Big Picture Focus

The secret to pass this exam successfully lies in mastering core security concepts and understanding their real-world applications. The AWS exam is not just about testing your theoretical knowledge; it evaluates whether you can design and execute secure cloud solutions that address real-world challenges.

Now that you are aware about the basic overview of the AWS Security Specialty exam, let us try to understand who can appear for it and why it is a valuable certification for cloud security professionals.

This Exam is Designed for:

The AWS Security Specialty exam is tailored for professionals experienced in securing AWS workloads and wish to validate their expertise. This is not a beginner-level certification–you have to build a solid understanding of AWS services and best practices in cloud security.

To Succeed, You Should:

- Have at least two years of hands-on experience working with AWS security services, including IAM, KMS, AWS WAF, Security Hub, and GuardDuty
- Must possess an in-depth knowledge of core security concepts, such as encryption, compliance, identity management, and risk assessment
- Be strategically aware about how to design architectures that strike a balance between security, cost-effectiveness, and operational efficiency
- Be able to work with hybrid architectures and securing data across cloud and on-premises environments
- Be familiar with automating security tasks using AWS tools and services such as Lambda, CloudFormation, and CI/CD pipelines

Hence, this exam is ideal for security engineers, architects, and consultants who want to validate their ability to implement and manage secure workloads on AWS. If you are confident about your skills and ready to take your cloud security expertise to the next level, this certification might be the perfect credential for you.

Exam Objectives

The AWS Security Specialty exam is designed to test your ability to identify and implement best practices to secure AWS workloads. The objectives are divided into key domains, with each one focusing on a critical aspect of cloud security.

Here is what you are expected to master for the exam:

- **Domain 1: Threat Detection and Incident Response (Weightage-14%)**
    - Analyze and respond to security events using services such as Amazon GuardDuty, Amazon Detective, AWS Security Hub, and AWS Config
    - Automate incident response using AWS Lambda, Amazon EventBridge, and Step Functions
    - Investigate potential threats and assess the impact of security incidents
- **Domain 2: Security Logging and Monitoring (Weightage-18%)**
    - Implement and configure logging using AWS CloudTrail, Amazon CloudWatch Logs, AWS Config, and VPC Flow Logs
    - Monitor AWS environments for suspicious activity or misconfigurations
    - Analyze logs and set up alerts to maintain visibility and respond to anomalies
- **Domain 3: Infrastructure Security (Weightage-20%)**
    - Design and implement secure network architectures using Amazon VPC, security groups, network ACLs, and VPC endpoints

    - Protect against DDoS and application layer attacks using AWS Shield, AWS WAF, and Route 53 Resolver DNS Firewall
    - Secure hybrid environments using AWS Direct Connect and VPN
- **Domain 4: Identity and Access Management (Weightage-16%)**
    - Manage IAM users, groups, roles, and policies to enforce least privilege access
    - Implement multi-factor authentication (MFA) and federated identity using AWS SSO and external identity providers
    - Evaluate permissions using IAM Access Analyzer and other tools to detect overly permissive policies
- **Domain 5: Data Protection (Weightage-18%)**
    - Encrypt data at rest and in transit using AWS Key Management Service (KMS), AWS Certificate Manager (ACM), and S3 default encryption
    - Configure and manage key rotation, access controls, and data classification policies
    - Address compliance requirements such as GDPR, HIPAA, or PCI DSS
- **Domain 6: Management and Security Governance (Weightage-14%)**
    - Establish governance using AWS Organizations, Service Control Policies (SCPs), and AWS Control Tower
    - Monitor account and resource compliance with AWS Config, AWS Audit Manager, and AWS License Manager
    - Implement guardrails and enforce security baselines across accounts

These objectives reflect the exam's emphasis on practical skills and real-world applications. By mastering these domains, you will be able to design and implement secure AWS solutions while confidently addressing cloud security challenges.

How This Book Will Guide You

Preparing for the **AWS Security Specialty** exam can be overwhelming, but this book is designed to be your **structured, step-by-step guide** to success. Whether you are a security professional, cloud architect, or a DevOps engineer, this book will provide you with the knowledge, strategies, and confidence required to pass the exam, while applying AWS security best practices to address real-world problems.

This Book Consists of:

- **A Comprehensive Coverage of Exam Domains:** Every chapter in this book is aligned with AWS exam objectives, and breaks down key security concepts, tools, and best practices for easy understanding

- **Real-World Scenarios and Case Studies:** Learn through **practical examples and security incidents that will help** you understand the real-life applications of AWS security environments
- **Exam-Style Questions and Practice Tests:** Test your knowledge with sample **questions similar to those in the actual exam**. Every question is solved with explanations for correct and incorrect answers
- **Practical Hands-On Guidance**: Gain experience with AWS security services via **hands-on exercises** that reinforce theoretical knowledge
- **Time-Saving Study Strategies**: Discover **exam tips, shortcuts, and study techniques** to maximize retention and prepare for the test efficiently

By following the structured approach in this book, you will not only be ready to ace the **AWS Security Specialty** exam but also develop the skills to design and implement secure AWS environments in your career towards your journey to become an AWS security expert!

The Importance of Cloud Security

As organizations increasingly migrate to the cloud, **security has become more critical than ever.** The shift from traditional on-premises infrastructure to cloud-based environments introduces new challenges, such as **data protection, identity management, compliance, and threat mitigation.** Without proper security measures, organizations run the risk of encountering **data breaches, service disruptions, financial losses, and incurring significant damage to their reputation.**

Why Cloud Security Matters

- **Protecting Sensitive Data**: Organizations store vast amounts of personal, financial, and proprietary data in the cloud. Without robust security controls, this data is vulnerable to breaches or unauthorized access attacks.
- **Mitigating Cyber Threats**: Cloud environments are the target of constant threats, such as **DDoS attacks, malware, insider scares, and phishing scams.** Strong security practices mitigate these threats, while making the environments safe to navigate.
- **Ensuring Compliance**: Many industries must adhere to **regulatory requirements** such as **GDPR, HIPAA, PCI-DSS, and SOC 2** to ensure compliance and avoid hefty penalties.
- **Maintaining Business Continuity**: Security incidents can disrupt operations, leading to downtime and loss of productivity. **Disaster recovery and high availability strategies** are essential for preventing them.
- **Building Customer Trust**: Organizations that prioritize security earn the trust of their customers and stakeholders, resulting in a stronger business rapport and credible brand reputation.

The Role of AWS in Securing Cloud Environments

AWS provides a **shared responsibility model** that **secures the infrastructur**e, while enabling the **customers to secure their workloads, applications, and data.** AWS offers **built-in security tools,** such as **Identity and Access Management (IAM), Key Management Service (KMS), AWS Shield, Security Hub, and GuardDuty,** to help organizations protect their cloud environments.

The Bottom Line

Cloud security is not optional, but a necessity. By implementing **strong security controls, continuous monitoring, and proactive threat management,** organizations can **protect their assets, comply with regulations, and ensure the integrity of their respective cloud environments.**

This book will guide you about AWS security best practices, helping you **build and maintain secure, scalable, and resilient cloud architectures.**

The AWS Shared Responsibility Model

When organizations move to the cloud from traditional infrastructures, their security commitments demonstrate a significant shift as well. The AWS Shared Responsibility Model clearly defines the security roles between AWS and its customers, providing clarity on who secures what in the cloud environment.

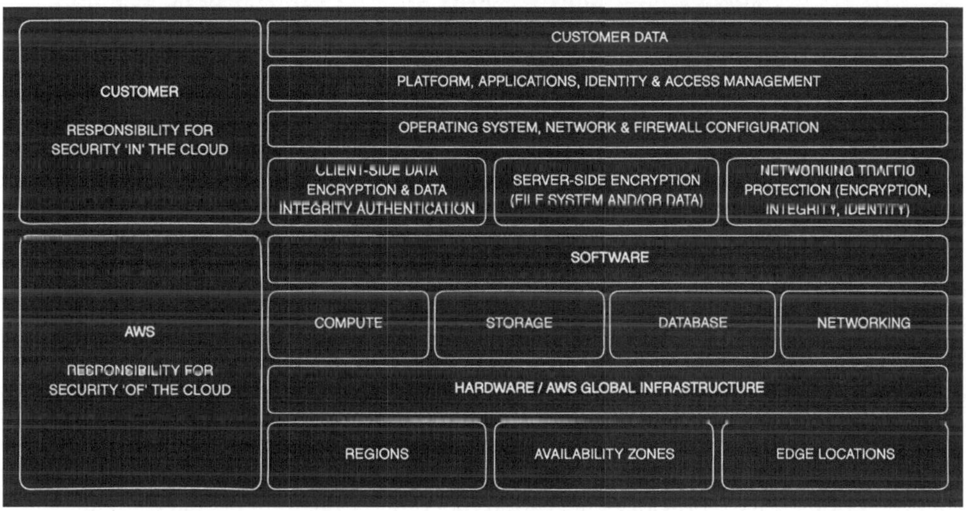

Figure 1.1: *AWS Shared Responsibility Model highlighting AWS vs. Customer Roles*

Understanding the Shared Responsibility Model

AWS operates under a shared security model, which means that security is a joint responsibility between AWS and the customer.

- **AWS is responsible for the security of the cloud:**
  - These include securing the physical infrastructure, hardware, software, networking, and data center operations.
  - AWS ensures global compliance certifications, continuous monitoring, and high availability of cloud services.
- **Customers are responsible for security in the cloud:**
  - These include managing guest OS, including updates and security patches, securing data, managing user access, configuring firewalls, and encrypting sensitive information.
  - Customers must implement security best practices based on their workloads to ensure proper configurations and access controls.

Breakdown of Responsibilities

The AWS Shared Responsibility Model outlines the division of security responsibilities between AWS and the customer. Understanding this division is crucial to know how secure workloads in the cloud properly.

Area	AWS Responsibility (Security of the Cloud)	Customer Responsibility (Security in the Cloud)
Physical Infrastructure	AWS secures data centers, networking, and global infrastructure	N/A (Managed entirely by AWS)
Hardware and Software	AWS maintains and patches underlying compute, storage, and network components	N/A
Operating System and Applications	Managed for AWS services (for example, AWS Lambda, S3, RDS)	Customer secures OS, patching, and applications running on EC2
Identity and Access Management	AWS provides IAM, MFA, and access management tools	Customers configure IAM roles, policies, and access controls
Data Protection	AWS provides encryption tools and key management (KMS)	Customers encrypt data, configure backups, and control data lifecycle policies

Network Security	AWS provides security groups, NACLs, and services such as AWS WAF and Shield.	Customers define security rules, VPN configurations, and VPC settings
Compliance and Auditing	AWS provides compliance reports and certifications (SOC 2, GDPR, HIPAA)	Customers ensure their workloads comply with regulations and audit logs regularly

Table 1.1: *AWS Shared Responsibility Model – Security of the Cloud vs. Security in the Cloud*

Key Takeaways:

- AWS secures the foundational infrastructure, but customers must configure their respective security settings based on best practices.
- Misconfigurations are the biggest security risk since several cloud security breaches result from improperly configured S3 buckets, IAM roles, or security groups.
- AWS provides powerful security services (such as AWS Security Hub, GuardDuty, and CloudTrail), but customers must use them effectively.

Understanding the AWS Shared Responsibility Model is essential for the AWS Security Specialty exam and real-world cloud security. It helps you identify which security tasks belong to AWS and which are your responsibility, crucial for avoiding misconfigurations. Mastery of this model enables you to design compliant, well-governed architectures using tools like AWS Config and Service Control Policies, ensuring secure and auditable workloads.

Understanding the Security Pillar of the AWS Well-Architected

The Security Pillar of the AWS Well-Architected Framework focuses on protecting data, systems, and assets through risk assessments and mitigation strategies. It emphasizes six core design principles.

- **Implementing a Strong Identity Foundation:** The Security Pillar employs the principle of least privilege and enforces a separation of duties with centralized identity management and multi-factor authentication.
- **Enabling Traceability:** The Security Pillar monitors, alerts, and audits actions and changes in real-time cloud environments via services like AWS CloudTrail and AWS Config.
- **Applying Security at All Layers:** The Security Pillar uses defense-in-depth approach where it applies security controls at every layer, including edge networks, VPC, instances, and application.

- **Automating Security Best Practices:** It is essential to automate security operations to reduce human error and ensure consistent, repeatable responses using tools like AWS Lambda, CloudFormation, and Config Rules.
- **Protecting Data in Transit and at Rest:** The Security Pillar uses encryption with AWS KMS to enforce access controls and protect sensitive data across several layers of storage and communication.
- **Preparing for Security Events:** It is highly advised to have an incident response plan and test it regularly. Use services like Amazon GuardDuty, Security Hub, and Detective for rapid detection and analysis.

Core AWS Security Services

AWS provides a **comprehensive suite of security services** that allow organizations to protect their cloud workloads, ensure compliance, detect threats, protect data, and secure their network. Understanding these **core security services** is essential for securing cloud environments and passing the **AWS Security Specialty exam**.

Identity and Access Management (IAM)

AWS **Identity and Access Management (IAM)** is the **foundation of AWS security**, as it controls **who can access what** within an AWS environment.

Key Features:

- **IAM Users, Groups, and Roles:** Define and manage access to AWS resources
- **IAM Policies:** Set fine-grained permissions using JSON-based policies
- **Multi-Factor Authentication (MFA):** Adds an extra layer of security for user authentication
- **Federated Access:** Integrate AWS IAM with external identity providers, such as Active Directory or Okta

Best Practices:

- Follow the **principle of least privilege**—grant only necessary permissions
- **Enable MFA** for all root users and privileged accounts
- Use **IAM Roles** instead of long-term access keys

AWS Key Management Service (KMS)

AWS **KMS** provides **encryption for data at rest and in-transit**, and ensures that **sensitive information** remains secure.

Key Features:

- **Symmetric and Asymmetric Encryption**: Secure data using AWS-managed or customer-managed keys
- **Automatic Key Rotation**: Reduces security risks by rotating encryption keys periodically
- **AWS Service Integration**: Works seamlessly with S3, RDS, Lambda, CloudTrail, and much more

Best Practices:

- Use **Customer-Managed Keys (CMKs)** for greater control
- **Enable key rotation** to minimize exposure in case of key compromise
- Restrict key access using **IAM policies and other key policies**

AWS Security Hub

AWS **Security Hub** provides a **centralized dashboard** for **security visibility and compliance monitoring**.

Key Features:

- **Aggregates security findings** from AWS services such as GuardDuty, Inspector, and IAM Access Analyzer
- **Compliance checks** using AWS security standards, such as **CIS AWS Foundations Benchmark**
- **Automated remediation** using AWS Lambda and Amazon EventBridge

Best Practices:

- Enable **Security Hub** to continuously monitor AWS security best practices
- Integrate it with **AWS Organizations** to assess security posture across multiple accounts
- Set up **automation rules** to remediate security threats in real-time

Amazon GuardDuty

AWS **GuardDuty** is an **intelligent threat detection service** that monitors AWS environments for malicious activity.

Key Features:

- **Analyzes AWS logs** (CloudTrail, VPC Flow Logs, DNS logs) to detect threats
- Identifies **unauthorized access, compromised credentials, and anomalies**

- **Integrates with Security Hub** and **AWS Lambda** for automated response

Best Practices:

- **Enable GuardDuty** across all AWS accounts and regions
- Configure **SNS notifications** for real-time security alerts
- Automate responses using **AWS Lambda** or **EventBridge rules**

AWS Web Application Firewall (AWS WAF)

AWS **WAF** protects web applications from **common attacks**, including **SQL injection, Cross-Site Scripting (XSS), and DDoS attacks.**

Key Features:

- **Blocks malicious traffic** using **pre-configured rule sets**
- **Integrates with CloudFront, ALB, and API Gateway** for application security
- **Supports custom rules** for IP blocking, request size limits, and bot mitigation

Best Practices:

- Deploy **AWS WAF** to protect public-facing web applications
- Use **AWS Managed Rules** for quick and effective security
- Enable **rate-based rules** to prevent brute-force and DDoS attacks

AWS Shield

AWS **Shield** provides **DDoS protection** for AWS applications, preventing **large-scale attacks**.

Key Features:

- **AWS Shield Standard:** Free, automatic **DDoS protection** for all AWS customers
- **AWS Shield Advanced:** Real-time **attack mitigation** with 24/7 security support
- **Automatic attack detection** and **mitigation** for volumetric and state-exhaustion attacks

Best Practices:

- Use **AWS Shield Advanced** for mission-critical applications
- Deploy **AWS WAF with Shield** to mitigate **application-layer threats**
- Integrate **AWS CloudFront and Route 53** for additional DDoS protection

AWS CloudTrail

AWS **CloudTrail** logs all AWS **API activity** to ensure security auditing and compliance tracking.

Key Features:

- **Records AWS API calls and user activity** for all AWS accounts
- **Stores logs in Amazon S3** for forensic analysis
- **Integrates with CloudWatch Logs** for real-time monitoring

Best Practices:

- **Enable CloudTrail** across all AWS accounts and regions
- Store logs in **S3 with encryption** and apply lifecycle policies
- Set up **CloudWatch Alarms** to detect suspicious activities

Amazon Macie

Amazon **Macie** is an **AI-powered security service** that can **detect sensitive data** in AWS environments **automatically**.

Key Features:

- Uses **machine learning** to identify **Personally Identifiable Information (PII),** such as credit card numbers, passwords, and financial data
- **Continuously monitors S3 buckets** for unauthorized access and data leaks
- **Generates security alerts** for exposure risks

Best Practices:

- Enable **Amazon Macie** to scan S3 buckets for sensitive data
- Restrict **public access** to sensitive S3 buckets
- Review and remediate **high-risk findings** immediately

AWS Config

AWS Config enables you to assess, audit, and evaluate the configurations of your AWS resources. It continuously monitors and records AWS resource configurations and allows you to automate the evaluation of recorded configurations according to the desired settings.

Key Features:

- **Configuration Recording:** Tracks changes to AWS resource configurations across environments
- **Compliance Rules:** Define AWS Config rules to evaluate whether resource configurations comply with best practices or organizational policies
- **Change History:** View detailed resource configuration history and snapshots to troubleshoot issues or support audits
- **Integration with AWS Services:** Works seamlessly with services like AWS CloudTrail, AWS Organizations, and AWS Systems Manager for centralized governance

Best Practices:

- Enable AWS Config across all accounts and regions using AWS Organizations for complete visibility
- Use managed rules provided by AWS to quickly enforce common compliance checks
- Aggregate configuration data across accounts and regions for centralized analysis
- Integrate with AWS Security Hub and Amazon CloudWatch for automated alerts and remediation workflows
- Regularly review compliance findings and investigate configuration drift to maintain a secure and compliant environment

Amazon Detective

Amazon Detective is a security service that helps you investigate and analyze potential security issues across your AWS environment. It automatically collects log data and uses machine learning and graph analysis to visualize and identify the root cause of suspicious activity.

Key Features:

- **Automated Data Ingestion:** Continuously pulls data from AWS CloudTrail, Amazon GuardDuty, and Amazon VPC Flow Logs
- **Security Investigation Graphs:** Visualizes relationships between resources and events to simplify root cause analysis
- **Context-Rich Insights:** Provides timelines, event summaries, and entity profiles (like user, IP, resource) for faster investigation
- **Seamless Integration:** Works directly with Amazon GuardDuty and AWS Security Hub to enhance threat response workflows

Best Practices:

- Enable Amazon Detective across all accounts and regions for a complete security investigation surface
- Use Detective alongside GuardDuty to pivot directly into deeper analysis of detected threats
- Leverage entity behavior modeling to understand baseline activity and quickly spot anomalies
- Grant access only to trained security analysts and restrict use through IAM roles and policies
- Regularly review investigation findings to identify trends and improve your incident response process

AWS Trusted Advisor

AWS Trusted Advisor is a real-time guidance service that helps you optimize your AWS environment by inspecting your account for security gaps, cost inefficiencies, performance bottlenecks, service limits, and fault tolerance issues.

Key Features:

- **Security Checks:** Flags exposed security groups, IAM access risks, MFA configurations, and S3 bucket permissions
- **Cost Optimization:** Identifies underutilized resources to reduce unnecessary spending
- **Performance and Fault Tolerance:** Recommends improvements for latency, resource limits, and backup strategies
- **Service Limits Monitoring:** Alerts you when you approach AWS service quotas to avoid interruptions
- **Integration with Organizations:** View and manage checks across all member accounts from a central dashboard

Best Practices:

- Regularly review Trusted Advisor's Security and Service Limits checks
- Automate remediation using AWS Lambda and EventBridge for certain actionable alerts
- Use the Trusted Advisor Organizational View to monitor multi-account environments
- Enable notifications to proactively respond to security and cost-related warnings

- Prioritize red and yellow check results for immediate attention

Amazon Inspector

Amazon Inspector is an automated vulnerability management service that scans AWS workloads such as EC2, Lambda, and container images for software vulnerabilities and unintended network exposure.

Key Features:

- **Automated Scanning:** Continuously scans EC2, Lambda, and container images stored in ECR
- **CVE Detection:** Identifies software vulnerabilities based on Common Vulnerabilities and Exposures (CVEs)
- **Network Reachability Analysis:** Flags exposed ports or internet-accessible services
- **Severity Scoring:** Uses CVSS-based risk scoring to prioritize remediation efforts
- **Event-Driven Scanning:** Triggers automatic scans when workloads change

Best Practices:

- Enable Inspector across all accounts and regions via AWS Organizations for unified coverage
- Integrate with AWS Security Hub to centralize vulnerability findings
- Prioritize remediation of critical and high-severity CVEs using Systems Manager Patch Manager
- Automate tagging of resources and use resource groups for targeted scanning
- Conduct periodic review of scan results and establish SLAs for addressing vulnerabilities

AWS Resilience Hub

AWS Resilience Hub helps you assess and improve the resilience of your applications running on AWS, ensuring they meet Recovery Time Objectives and Recovery Point Objectives (RTO/RPO).

Key Features:

- **Resilience Assessment:** Automatically analyzes applications for potential resilience gaps
- **Recovery Recommendations:** Offers guidance to meet defined RTO and RPO goals

- **Policy-Driven Validation:** Lets you define and enforce resilience policies for business-critical applications
- **Integration with AWS Fault Injection Simulator:** Validates how applications behave under failure conditions
- **Resilience Score:** Quantifies the readiness of your applications to recover from disruptions

Best Practices:

- Define application resilience requirements in line with business continuity goals.
- Use application templates and tagging to organize and assess related AWS resources
- Regularly review Resilience Hub findings and implement suggested architecture changes
- Run chaos engineering experiments with Fault Injection Simulator to validate assumptions
- Use Resilience Hub reports to demonstrate compliance with operational resilience frameworks

AWS provides a **powerful set of security services**, however, **proper configuration and continuous monitoring** are critical to prevent security breaches that occur due to **misconfigurations, weak access controls, or lack of monitoring.**

By leveraging **IAM, GuardDuty, Security Hub, WAF, KMS, CloudTrail, and other security services**, organizations can **enhance cloud security, mitigate threats, and maintain compliance** in AWS.

For the **AWS Security Specialty exam**, understanding these **core AWS security services along with t**heir **capabilities, integrations, and best practices** is essential to passing the exam and learning how to secure real-world cloud environments.

Common Cloud Security Challenges

As organizations increasingly opt for cloud computing, they face **unique security challenges** that differ from traditional on-premises environments. While AWS provides a secure foundation, **misconfigurations, compliance risks, insider threats, and evolving cyberattacks** can compromise cloud security, if they are not managed properly. Therefore, understanding these **common cloud security challenges** is important for building resilient cloud architectures and passing the **AWS Security Specialty exam**.

Misconfiguration and Human Errors

One of the leading causes of cloud security breaches is **misconfiguration**, which often occurs due to **human errors, lack of knowledge, or improper access controls.**

Common Misconfigurations:

- **Publicly exposed S3 buckets**: Storing sensitive data in misconfigured and publicly accessible S3 buckets
- **Overly permissive IAM policies**: Granting excessive permissions like AdministratorAccess to all users
- **Unrestricted security groups**: Leaving SSH (22) and RDP (3389) ports open on the internet
- **Disabled logging and monitoring**: Failing to enable CloudTrail, GuardDuty, or VPC Flow Logs for tracking suspicious activities

Best Practices:

- Use **AWS IAM best practices** (least privilege, role-based access, MFA)
- Enable **AWS Config and Security Hub** to continuously monitor misconfigurations
- Implement **S3 Bucket Policies and Access Analyzer** to prevent data exposure
- Regularly perform **security audits and penetration testing**

Insider Threats and Unauthorized Access

Not all cloud security concerns emerge from external hackers–**insider threats** also pose a serious risk. Unauthorized access to credentials and accounts from malicious employees can result in **data leaks, privilege abuse, or sabotage**.

Insider Threat Scenarios:

- **Former employees retaining access** to AWS accounts and data
- **Compromised IAM credentials** leading to unauthorized access
- **Misuse of privileged access** by administrators or developers

Best Practices:

- Implement **IAM Role-Based Access Control (RBAC)** instead of using root users
- Enforce **MFA for all privileged accounts**
- Use **AWS CloudTrail and GuardDuty** to monitor user activity and detect anomalies

- Rotate access keys and **automate IAM credential revocation** upon employee termination

Insecure APIs and Unprotected Endpoints

APIs are a **critical attack vector** in cloud security. If not secured well, **unauthorized users or attackers** can exploit **public APIs** to gain access to cloud resources.

API Security Risks:

- **Exposed API keys** in GitHub repositories or code repositories
- **Lack of authentication** for API endpoints
- **Unrestricted CORS (Cross-Origin Resource Sharing)** policies exposing APIs to the internet

Best Practices:

- Use **AWS API Gateway** with **IAM authentication, AWS WAF, and WebACLs**
- **Encrypt API data** in transit with TLS (HTTPS) and at rest with AWS KMS
- Enable **CloudWatch Logging and AWS X-Ray** for API activity monitoring
- Regularly scan for **exposed credentials using AWS Secrets Manager and CodeGuru**

Data Breaches and Leaks

Cloud storage is often targeted for **data breaches** due to **weak encryption policies, misconfigured access controls, and publicly exposed assets**.

Common Causes of Data Leaks:

- **Publicly accessible S3 buckets** that might expose confidential information
- **Lack of encryption for sensitive data** stored in databases or backups
- **Weak IAM policies** that grant excessive permissions to users and applications

Best Practices:

- Use **AWS KMS** to encrypt data at rest and enforce server-side encryption for S3
- Apply **VPC endpoint policies** to restrict access to S3 and RDS
- Regularly scan and audit sensitive data with **Amazon Macie**
- Enable **AWS Shield and GuardDuty** to monitor and mitigate threats

Compliance and Regulatory Challenges

Organizations in **regulated industries**, such as healthcare, finance, government, and others, must adhere to compliance frameworks such as **GDPR, HIPAA, PCI-DSS, and SOC 2**. Failure to meet these **compliance requirements** can result in punitive **fines, legal action, and loss of customer trust**.

Common Compliance Issues:

- Storing customer data in unauthorized regions
- Failure to meet encryption and access control requirements
- Inadequate logging and monitoring for compliance audits

Best Practices:

- Use **AWS Artifact** to access compliance reports and certifications
- Enable **AWS Config and Security Hub** to monitor compliance status
- Store logs securely in **S3 with retention policies and encryption**
- Implement **audit trails with CloudTrail and AWS Organizations**

Distributed Denial-of-Service (DDoS) Attacks

Cloud applications face **constant DDoS threats**, where attackers attempt to **overwhelm resources, causing downtime and resulting in degraded performance**.

Common DDoS Attack Methods:

- **Volumetric Attacks**: Flooding networks with high traffic to consume bandwidth
- **State-Exhaustion Attacks**: Overloading firewalls or load balancers
- **Application-Layer Attacks**: Exploiting web applications through bot traffic

Best Practices:

- Use **AWS Shield Advanced** to protect against large-scale DDoS attacks
- Deploy **AWS WAF** to filter malicious traffic and block attack patterns
- Implement **CloudFront with Origin Shield** to reduce the attack surface
- Set up **Auto Scaling** to handle sudden traffic spikes automatically

Weak Incident Response and Security Monitoring

Without a **well-defined incident response plan**, organizations struggle to **detect, contain, and recover from security breaches**.

Common weaknesses in incident response include:

- Lack of centralized monitoring and alerting
- Delayed response to security threats
- No automated remediation mechanisms

Best Practices:

- Implement **AWS Security Hub** for a centralized security view
- Use **Amazon Detective** to investigate security incidents
- Automate threat response using **AWS Lambda** and **EventBridge**
- Conduct **regular incident response drills** using AWS Resilience Hub

Securing cloud environments requires **proactive monitoring and instituting stronger access controls, encryption, and automated security mechanisms** to prevent the risks stemming from m**isconfigurations, insider threats, API vulnerabilities, and DDoS attacks**.

By leveraging **AWS security best practices and services**, including **IAM, Security Hub, GuardDuty, WAF, Macie, and AWS Shield**, organizations can **mitigate risks, maintain compliance, and strengthen their cloud security posture**.

You must understand and study these **common cloud security challenges** for the **AWS Security Specialty exam** to demonstrate your real-world expertise in securing AWS workloads.

Core AWS Security Services: Practical Use Cases

AWS offers a wide range of security services designed to protect identities, data, networks, and applications. Understanding their practical use cases helps you choose the right tools for specific scenarios and apply them effectively in both the AWS Security Specialty exam and real-world cloud environments.

AWS Service	Primary Function	Best Use Case
AWS Identity and Access Management (IAM)	Manages user identities, roles, and permissions	Enforcing least privilege access across AWS resources
AWS Key Management Service (KMS)	Encrypts data at rest and in-transit using managed keys	Encrypting sensitive data stored in S3, RDS, and EBS volumes
AWS Security Hub	Centralized security monitoring and compliance checks	Aggregating security alerts from multiple AWS accounts

Amazon GuardDuty	Threat detection using AI and anomaly detection	Identifying suspicious activity such as compromised credentials
AWS Web Application Firewall (WAF)	Protects web applications from common threats such as SQL injection and XSS	Blocking malicious traffic for APIs and websites
AWS Shield	Provides DDoS protection for applications and AWS services	Preventing large-scale DDoS attacks on AWS-hosted applications
AWS CloudTrail	Logs AWS API activity for auditing and compliance	Tracking user actions and detecting unauthorized access
Amazon Macie	Uses machine learning to discover and classify sensitive data	Detecting personal identifiable information (PII) in S3 buckets
AWS Inspector	Performs automated vulnerability scanning on workloads	Identifying misconfigurations and security weaknesses in EC2 instances
AWS Systems Manager Patch Manager	Automates patching of EC2 instances and on-premises servers	Ensuring compliance by applying security updates automatically
AWS Config	Monitors AWS resource configurations for compliance	Detecting non-compliant security settings in AWS environments
AWS Certificate Manager (ACM)	Manages SSL/TLS certificates for secure web applications	Encrypting data in transit for HTTPS-enabled websites
Amazon Detective	Investigates and visualizes security incidents in AWS	Analyzing attack patterns and suspicious user behavior
AWS Secrets Manager	Securely manages and rotates database and application credentials	Storing and automatically rotating sensitive API keys and passwords

Table 1.2: *Overview of Core AWS Security Services, Their Primary Functions, and Best Use Cases*

Common Cloud Security Challenges: Real-World Case Studies

Cloud security breaches are not just theoretical risks—they come with **real consequences like financial losses, reputational damage, and legal liabilities**.

To explain this further, we have mentioned two major AWS-related security incidents (with company names masked) in the following sections to highlight the importance of **proper security configurations and proactive monitoring**.

Financial Institution's Cloud Data Breach (2019)

A cloud engineer exploited **a misconfigured Identity and Access Management (IAM) role** to access **sensitive customer data** stored in an object storage service. The attacker was able to execute commands on a cloud-based virtual machine using a **Server-Side Request Forgery (SSRF) vulnerability**, which provided them unauthorized access to storage resources.

Security Lessons Learned:

- **Least Privilege Access Principle:** IAM roles should follow the principle of **least privilege access**—the compromised role had excessive permissions, which allowed the attacker to retrieve credentials to access storage resources.
- **Storage Security:** Storage buckets **should not be publicly accessible** unless absolutely necessary. Furthermore, **Access Control Lists (ACLs)** should be properly configured.
- **Monitoring and Logging:** Cloud security monitoring tools could have helped detect unusual API activity sooner. **Automated anomaly detection** is crucial for identifying unauthorized access attempts.

How Cloud Security Services Could Have Helped:

- **Using IAM Access Analyzer:** Would have identified the **overly permissive IAM policy** that allowed unauthorized access
- **Employing Sensitive Data Discovery Tools:** Could have detected **exposed personally identifiable information (PII)** and triggered alerts on unauthorized access
- **Cloud Security Hub:** Could have **aggregated threat detection and access logs**, enabling faster detection and response

Tech Company's Cloud Cryptojacking Attack (2018)

A tech company's cloud environment was compromised after hackers **discovered an exposed Kubernetes dashboard** without any authentication. Once they got inside, they deployed **cryptojacking scripts** to mine cryptocurrency using the company's cloud resources.

Security Lessons Learned:

- **Securing Kubernetes:** Kubernetes dashboards should **not be publicly accessible** without authentication. Using **IAM roles and service accounts** for access control is essential for:

- **Secret Management:** Hardcoded credentials should be avoided. **Cloud-based secret management tools** or **IAM roles** should be used instead.
- **Network Security:** Virtual Private Cloud (VPC) security groups should **restrict access to internal services**, preventing unauthorized external access.

How Cloud Security Services Could Have Helped:

- **Web Application Firewall (WAF):** Could have blocked unauthorized access to the Kubernetes dashboard
- **Threat Detection Service:** Would have detected unusual API calls and potential **cryptojacking activity**
- **Cloud Configuration Auditing**: Could have flagged **misconfigured Kubernetes security settings**

Key Takeaways from These Security Incidents

Misconfigurations are one of the biggest security risks to cloud environments. As observed above, cloud breaches can occur due to **poor IAM policies, exposed storage, or weak access controls.**

Regular security audits are essential. Organizations should conduct **automated security scans** to detect vulnerabilities before attackers can.

Cloud providers offer strong security tools–but they must be used properly. Services such as **IAM Access Analyzer, Threat Detection, Security Monitoring, and Sensitive Data Discovery** help organizations **monitor and mitigate threats proactively**.

By studying these incidents, cloud security professionals can **learn from past mistakes and strengthen their own cloud security posture**.

AWS Security Specialty Exam: 8-Week Study Plan

A structured study plan is key to mastering the AWS Security Specialty exam. The following 8-week plan provides a focused approach to cover all exam domains systematically, balancing theoretical learning with hands-on practice to build both confidence and competence.

Week	Focus Area	Topics to Cover	Hands-on Labs
Week 1 and 2	AWS Security Fundamentals and IAM	AWS Shared Responsibility Model IAM Policies, Roles, and Permissions Multi-Factor Authentication (MFA) and Federation IAM Access Analyzer and AWS Organizations AWS Security Token Service (STS)	Create and manage IAM users, groups, and roles Configure IAM policies with the least privilege access Set up IAM federation with an external identity provider
Week 3 and 4	Data Protection and Compliance	AWS Key Management Service (KMS) AWS Certificate Manager (ACM) Data Encryption (S3, EBS, RDS, DynamoDB) AWS Secrets Manager and Parameter Store Compliance and Regulatory Standards (GDPR, HIPAA, PCI-DSS)	Encrypt an S3 bucket using AWS KMS Configure SSL/TLS certificates using ACM Use AWS Secrets Manager to store and retrieve credentials securely
Week 5 and 6	AWS Security Services and Incident Response	AWS Security Hub, AWS Config, and AWS Inspector AWS GuardDuty and Amazon Detective AWS Shield and AWS Web Application Firewall (WAF) Incident Response and Forensics in AWS AWS CloudTrail and VPC Flow Logs	Enable AWS Security Hub and analyze findings Configure AWS WAF rules to block SQL injection attacks Investigate security incidents using AWS GuardDuty and CloudTrail logs
Week 7	Exam Strategy and Practice Tests	Exam Format and Question Types (Multiple Choice versus Multiple Response) Time Management and Question Elimination Strategies Reviewing Common Exam Traps	Take 1-2 full-length practice exams under timed conditions. Analyze mistakes and revisit weak areas
Week 8	Final Review and Mock Exams	Quick Review of Core AWS Security Services Memorization of Key IAM and Encryption Concepts Reviewing Hands-On Labs and Practical Scenarios	Take a final full-length mock exam and review incorrect answers Revise AWS Well-Architected Framework – Security Pillar

Table 1.3: *8-Week Study Plan for AWS Certified Security – Specialty Exam Preparation*

Conclusion

As this chapter comes to a close, it is time to have a look at some important insights and prepare for your journey ahead.

- **The Importance of AWS Security**

  Cloud security is **non-negotiable** in today's digital landscape. Organizations must protect sensitive data, ensure compliance, and mitigate threats like **misconfigurations, insider risks, API vulnerabilities, and DDoS attacks**. AWS provides robust security tools, but **security is a responsibility** shared among AWS and customers.

- **Core AWS Security Services**

  AWS offers a wide range of security services to help secure cloud workloads that include:

  - **Identity and Access Management (IAM)**: Controls access and permissions
  - **AWS Key Management Service (KMS)**: Encrypts data at rest and in transit
  - **AWS Security Hub and GuardDuty**: Centralized threat detection and monitoring
  - **AWS Web Application Firewall (WAF) and Shield**: Protects against cyber threats such as SQL injection and DDoS attacks
  - **AWS CloudTrail and Macie**: Enables security auditing, compliance tracking, and sensitive data discovery
  - **AWS Config:** Continuously monitors and evaluates AWS resource configurations for compliance
  - **Amazon Detective:** Helps investigate and analyze security incidents using data visualizations and behavioral analytics

To secure AWS environments, organizations must **properly configure and continuously monitor** these security tools.

- **Exam Preparation Tips**

  If you are preparing for the **AWS Certified Security-Specialty** exam, here are some practical steps for you to follow and get a head start on it:

  - **Understand the AWS Shared Responsibility Model**: A crucial exam topic
  - **Master key AWS security services**: Hands-on experience is essential
  - **Learn incident response strategies**: Security breaches and their remediation are core exam areas

  - **Use AWS documentation and whitepapers**: AWS Security Best Practices and Well-Architected Framework provide valuable insights
  - **Take practice exams**: Simulate real exam scenarios to assess your readiness

Next Steps

Now that you have a solid understanding of **AWS security fundamentals**. you must:

- **Dive deeper into individual security services** in the upcoming chapters
- **Practice hands-on labs** using AWS Free Tier to gain real-world experience
- **Familiarize yourself with real-world security case studies** to enhance problem-solving skills

References

- AWS Certified Security – Specialty Official Page: https://aws.amazon.com/certification/certified-security-specialty/
- AWS Certified Security – Specialty Exam Guide (PDF): https://d1.awsstatic.com/training-and-certification/docs-security-spec/AWS-Certified-Security-Specialty_Exam-Guide.pdf
- AWS Certified Security – Specialty Sample Questions: https://d1.awsstatic.com/training-and-certification/docs/AWS_Certified_Security_Specialty_Sample_Questions.pdf
- AWS Identity and Access Management (IAM) User Guide: https://docs.aws.amazon.com/IAM/latest/UserGuide/introduction.html
- AWS Key Management Service Developer Guide: https://docs.aws.amazon.com/kms/latest/developerguide/
- Amazon S3 Encryption: https://docs.aws.amazon.com/AmazonS3/latest/dev/UsingEncryption.html
- Amazon RDS Encryption: https://docs.aws.amazon.com/AmazonRDS/latest/UserGuide/Overview.Encryption.html
- Amazon EBS Encryption: https://docs.aws.amazon.com/AWSEC2/latest/UserGuide/EBSEncryption.html
- AWS Certificate Manager User Guide: https://docs.aws.amazon.com/acm/latest/userguide/
- AWS CloudHSM User Guide: https://docs.aws.amazon.com/cloudhsm/latest/userguide/
- AWS Security Hub User Guide: https://docs.aws.amazon.com/securityhub/latest/userguide/what-is-securityhub.html

- Amazon GuardDuty User Guide: https://docs.aws.amazon.com/guardduty/latest/ug/what-is-guardduty.html
- AWS WAF and AWS Shield Developer Guide: https://docs.aws.amazon.com/waf/latest/developerguide/waf-chapter.html
- Amazon Macie User Guide: https://docs.aws.amazon.com/macie/latest/user/what-is-macie.html
- AWS CloudTrail User Guide: https://docs.aws.amazon.com/awscloudtrail/latest/userguide/cloudtrail-user-guide.html
- Amazon Inspector User Guide: https://docs.aws.amazon.com/inspector/latest/user/introduction.html
- AWS Config Developer Guide: https://docs.aws.amazon.com/config/latest/developerguide/WhatIsConfig.html
- Amazon Detective Admin Guide: https://docs.aws.amazon.com/detective/latest/adminguide/what-is-detective.html
- AWS Trusted Advisor User Guide: https://docs.aws.amazon.com/awssupport/latest/user/trusted-advisor.html
- AWS Resilience Hub User Guide: https://docs.aws.amazon.com/resilience-hub/latest/userguide/what-is.html
- AWS Well-Architected Framework – Security Pillar: https://docs.aws.amazon.com/wellarchitected/latest/security-pillar/welcome.html
- AWS Security Best Practices Whitepaper (PDF): https://docs.aws.amazon.com/pdfs/whitepapers/latest/aws-security-best-practices/aws-security-best-practices.pdf
- AWS Compliance Programs: https://aws.amazon.com/compliance/programs

CHAPTER 2
Identity and Access Management (IAM)

Introduction

AWS Identity and Access Management (IAM) is a fundamental service that enables you to securely control access to AWS resources. This chapter provides you an in-depth understanding of IAM concepts, best practices, and hands-on guidance that will enable you to configure IAM securely.

Identity and Access Management (IAM) is the cornerstone of cloud security and a critical component for achieving compliance in AWS environments. It governs who can access what, while ensuring that only authorized users, roles, and applications interact with specific resources. In dynamic and scalable cloud environments, the significance of an effective IAM becomes even more crucial. Misconfigurations in IAM policies can result in serious vulnerabilities such as privilege escalation, data breaches, and non-compliance with regulatory standards. By implementing IAM best practices, organizations can significantly reduce their attack surface, while maintaining least privilege access and strengthening their overall security posture.

Structure

In this chapter, we will cover the following topics:

- IAM Roles, Policies, and Permission Boundaries
    - What Are IAM Roles and How They Work
    - Identity-Based and Resource-Based Policies
    - Types of IAM Policies (AWS-Managed, Customer-Managed, Inline)
    - Permission Boundaries and Their Use Cases
    - Best Practices for Implementing IAM Policies
- User and Group Management
    - Creating and Managing IAM Users

  - Types of IAM Credentials
  - Managing IAM Groups and Their Permissions
  - Best Practices for User and Group Management
- Cross-Account Access and Identity Federation
  - Cross-Account Role Assumption and Trust Policies
  - Federated Access Using SAML, Web Identity, and AWS IAM Identity Center
  - Best Practices for Cross-Account Access and Federation
- Multi-Factor Authentication (MFA)
  - Importance of MFA in AWS
  - Types of MFA Devices (Virtual, Hardware, FIDO2)
  - Enforcing MFA Using IAM Policies
  - Best Practices for MFA Implementation
- Auditing IAM Configurations with AWS Config
  - Monitoring and Evaluating IAM Resource Configurations
  - Using Managed and Custom Config Rules
  - Automating Compliance and Remediation
- Hands-on Lab: Setting up Secure IAM Roles and Policies
  - Creating IAM Roles with Least Privilege
  - Applying Permission Boundaries and MFA Enforcement
  - Validating Configurations Using AWS Config

IAM Roles, Policies, and Permission Boundaries

IAM roles, policies, and permission boundaries form the foundation of access control in AWS. Understanding how these elements interact is crucial for defining secure, least-privilege permissions and ensuring that users, applications, and services access only what they need.

IAM Roles

IAM roles are a secure way to grant permissions to AWS services, applications, and users **without requiring long-term credentials**. Unlike IAM users, which have **persistent access keys**, IAM roles issue **temporary security credentials** that expire after a set duration.

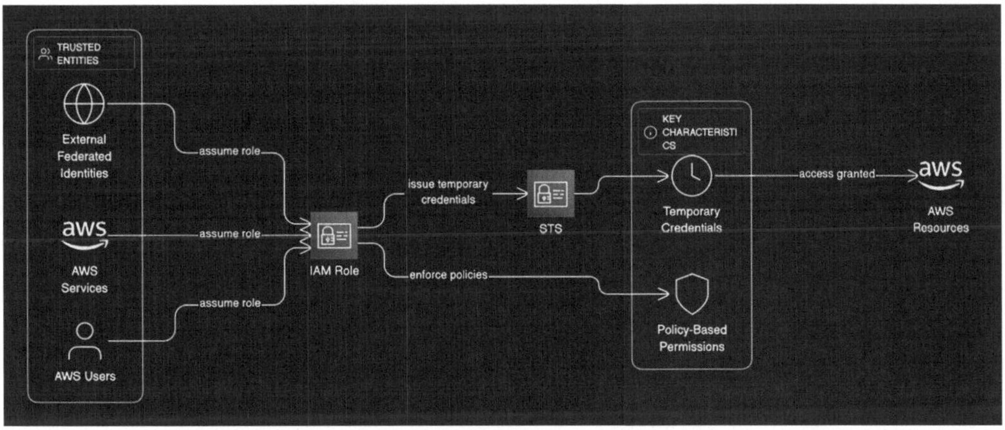

Figure 2.1: *AWS role assumption flow: trusted entities use STS to get temporary, policy-based access to resources*

Key Characteristics of IAM Roles

- **Temporary Credentials:** Provided by AWS Security Token Service (STS), reducing the risk of credential exposure
- **Assumable by Trusted Entities:** AWS services, users, and external federated identities can assume roles
- **Policy-Based Permissions:** Roles follow IAM policies defining allowed actions and resources

Use Cases for IAM Roles

IAM roles play a critical role in delegating secure access to AWS resources without relying on long-term credentials. They provide temporary security credentials and can be assumed by trusted entities such as AWS services, IAM users, and federated identities.

The flexibility and security of IAM roles make them ideal for various scenarios, where permissions need to be granted dynamically or across different accounts and identity providers. The following are some of the most common and impactful use cases for implementing IAM roles in AWS environments:

- **Assigning Permissions to AWS Services:** AWS services such as Lambda, EC2, and ECS often need access to S3, DynamoDB, or SNS. IAM roles enable these services to securely assume permissions without storing credentials.
- **Cross-Account Access:** In multi-account setups, IAM roles allow users in one AWS account to access resources in another without creating IAM users in multiple accounts.

- **Federated Access:** Organizations using external identity providers (for example, Active Directory, Okta) can assign IAM roles to users authenticated outside AWS.
- **IAM Role Anywhere: Access for External Workloads:** For workloads that run outside of AWS such as in on-premises data centers, edge locations, or hybrid environments, IAM Role Anywhere allows them to assume IAM roles using X.509 certificates issued by a trusted certification authority.

This enables secure, credential-free access to AWS services like Secrets Manager, S3, or CloudWatch from external environments, and is ideal for highly regulated industries or hybrid cloud deployments.

Identity-Based Policies

Identity-based policies define the actions an IAM user/group/ role can perform on AWS resources. These policies are written in JSON and attached directly to IAM identities.

Structure of an IAM Policy

A typical IAM policy consists of:

- **Version:** Specifies the policy language version
- **Statement:** Defines a permission rule, including:
  - **Effect:** Allow or Deny
  - **Action:** AWS service actions (for example, `s3:PutObject`)
  - **Resource:** AWS resource ARNs (for example, `arn:aws:s3:::my-bucket/*`)
  - **Condition (Optional):** Additional constraints (for example, IP address restrictions)

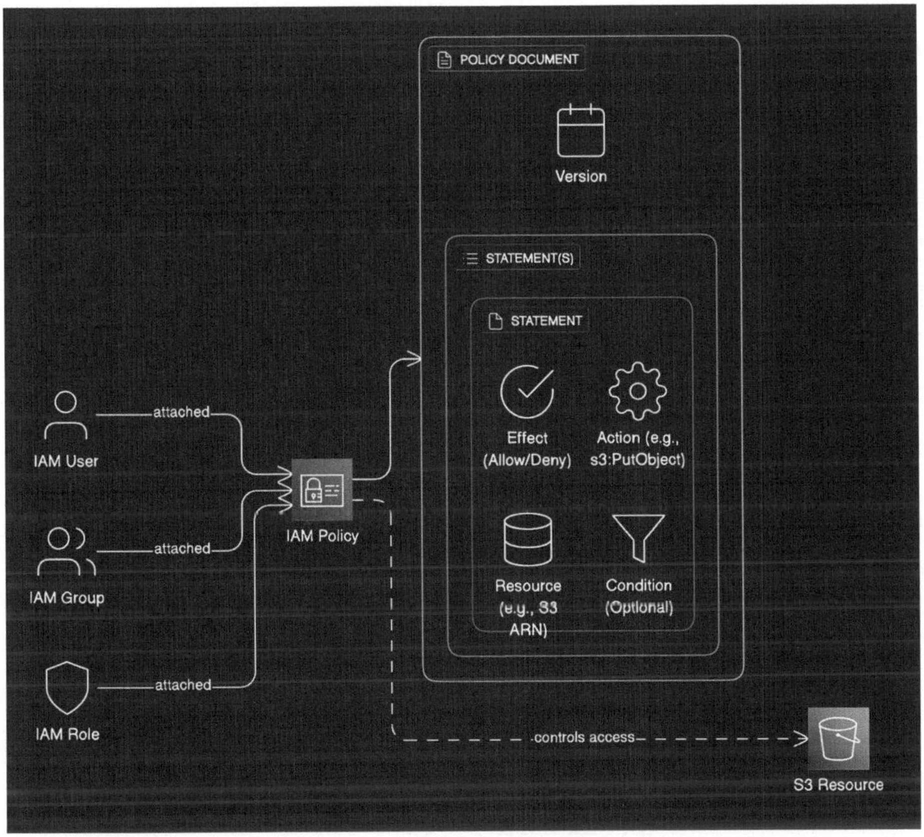

***Figure 2.2:** AWS IAM policy structure showing how users, groups, and roles use policy statements to control S3 resource access*

Example: Read-Only Access to S3

```
{
    "Version": "2012-10-17",
    "Statement": [
        {
            "Effect": "Allow",
            "Action": [
                "s3:GetObject",
                "s3:ListBucket"
            ],
            "Resource": [
                "arn:aws:s3:::example-bucket",
                "arn:aws:s3:::example-bucket/*"
            ]
        }
    ]
}
```

Types of IAM Policies

AWS provides different types of IAM policies to suit various access management needs. Each type offers a different level of control, flexibility, and maintenance responsibility, allowing you to choose the best fit for your organization's security requirements.

- **AWS-Managed Policies:** Predefined policies managed by AWS
- **Customer-Managed Policies:** Custom policies created by users
- **Inline Policies:** Policies directly attached to a single user, group, or role

Feature / Criteria	AWS-Managed Policies	Customer-Managed Policies
Definition	Predefined policies created and maintained by AWS	Custom policies created and maintained by the user
Customization	Not customizable	Fully customizable
Maintenance Responsibility	AWS	Customer
Use Case Examples	AmazonEC2ReadOnlyAccess, AmazonS3FullAccess	Granting specific actions on a custom resource
Best For	Common, general-purpose access scenarios	Tailored access for teams, applications, or regulatory needs
Policy Versioning	No (AWS updates are automatic and invisible to the user)	Yes (you control and manage versions)
Risk of Misconfiguration	Low (controlled by AWS)	Medium to High (requires IAM expertise)
Tagging Support	Not taggable	Supports resource tagging
Use in Fine-Grained Access	Limited	Ideal for least-privilege design and fine-tuned permissions
Auditing & Governance	Basic	Enhanced (supports tagging, naming conventions, and so on)

Table 2.1: *Comparison of AWS-Managed and Customer-Managed IAM Policies*

Policy Evaluation Logic

IAM follows a **default-deny** model. An action is only permitted if an explicit `"Allow"` policy is applied and no explicit `"Deny"` overrides it.

Permission Boundaries

Permission boundaries are an advanced IAM feature that **restrict the maximum number of permissions** an IAM role or user can receive. Even if a policy grants more permissions than the ordinary, the boundaries enforce the upper limit.

Working of Permission Boundaries

Permission boundaries are **not standalone policies**, but are used in conjunction with identity-based policies. AWS evaluates permissions by checking:

- Identity-based policies
- Permission boundaries (if applied)
- Resource-based policies
- Service control policies (SCPs) in AWS Organizations

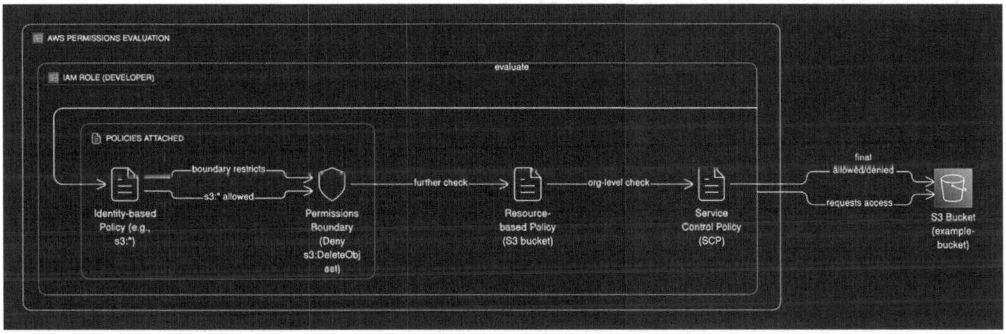

Figure 2.3: *AWS permissions evaluation flow showing how identity-based policies, permission boundaries, resource-based policies, and service control policies determine S3 bucket access*

Example: Restricting S3 Access

A developer role needs access to multiple services but must be restricted from deleting S3 objects. The following permission boundary can be applied:

```
{
    "Version": "2012-10-17",
    "Statement": [
        {
            "Effect": "Deny",
            "Action": "s3:DeleteObject",
            "Resource": "arn:aws:s3:::example-bucket/*"
        }
    ]
}
```

Even if an identity-based policy grants **`s3:*`** permissions, the boundary ensures **`s3:DeleteObject`** is never allowed.

Use Cases for Permission Boundaries

Permission boundaries help enforce the maximum level of access an IAM user or role can have. They are especially useful in large organizations where delegated administrators or development teams need flexibility without exceeding defined security limits.

- Restricting excessive privileges for IAM users and roles
- Ensuring compliance with security best practices
- Applying consistent permission control across an organization

Best Practices for IAM Roles, Policies, and Permission Boundaries

Following best practices for IAM roles, policies, and permission boundaries ensures that access within your AWS environment remains controlled, auditable, and aligned with the principle of least privilege. Implementing these guidelines reduces the risk of privilege escalation and accidental exposure of critical resources.

- **Follow the Principle of Least Privilege**

  Grant users and roles only the permissions they need to perform their tasks—nothing more. This minimizes the risk of accidental or malicious misuse. Regularly reviewing and refining IAM policies ensures access stays tightly controlled as roles and responsibilities evolve.

- **Use IAM Roles Instead of IAM Users**

  IAM users rely on long-term credentials (like access keys), which can be a security risk if leaked or forgotten. IAM roles provide **temporary credentials**, making them ideal for AWS services and applications. This reduces exposure and supports better access management.

- **Implement Permission Boundaries for Controlled Access**

  Permission boundaries define the **maximum set of permissions** an IAM role or user can have, even if more permissions are granted via policies. This helps prevent privilege escalation and enforces stricter controls across your organization.

- **Enable Multi-Factor Authentication (MFA)**

  MFA adds a second layer of authentication (like a code from a phone app) in addition to a password. It's especially important for admin users or those with sensitive access, as it significantly reduces the risk of unauthorized access—even if credentials are compromised.

- **Monitor IAM Activities Using AWS CloudTrail**

  AWS CloudTrail records all IAM-related activities, such as user logins, policy changes, and role assumptions. Monitoring these logs helps detect suspicious behavior early, supports audits, and improves your ability to respond quickly to security incidents.

- **Tagging IAM Roles and Policies**

  Tags help organize IAM resources by assigning key-value pairs such as **`Environment=Prod`** or **`Owner=SecurityTeam`**. They improve visibility and support functions such as cost allocation, policy enforcement, and compliance auditing across your AWS environment.

- **External IDs**

  External IDs add a layer of security when granting IAM role access to third parties. They prevent the confused deputy problem by ensuring that only the authorized external entity can assume the role, even when the role's ARN is known.

IAM Users

IAM users are **individual identities** that are created within AWS to represent real people or applications that require access to resources. Each IAM user has a unique **name and credentials**, such as a password for AWS Management Console access or keys for programmatic access.

Key Characteristics of IAM Users

- **Unique identities:** Each user is assigned a specific username.
- **Credential-based authentication:** Users authenticate via passwords or access keys.
- **Policy-based permissions:** Users require explicitly assigned IAM policies to access AWS services.

Types of IAM User Credentials

- **Console Password:** Used to log in to the AWS Management Console
- **Access Keys:** Used for CLI, SDK, or API access
- **SSH Keys:** Used for specific AWS services such as AWS CodeCommit
- **Multi-Factor Authentication (MFA):** Enhances security by requiring a second authentication factor

Example: Creating an IAM User

1. Navigate to the IAM Console
2. Select **`Users`** and click **`Add User`**
3. Choose authentication type (password or access keys)

4. Attach policies or add the user to a group
5. Enable MFA for enhanced security

Use Cases for IAM Users

- **Developers needing CLI/API access** to AWS services
- Administrators managing AWS resources
- **Service accounts for applications** requiring API interaction with AWS

IAM Groups

IAM groups are **collections of IAM users** that share the same permissions. Instead of assigning policies to individual users, groups allow centralized management of permissions.

Key Characteristics of IAM Groups

- **Simplifies permission management:** Policies are applied at the group level.
- **Users can belong to multiple groups:** A user can be a member of multiple groups, inheriting permissions from all.
- **Easier administration:** Instead of updating policies for individual users, modifying a group policy updates permissions for all members.

Example: Creating an IAM Group

1. Navigate to the IAM Console
2. Select **Groups** and click **Create New Group**
3. Assign an appropriate name (for example, `Developers` or `Admins`)
4. Attach policies defining group permissions
5. Add users to the group

Use Cases for IAM Groups

- **Developers:** A group with access to development resources
- **Administrators:** A group with full AWS management privileges
- **Read-Only Auditors:** A group with permissions to view resources but not modify them

Authentication and Security Best Practices

Strong authentication and security practices are essential to protect AWS accounts and resources from unauthorized access. Implementing these measures ensures that only verified users can perform actions within your environment, significantly reducing the risk of credential misuse or compromise.

- **Enforce Multi-Factor Authentication (MFA)**
  - Require MFA for IAM users, especially those with administrative privileges
  - Use hardware MFA devices or virtual MFA applications such as **Google Authenticator** or **AWS MFA**
- **Use IAM Groups Instead of Individual Policies**
  - Assign permissions to groups rather than individual users to simplify management
- **Rotate and Manage Access Keys**
  - Avoid long-term access keys. If required, rotate them regularly and track usage
  - Use AWS Secrets Manager or AWS IAM Access Analyzer to monitor key usage
- **Implement Least Privilege Access**
  - Grant only the permissions necessary for a user's role
  - Regularly review and audit IAM permissions
- **Use IAM Roles Instead of IAM Users for Applications**
  - Applications should assume IAM roles instead of using long-term credentials.
  - AWS services like EC2 and Lambda should be assigned IAM roles with scoped permissions.
- **Monitor IAM Activity with AWS CloudTrail**
  - Enable AWS CloudTrail to log all IAM-related activities
  - Analyze logs for unauthorized access attempts or unusual activity

Managing User Access with IAM Policies

In AWS, controlling the user's access to specific resources and determining what actions they can perform is important to maintain a secure environment. IAM policies are the core mechanism used to manage this access. These JSON-based documents define permissions for IAM users, groups, and roles by specifying permitted and denied actions on specific AWS resources. By attaching the appropriate policies to identities, you can enforce fine-grained access control across your AWS environment.

This section explains different types of IAM policies, their functions, and how you can use them effectively to align with security best practices.

Example: Administrator Access Policy

This policy grants full administrative access to a user or group:

```
{
    "Version": "2012-10-17",
    "Statement": [
        {
            "Effect": "Allow",
            "Action": "*",
            "Resource": "*"
        }
    ]
}
```

Example: Read-Only Access Policy

This policy allows a user or group to view AWS resources without making changes:

```
{
    "Version": "2012-10-17",
    "Statement": [
        {
            "Effect": "Allow",
            "Action": [
                "ec2:Describe*",
                "s3:List*",
                "rds:Describe*"
            ],
            "Resource": "*"
        }
    ]
}
```

Best Practices for User and Group Management

Effectively managing IAM users and groups is essential to maintain secure and scalable access control within AWS. By organizing users into groups and assigning permissions at the group level, you can simplify permission management and reduce the risk of misconfigurations. Following best practices, such as enforcing strong authentication, minimizing the use of long-term credentials, and regularly reviewing user activity ensures that only authorized individuals have appropriate access to AWS resources.

The following section outlines key recommendations to manage users and groups securely while aligning with the principle of least privilege.

- **Use AWS IAM Identity Center (SSO) for Centralized Access Management**
  - AWS IAM Identity Center (formerly AWS SSO) provides **federated access** and simplifies user management across multiple AWS accounts
- **Regularly Review and Deactivate Unused IAM Users**
  - Use AWS IAM **Access Analyzer** to identify inactive users
  - Disable or remove IAM users that no longer require access
- **Implement Role-Based Access Control (RBAC)**
  - Define roles with specific permissions and assign users to appropriate groups based on their job function
- **Avoid Using Root User for Daily Tasks**
  - The AWS root account has unrestricted access and should only be used for essential administrative tasks
  - Create IAM users with admin privileges instead of using the root account

Cross-Account Access

In modern AWS architectures, organizations often operate multiple AWS accounts for different teams, business units, or environments like development, testing, and production. Therefore, managing secure access across accounts is critical to the process. AWS provides **cross-account access** using IAM roles and **identity federation** to enable external authentication from third-party identity providers (IdPs). This chapter explores these concepts in detail along with examples and best practices.

Cross-account access allows AWS users, applications, or services in one AWS account (**Account A**) to access resources in another AWS account (**Account B**) without needing separate IAM users in both accounts.

Working of Cross-Account Access

Cross-account access allows users, applications, or services in one AWS account to securely access resources in another without the need to create duplicate IAM users. This approach streamlines access management across multi-account environments while maintaining strong security boundaries.

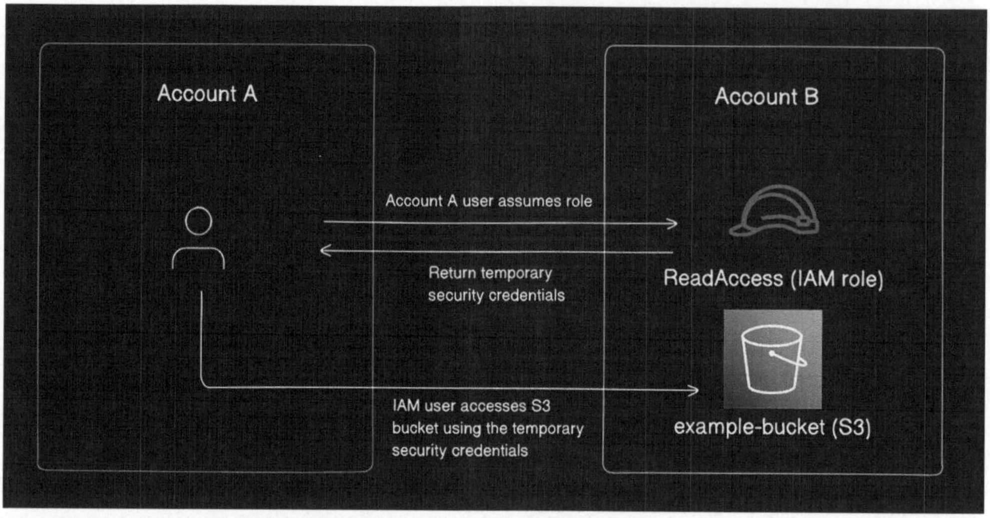

Figure 2.4: *Cross-account S3 access flow where a user in Account A assumes a role in Account B to obtain temporary credentials for accessing an S3 bucket*

Steps to Configure Cross-Account Access

1. **Create an IAM Role in Account B** with the necessary permissions
2. **Define a Trust Policy** that allows users from Account A to assume the role
3. **Use STS AssumeRole API** to obtain temporary security credentials
4. **Access Resources in Account B** using the assumed role

Example: Allowing Users from Account A to Assume a Role in Account B

Step 1: Create an IAM Role in Account B

Navigate to the IAM console in Account B and create a role with the following trust policy:

```
{
    "Version": "2012-10-17",
    "Statement": [
        {
            "Effect": "Allow",
            "Principal": {
                "AWS": "arn:aws:iam::111122223333:root"
            },
            "Action": "sts:AssumeRole"
        }
    ]
}
```

- Replace **111122223333** with the AWS Account ID of Account A
- This allows users from Account A to assume the role

Step 2: Attach a Permissions Policy to the Role

Example policy to allow read access to an S3 bucket in Account B:

```
{
    "Version": "2012-10-17",
    "Statement": [
        {
            "Effect": "Allow",
            "Action": [
                "s3:ListBucket",
                "s3:GetObject"
            ],
            "Resource": [
                "arn:aws:s3:::example-bucket",
                "arn:aws:s3:::example-bucket/*"]
        }
    ]
}
```

Step 3: Assume the Role from Account A

A user in Account A can assume the role using AWS CLI:

```
aws sts assume-role --role-arn arn:aws:iam::222233334444:role/
CrossAccountReadOnly --role-session-name MySession
```

This returns temporary security credentials that allow the user to access resources in Account B.

Use Cases for Cross-Account Access

Cross-account access is widely used in multi-account AWS environments to simplify management and maintain security boundaries. The following are common scenarios where implementing cross-account roles provides operational efficiency and centralized control.

- **Centralized Logging:** An AWS account collects logs from multiple accounts.
- **Shared Services:** A central account hosts services accessed by multiple business units.
- **Third-Party Access:** Vendors or partners access specific AWS resources without creating IAM users.

Identity Federation

Identity federation allows external users from an **Identity Provider (IdP)**, such as **Active Directory, Okta, Google, or SAML-based providers**, to authenticate into AWS **without creating IAM users**.

AWS supports the following federation methods:

- **SAML 2.0 Federation:** Uses Security Assertion Markup Language (SAML) to authenticate users
- **Web Identity Federation:** Enables authentication via third-party identity providers like Google, Facebook, or Amazon Cognito
- **AWS IAM Identity Center (SSO):** Provides centralized login and access management

SAML-Based Federation Example

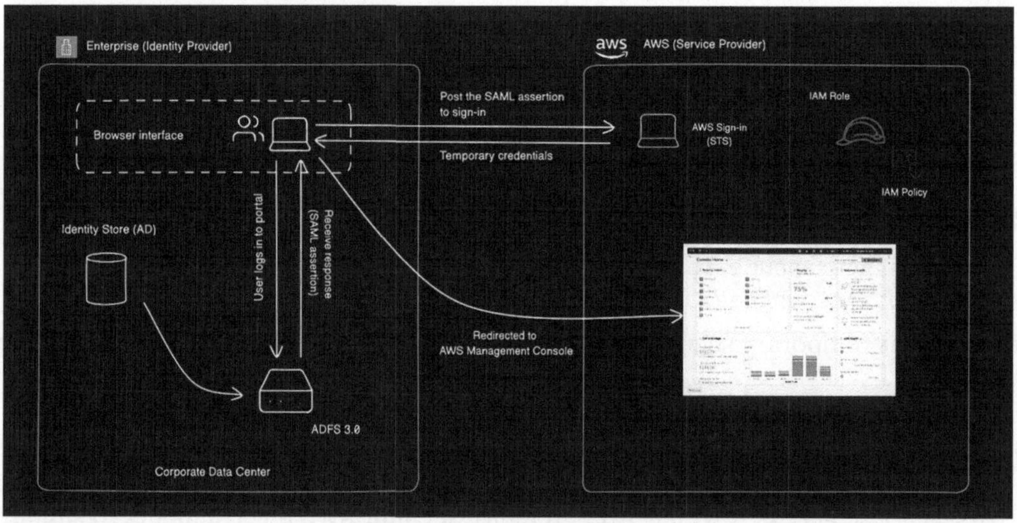

Figure 2.5: *AWS Federated Authentication with Active Directory Federation Services (AD FS)*

Step 1: Configure a SAML Identity Provider in AWS IAM

1. Go to **`AWS IAM Console → Identity Providers`**
2. Choose **`Create Provider`** and select **`SAML`**
3. Upload the SAML metadata file from your IdP (for example, Okta, Active Directory Federation Services)
4. Define the provider name (for example, **`CorporateSAMLProvider`**)

Step 2: Create an IAM Role for Federated Users

Create an IAM role with a trust relationship for the SAML IdP:

```
{
    "Version": "2012-10-17",
    "Statement": [
        {
            "Effect": "Allow",
            "Principal": {
                "Federated": "arn:aws:iam::123456789012:saml-provider/CorporateSAMLProvider"
            },
            "Action": "sts:AssumeRoleWithSAML",
            "Condition": {
                "StringEquals": {
                    "SAML:aud": "https://signin.aws.amazon.com/saml"
                }
            }
        }
    ]
}
```

Step 3: Assign the Role in the Identity Provider

- In your IdP (for example, Okta, Active Directory), assign the IAM role to user groups.
- Users logging in via the IdP can now assume this role.

Step 4: Login to AWS via SAML

Users can authenticate using their corporate credentials and receive a temporary AWS session, allowing them access without providing them IAM user credentials.

Web Identity Federation Example (Amazon Cognito)

1. Set up **Amazon Cognito** as the IdP
2. Configure supported providers (Google, Facebook, Apple)
3. Map identity attributes to IAM roles
4. Users authenticate via third-party login and obtain temporary AWS credentials

Use Cases for Identity Federation

Identity federation enables seamless and secure authentication for users from external identity providers. The following use cases highlight how organizations leverage federation to simplify access management and improve user experience across AWS environments.

- **Enterprise SSO:** Organizations integrate AWS authentication with corporate directories.
- **Mobile & Web Applications:** Apps authenticate users via third-party login.
- **Temporary Access to AWS Resources:** External users access AWS services without creating IAM users.

Best Practices for Cross-Account Access and Federation

In multi-account AWS environments where you are integrating external identity providers, securing access control becomes a highly complex exercise. The best practices listed in the following section ensure that cross-account access and identity federation are implemented in a secure, auditable, and manageable way:

- **Use IAM Roles Instead of IAM Users**

  Creating IAM users for external entities (like vendors or other teams) introduces the risk of long-term credentials being lost, leaked, or misused. Instead:

  - Use **IAM roles with temporary credentials** provided by AWS Security Token Service (STS).
  - Trusted users or services can assume roles via **`sts:AssumeRole`**, ensuring time-bound and auditable access.
  - This approach eliminates the need to manage and rotate static credentials.

  Example: A partner company can access your S3 bucket by assuming a role in your account instead of having a persistent IAM user created for them.

- **Implement Least Privilege Access**

  Doing so only granst the minimum set of permissions required for a user or application to perform its job.

  - Define **narrow-scope IAM policies** for cross-account roles
  - Use **resource-based policies** (for example, S3 bucket or KMS key policies) to allow access only to specific resources
  - Combine identity-based and resource-based policies to enforce multiple layers of control

Example: A billing dashboard role only needs **`s3:GetObject`** and **`cloudwatch:GetMetricData`**—not complete administrative access.

- **Enable Multi-Factor Authentication (MFA)**

  Adding MFA increases the security of cross-account access and ensures that even if credentials are stolen, further unauthorized access can be prevented.

  - **Require MFA for privileged roles** such as administrator or billing roles
  - Use IAM policies with Condition blocks that enforce MFA:

    ```
    "Condition": {
        "BoolIfExists": {
            "aws:MultiFactorAuthPresent": true
        }
    }
    ```

  Example: A cross-account administrator role can only be assumed if the user has MFA enabled on their account.

- **Monitor IAM Activity with AWS CloudTrail**

  Logging and monitoring are essential for detecting abuse or misconfigurations.

  - **Enable AWS CloudTrail** to log all IAM and STS activities across accounts
  - Use **Amazon GuardDuty** to detect anomalous behaviors, such as:
    - Unexpected role assumptions
    - Unusual access patterns
    - Suspicious API activity

  Example: If GuardDuty detects that a developer account is unexpectedly accessing resources in production, it can trigger an alert or generate an automated response.

- **Rotate and Audit Access Credentials**

  Regular audits ensure that cross-account access stays aligned with business needs and security policies.

  - **Rotate IAM roles and permissions periodically**, especially if requirements change, or if there are personnel shifts
  - Review trust relationships and ensure that only intended external accounts or IdPs are listed
  - Decommission unused roles and clean up outdated trust policies

Example: If a third-party consultant's engagement ends, their ability to assume roles in your account should be revoked immediately.

Cross-account access and identity federation are essential to secure AWS environments with multiple accounts or external identities. IAM roles facilitate **secure access between AWS accounts**, while identity federation integrates **corporate authentication systems** with AWS. By following best practices, organizations can **enhance security, minimize credential exposure, and streamline access management**.

Multi-Factor Authentication (MFA)

Security is a critical aspect of managing AWS environments. To enhance euthentication security, Multi-Factor Authentication (MFA) is a key mechanism, which adds an extra layer of security as it requires users to provide two or more authentication factors before gaining access to AWS resources. This chapter explores MFA in AWS, its types, implementation strategies, and best practices.

Understanding MFA

Multi-Factor Authentication (MFA) is a method that requires users to provide **two or more verification factors** to log in, thereby reducing the risk of unauthorized access.

Authentication Factors

MFA typically involves the following authentication factors:

- **Something You Know:** Password or PIN
- **Something You Have:** Security token, mobile device, or smart card
- **Someone You Are:** Biometric verification, such as fingerprints or facial recognition

Importance of MFA in AWS

- Protects against compromised credentials
- Enhances security for AWS Management Console, CLI, and API access
- Reduces the risk of account takeover due to phishing or credential leaks

Implementing MFA in AWS

Implementing Multi-Factor Authentication (MFA) in AWS is a critical step in strengthening account security. It ensures that users verify their identity through multiple factors, reducing the risk of unauthorized access even if credentials are exposed.

- **Enabling MFA for IAM Users**

  Multi-Factor Authentication (MFA) adds an extra layer of security to user logins by requiring a second factor like a code from a mobile app, besides the usual username and password. This prevents unauthorized access even if the password is compromised.

Step 1: Navigate to the IAM Console

1. Sign in to the **`AWS Management Console`**
2. Go to **`IAM → Users`**
3. Select the user to enable MFA

Step 2: Assign an MFA Device

1. Click **`Security credentials`**
2. Under **`Multi-factor authentication (MFA)`**, click **`Assign MFA device`**
3. Choose the type of MFA (Virtual, Hardware, or FIDO2)

Step 3: Complete MFA Setup

1. For virtual MFA, scan the QR code with your authenticator app
2. Enter two consecutive MFA codes from the app
3. Click **`Assign MFA`** to complete the process

Step 4: Test MFA

1. Log out and try logging in again
2. Enter your username and password
3. Provide the MFA code from your device

- **Enforcing MFA Using IAM Policies**

  Organizations can enforce MFA for users accessing AWS resources. The following is an IAM policy that requires MFA for all actions, except for IAM operations:

```
{
    "Version": "2012-10-17",
    "Statement": [
        {
            "Effect": "Deny",
```

```
                "Action": "*",
                "Resource": "*",
                "Condition": {
                    "BoolIfExists": {
                        "aws:MultiFactorAuthPresent": false
                    }
                }
            }
        ]
    }
```

This policy ensures that users **must use MFA** to perform any AWS actions.

MFA for Root and Federated Users

The AWS **root user** is the most powerful account in any AWS environment. It has unrestricted access to all resources and billing features, which makes it a high-value target for attackers. Therefore, enabling **Multi-Factor Authentication (MFA)** for the root user is a critical security best practice.

- **Enabling MFA for the AWS Root User**

  The root user has complete access to an AWS account and should be protected with MFA.

Steps:

1. Log in to the AWS **`Management Console`** as the root user
2. Navigate to **`IAM → Security Credentials`**
3. Under **`Multi-Factor Authentication (MFA)`**, click **`Enable MFA`**
4. Choose a **virtual or hardware MFA device** and complete the setup

- **MFA for Federated Users**

  For organizations using **AWS IAM Identity Center (SSO)** or **SAML Federation**, MFA can be enforced at the **identity provider (IdP) level**. A few examples of IdPs are:

  - Microsoft Active Directory
  - Okta
  - Google Workspace

Steps to Enforce MFA in AWS IAM Identity Center

1. **Enable MFA** in your IdP settings
2. Configure AWS IAM Identity Center to require MFA for user authentication

3. Use **Conditional Access Policies** to enforce MFA for specific users or groups

Best Practices for MFA in AWS

Implementing strong Multi-Factor Authentication (MFA) practices in AWS is essential for securing accounts and services. Require MFA for all IAM users, especially administrators, and use FIDO2 hardware keys for the highest level of protection. Regularly test and rotate MFA devices to maintain reliability. Enforce MFA through IAM policies and monitor usage with AWS CloudTrail and GuardDuty for suspicious activity. Prepare for lost devices with backup options or break-glass procedures. Finally, mandate MFA for sensitive services such as AWS Billing, IAM, and data stores such as S3, RDS, and DynamoDB to prevent unauthorized access and data breaches.

- **Require MFA for All IAM Users**
  - Enforce MFA for all IAM users, especially those with administrative privileges
- **Use FIDO2 Security Keys for Maximum Security**
  - Hardware security keys offer the strongest protection against phishing
- **Regularly Rotate and Test MFA Devices**
  - Conduct a periodic review to determine if MFA devices are working properly
  - Replace outdated hardware tokens
- **Implement IAM Policies to Enforce MFA**
  - Use AWS IAM policies to **deny actions unless MFA is present**
- **Monitor MFA Usage with AWS CloudTrail**
  - Track user login attempts and detect non-MFA logins
  - Set up **Amazon GuardDuty** to alert on suspicious authentication attempts
- **Have a Backup Plan for Lost MFA Devices**
  - Configure backup MFA devices or **use IAM break-glass procedures**
- **Require MFA for Sensitive AWS Services**
  - Enforce MFA for access to:
    - **AWS Billing** (to prevent account hijacking)
    - **IAM and Security services** (to avoid privilege escalation)
    - **Data-sensitive services** like **S3, RDS, and DynamoDB**

Multi-Factor Authentication (MFA) is a critical security measure in AWS environments, as it provides an additional layer of protection against unauthorized access. By implementing **virtual MFA, hardware security keys, and IAM enforcement policies**, organizations can strengthen security for IAM users, federated users, and AWS accounts. Following the **best practices**, such as monitoring MFA usage and enforcing least privilege access, you can ensure that your cloud infrastructure is secure.

Auditing IAM Configurations with AWS Config

Effective security and compliance management in AWS requires you to monitor IAM configurations continuously. **AWS Config** is a powerful service that enables organizations to track changes, audit IAM settings, and ensure compliance with security best practices. This chapter explores **AWS Config**, its role in auditing IAM configurations, and how can you use it effectively with the aid of practical examples.

Understanding AWS Config

AWS Config is a **managed service** that provides detailed visibility into **AWS resource configurations** and tracks changes over time. It allows users to:

- Continuously monitor IAM configurations
- Detect and remediate non-compliant IAM policies, roles, and users
- Generate compliance reports for regulatory requirements

Working of AWS Config

Understanding how AWS Config works is essential for maintaining visibility and compliance across your AWS environment. It tracks configuration changes, evaluates them against defined rules, and helps identify or automatically remediate non-compliant resources.

- AWS Config continuously records changes to IAM resources (for example, users, roles, and policies).
- Predefined or custom rules evaluate the configurations against security policies.
- Alerts and remediation actions trigger when violations occur.
- Historical logs help audit security changes over time.

Key Benefits

AWS Config provides several key benefits that enhance governance, visibility, and security automation. These advantages help organizations maintain continuous compliance and streamline auditing across multiple AWS accounts.

- **Automated Compliance:** Continuously evaluates IAM settings against security policies
- **Audit Trail:** Tracks and stores configuration changes
- **Integration with AWS Security Tools:** Works with AWS Security Hub, CloudTrail, and AWS Organizations

Setting Up AWS Config for IAM Auditing

Setting up AWS Config for IAM auditing allows you to monitor changes to identities, roles, and policies in real time. The following steps outline how to enable and configure AWS Config to capture and store IAM-related activity for continuous compliance tracking.

Step 1: Enable AWS Config

1. Sign in to the `AWS Management Console`
2. Navigate to `AWS Config`
3. Click `Get started` and choose `Set up AWS Config`
4. Select a `S3 bucket` for configuration history storage
5. Enable `AWS Config recording` for IAM resources (Users, Roles, Policies)

Step 2: Define AWS Config Rules for IAM Security

AWS Config uses **rules** to assess IAM settings. You can choose from AWS **managed rules** or create **custom rules**.

Example: Enforcing IAM MFA Usage

AWS provides a **managed rule** (`iam-user-mfa-enabled`) to ensure that IAM users have enabled MFA.

Steps to Enable Rule:

1. Go to `AWS Config → Rules`
2. Click `Add Rule`
3. Search for `iam-user-mfa-enabled`
4. Select the rule and click `Save`
5. AWS Config can now monitor users without MFA and mark them as **non-compliant**

Example: Preventing IAM Policies with Wildcards (*)

AWS Config has a managed rule (**`iam-policy-no-statements-with-admin-access`**) to detect IAM policies that grant full access.

Steps to Enable Rule:

1. Navigate to AWS Config → Rules
2. Click **`Add Rule`**
3. Select **`iam-policy-no-statements-with-admin-access`**
4. Save the rule
5. AWS Config will flag any IAM policy that allows full access (*)

Auditing IAM Changes Using AWS Config

AWS Config enables you to audit IAM changes by providing a detailed timeline of configuration updates to IAM roles, users, and policies. You can track changes by navigating AWS Config, selecting the IAM resource, and reviewing the Configuration Timeline to detect unauthorized modifications.

For instance, AWS Config can help you identify when an overly permissive policy is attached or when an IAM user is deleted, showing who made the change and at what time. This visibility enables security teams to respond quickly to suspicious activity and maintain compliance.

Viewing IAM Configuration Changes

AWS Config provides a timeline of changes to IAM resources.

Steps to View IAM Change History:

1. Navigate to **`AWS Config → Resources`**
2. Select **`IAM Role/User/Policy`**
3. Click a resource to view **`Configuration Timeline`**
4. Compare changes to detect unauthorized modifications

Example: Detecting Unauthorized IAM Policy Changes

1. A **security team reviews AWS Config logs**.
2. They notice a **user attached an overly permissive IAM policy**.

3. AWS Config **flags the change** and provides details.
4. Security **removes the policy** and investigates the incident.

Example: Tracking Deleted IAM Users

If an IAM user is deleted, AWS Config logs provide historical details:

1. Navigate to **`AWS Config → Resources`**
2. Search for the deleted IAM user
3. Review the **`Change Timeline`** to identify who deleted the user and when

Automating IAM Compliance with AWS Config and AWS Lambda

Automating IAM compliance using AWS Config and AWS Lambda helps maintain a secure and consistent access environment. This integration enables real-time detection and automatic remediation of IAM misconfigurations without manual intervention.

Setting Up Automatic Remediation

AWS Config can trigger **AWS Lambda functions** to **remediate IAM misconfigurations**.

Example: Auto-Enforcing MFA for IAM Users

If AWS Lambda detects an IAM user without MFA, it can:

- Send an **email notification** to the user
- Automatically **disable the user's access**

Steps to Set Up Automation:

1. **Create an AWS Lambda function** to check IAM user MFA status
2. Configure AWS Config to **trigger the Lambda function** whenever a violation occurs
3. Lambda will enforce the required security action (like notifying or disabling the user)

Sample Lambda Code to Enforce MFA

```
import boto3

iam = boto3.client('iam')
```

```
def lambda_handler(event, context):
    user = event['detail']['configuration']['userName']
    response = iam.list_mfa_devices(UserName=user)
    if not response['MFADevices']:
        print(f"User {user} has no MFA. Taking action.")
        iam.update_login_profile(UserName=user, PasswordReset
Required=True)
```

This function forces a **password reset** for users without MFA.

Best Practices for IAM Auditing with AWS Config

Following the best practices for IAM auditing with AWS Config ensures consistent monitoring, streamlined compliance, and early detection of security gaps. Implementing these measures strengthens identity governance across all AWS accounts.

- **Enable AWS Config across All AWS Accounts**
  - Use **AWS Organizations** to enable AWS Config in multiple accounts
  - Store AWS Config logs in a **centralized S3 bucket**
- **Implement Custom AWS Config Rules for IAM Security**
  - Use AWS Lambda to create **custom rules** tailored to your security policies
  - Example: Flag IAM users **without access key rotation** in 90 days
- **Regularly Review Compliance Reports**
  - Schedule periodic reviews of **non-compliant IAM users and roles**
  - Use AWS Security Hub to **aggregate IAM security findings**
- **Integrate AWS Config with CloudTrail**
  - **AWS CloudTrail** records IAM API calls, while **AWS Config tracks resource changes**
  - Use **Amazon GuardDuty** to detect suspicious IAM activities
- **Automate IAM Policy Remediation**
  - Use AWS Lambda and AWS Config to **auto-revoke overly permissive IAM policies**
  - Implement least privilege access policies to secure access

AWS Config is a powerful tool for **auditing IAM configurations**, detecting unauthorized changes, and ensuring compliance. By implementing **AWS Config rules, automation with AWS Lambda, and periodic reviews**, organizations can maintain a secure IAM posture. Integrating AWS Config with **AWS CloudTrail, AWS**

Security Hub, and AWS Organizations further strengthens security across AWS accounts.

Hands-on Lab: Setting Up Secure IAM Roles and Policies

In this hands-on lab, we will walk you through the process of setting up **secure IAM roles and policies** in AWS. IAM roles allow AWS services and applications to interact securely, while IAM policies define **permissions and access control**. By the end of this lab, you will be able to:

- Create **secure IAM roles** for different AWS services
- Implement **least privilege access** with IAM policies
- Test and verify role-based access control

Prerequisites

Before getting started, make sure that you have the following:

- **An AWS account** with administrator access.
- **AWS CLI installed** on your local machine.
- **IAM permissions** to create roles and policies, and attach them.

Step 1: Creating an IAM Role for EC2

1. **Navigate to IAM Role Creation**
    a. Sign in to the **`AWS Management Console`**
    b. Go to **`IAM → Roles`**
    c. Click **`Create Role`**
2. **Choose Trusted Entity**
    a. Select **`AWS Service`**
    b. Choose **`EC2`** as the trusted service
    c. Click **`Next`**
3. **Attach a Policy**

For secure access, create a **custom policy** that grants read-only access to Amazon S3.

Example IAM Policy (s3-readonly-policy)

```
{
    "Version": "2012-10-17",
    "Statement": [
        {
            "Effect": "Allow",
            "Action": ["s3:GetObject", "s3:ListBucket"],
            "Resource": ["arn:aws:s3:::example-bucket",
"arn:aws:s3:::example-bucket/*"]
        }
    ]
}
```

Steps to Create and Attach an IAM Policy

1. Click `Create Policy` and paste the JSON above
2. Name the policy `s3-readonly-policy`
3. Attach this policy to the role

4. **Create the Role**
    a. Name the role `ec2-s3-readonly-role`
    b. Click `Create Role`

Step 2: Attaching the IAM Role to an EC2 Instance

1. Launch an **EC2 instance** from the AWS Console
2. Under **IAM role**, select `ec2-s3-readonly-role`
3. Complete the instance setup and launch it
4. SSH into the EC2 instance and verify access:

    ```
    aws s3 ls s3://example-bucket
    ```
5. If access is denied, review the policy and role assignment.

Step 3: Creating an IAM Role for Lambda

1. **Create a New Role**
    a. Go to `IAM → Roles → Create Role`
    b. Select `AWS Service → Lambda`
2. **Attach a Custom Policy for Logging**

Lambda functions often need to log events in **Amazon CloudWatch**. Create this policy:

Example IAM Policy (lambda-logging-policy)

```
{
    "Version": "2012-10-17",
    "Statement": [
        {
            "Effect": "Allow",
            "Action": ["logs:CreateLogGroup", "logs:Create
LogStream", "logs:PutLogEvents"],
            "Resource": "arn:aws:logs:*:*:*"
        }
    ]
}
```

3. **Assign the Role to Lambda**
   a. Create a Lambda function in AWS Console
   b. Under **Permissions**, select **`Lambda-Logging-Role`**
   c. Deploy a test function and verify logs in **Amazon CloudWatch**

Step 4: Testing and Verifying IAM Roles

To verify access:

a. Use **AWS CLI** or **AWS SDK** to assume roles
b. Check permissions using AWS STS **`get-caller-identity`**
c. Test unauthorized actions to ensure proper restrictions

Best Practices for Secure IAM Roles and Policies

Adhering to best practices for IAM roles and policies helps maintain strong access controls and minimizes the risk of unauthorized actions. Implementing these measures ensures secure, compliant, and well-managed IAM configurations across your AWS environment.

- **Follow Least Privilege**: Grant only required permissions
- **Enable MFA** for sensitive roles
- **Monitor Role Activity**: Use AWS CloudTrail for auditing
- Rotate IAM Credentials Regularly

You have successfully set up **secure IAM roles and policies** for AWS services like **EC2 and Lambda**. These configurations enhance security and help one follow AWS best practices to establish access control. It is advised to always review IAM policies if you want to **minimize risk and enforce the least privilege access principle**.

Conclusion

This chapter explored the essential best practices for securing AWS environments using Identity and Access Management (IAM). From establishing granular roles and policies, to implementing permission boundaries, these elements work together to enforce the principle of least privilege. We also emphasized the importance of centralized user and group management, password policies, and using temporary credentials to reduce long-term security risks. These strategies ensure that access is both secure and manageable across a growing cloud infrastructure.

We also covered the critical role of Multi-Factor Authentication (MFA) in reducing the risk of compromised credentials, besides the value of auditing IAM changes using AWS Config to maintain visibility and detect misconfigurations. The section on hands-on guidance reinforced how to apply these concepts in real AWS environments. Considered together, these IAM best practices create a strong foundation for cloud security.

In the next chapter on **Data Protection and Encryption**, we will explore how to safeguard sensitive data using encryption at rest and in-transit, AWS Key Management Service (KMS), and data classification strategies to meet compliance and regulatory requirements.

References

- AWS Identity and Access Management (IAM) User Guide: https://docs.aws.amazon.com/IAM/latest/UserGuide/introduction.html
- AWS IAM Policy Reference: https://docs.aws.amazon.com/IAM/latest/UserGuide/reference_policies.html
- AWS Policy Examples: https://docs.aws.amazon.com/IAM/latest/UserGuide/access_policies_examples.html
- IAM JSON Policy Elements: https://docs.aws.amazon.com/IAM/latest/UserGuide/reference_policies_elements.html
- AWS STS AssumeRole API: https://docs.aws.amazon.com/STS/latest/APIReference/API_AssumeRole.html
- AWS IAM Role Anywhere: https://docs.aws.amazon.com/rolesanywhere/latest/userguide/introduction.html
- AWS IAM Identity Center (SSO): https://docs.aws.amazon.com/singlesignon/latest/userguide/what-is.html

- AWS Multi-Factor Authentication (MFA): https://docs.aws.amazon.com/IAM/latest/UserGuide/id_credentials_mfa.html
- IAM Best Practices: https://docs.aws.amazon.com/IAM/latest/UserGuide/best-practices.html
- AWS Access Analyzer: https://docs.aws.amazon.com/IAM/latest/UserGuide/access-analyzer.html
- AWS Config: https://docs.aws.amazon.com/config/latest/developerguide/WhatIsConfig.html
- AWS Config Rules: https://docs.aws.amazon.com/config/latest/developerguide/evaluate-config.html
- AWS Lambda Developer Guide: https://docs.aws.amazon.com/lambda/latest/dg/welcome.html
- Cross-Account Access Using IAM Roles: https://docs.aws.amazon.com/IAM/latest/UserGuide/id_roles_common-scenarios_aws-accounts.html
- IAM Federation Using SAML 2.0: https://docs.aws.amazon.com/IAM/latest/UserGuide/id_roles_providers_saml.html
- Web Identity Federation with Cognito: https://docs.aws.amazon.com/cognito/latest/developerguide/cognito-identity.html
- AWS Security Best Practices Whitepaper: https://docs.aws.amazon.com/pdfs/whitepapers/latest/aws-security-best-practices/aws-security-best-practices.pdf
- AWS Well-Architected Framework – Security Pillar: https://docs.aws.amazon.com/wellarchitected/latest/security-pillar/welcome.html

CHAPTER 3
Data Protection and Encryption

Introduction

Data protection has become the foremost priority for organizations operating in the cloud. AWS offers a comprehensive suite of services designed to secure data, which is an invaluable asset for companies today. This chapter explores the tools, techniques, and best practices for protecting data in AWS environments, while emphasizing encryption mechanisms that safeguard information at rest and in transit.

As organizations migrate sensitive workloads to the cloud, ensuring proper data protection is a legal and regulatory necessity, besides being an important technical requirement. Protecting sensitive information like financial records, customer information, healthcare data, and intellectual property requires a strategic approach that combines AWS services with well-designed security controls.

We will learn about AWS Key Management Service (KMS)—the centrepiece of AWS's encryption capabilities, and how it integrates with services like Amazon S3, RDS, and EBS to provide seamless protection. In further sections of this chapter, you will also learn about encryption types, key management strategies, and compliance frameworks that govern data protection. By the end of it, you will be equipped with the knowledge to implement robust data protection mechanisms that align with industry best practices and regulatory requirements.

Structure

In this chapter, we will cover the following topics:

- Data Protection Fundamentals in AWS
    - Shared Responsibility Model for Data Protection
    - The CIA Triad in Cloud Data Security
    - Data States That Require Protection (At Rest, In Transit, In Use)

- Data Classification in AWS
- Key Encryption Concepts (Symmetric, Asymmetric, and Envelope Encryption)

- AWS Key Management Service (KMS)
  - Core Components of KMS (CMKs, Key Policies, Grants, Data Keys)
  - How KMS Works: Envelope Encryption
  - Key Rotation and Lifecycle Management
  - KMS Integration with AWS CloudTrail
  - Creating and Managing KMS Keys
  - Monitoring and Pricing Considerations
- Encryption for AWS Services
  - S3 Encryption Mechanisms (SSE-S3, SSE-KMS, SSE-C, and Client-Side Encryption)
  - RDS Encryption Options (At Rest, In Transit, and TDE)
  - EBS Volume Encryption (Working, Benefits, and Best Practices)
- Securing Data In-Transit
  - TLS/SSL Encryption for Network Communication
  - VPN and Direct Connect Encryption Options
  - Using AWS Certificate Manager (ACM) for Managing Certificates
- Compliance and Regulatory Considerations
  - Understanding Data Protection Regulations (GDPR, HIPAA, PCI DSS)
  - Mapping AWS Services to Compliance Controls
  - Implementing Auditing and Reporting for Encrypted Resources
- Key Management Best Practices
  - Enforcing Least Privilege for Key Usage
  - Automating Key Rotation and Revocation
  - Monitoring Key Access with CloudTrail and CloudWatch
  - Using Customer-Managed Keys for Sensitive Workloads

Data Protection Fundamentals in AWS

Before diving into specific AWS encryption services, it is essential to understand the foundational concepts that drive data protection in cloud environments. These fundamentals guide the design and implementation of security controls that safeguard an organization's information.

Shared Responsibility Model for Data Protection

AWS operates under a **shared responsibility model**, where both AWS and the customer have distinct roles in securing data. For data protection:

- **AWS is responsible for**: Securing the underlying infrastructure that runs all AWS services, including physical security of data centres, hardware maintenance, and implementing base-level security for managed services
- **Customers are responsible for**: Protecting their data, encrypting content, managing encryption keys, implementing identity and access controls, and configuring individual AWS services securely

Example: While AWS ensures that S3 is secure, customers must decide the encryption methods to apply to their S3 buckets, who can access the data, and how long do they want to retain sensitive information.

The CIA Triad in Cloud Data Security

The CIA triad–**Confidentiality**, **Integrity**, and **Availability**–forms the backbone of data security principles:

- **Confidentiality**: Ensuring that data is accessible only to authorized individuals. In AWS, confidentiality is maintained through encryption, proper IAM policies, and secure key management
- **Integrity**: Guaranteeing that data remains accurate and unaltered during storage, processing, and transmission. AWS supports integrity through checksums, version controls, and secure API calls
- **Availability**: Making sure data is accessible when needed. AWS provides high availability through redundant systems, multi-AZ deployments, and disaster recovery options

Data States That Require Protection

Data exists in three states, with each requiring specific protection mechanisms:

- **Data at Rest**: Refers to information stored in persistent storage systems (S3 buckets, EBS volumes, RDS databases)
    - **Protection mechanisms**: Server-side encryption, client-side encryption, key management

- **Data In-Transit**: Refers to information moving from one location to another (between services, to/from the internet)
    - **Protection mechanisms**: TLS/SSL encryption, VPN connections, AWS PrivateLink
- **Data In-Use**: Information being processed in memory
    - **Protection mechanisms**: Secure enclaves, memory encryption, trusted execution environments

Data Classification in AWS

Implementing effective data protection begins with proper classification. By categorizing data according to sensitivity and criticality, you can apply appropriate protection measures where they matter most.

AWS recommends classifying data into categories such as:

- **Public**: Information that poses no risk if it is disclosed
- **Internal**: Non-sensitive information meant for use within the organization
- **Confidential**: Sensitive information that can cause harm if exposed
- **Restricted**: Highly sensitive information requiring the strictest controls

This classification informs your encryption strategy, access controls, and monitoring requirements for different data types.

Key Encryption Concepts

Before exploring AWS encryption services, let's establish some foundational encryption concepts:

- **Symmetric Encryption**: Uses a single key for both encryption and decryption. It is faster than other methods listed here but requires secure key distribution
- **Asymmetric Encryption**: Uses a key pair (public and private keys), where the public key encrypts data, while the private key decrypts it. This approach solves key distribution challenges but is more computationally intensive
- **Envelope Encryption**: A practice of encrypting data with a data key, then encrypting the data key with a master key. AWS KMS uses this approach to provide scalable key management
- **Key Management**: The process of generating, storing, rotating, and deleting encryption keys securely
- **Key Material:** This is the actual cryptographic secret used for encryption and decryption. In AWS KMS, key material can be generated by AWS (default),

imported by the customer (imported key material), or generated in AWS CloudHSM via a custom key store. Understanding key material is crucial when configuring key rotation, compliance with external requirements, or using multi-tenant vs. single-tenant HSMs

AWS Key Management Service (KMS)

AWS Key Management Service (KMS) is a managed tool that simplifies the process of creating and controlling the keys used to encrypt data. KMS is integrated with many AWS services, providing centralized control over the entire lifecycle of cryptographic keys.

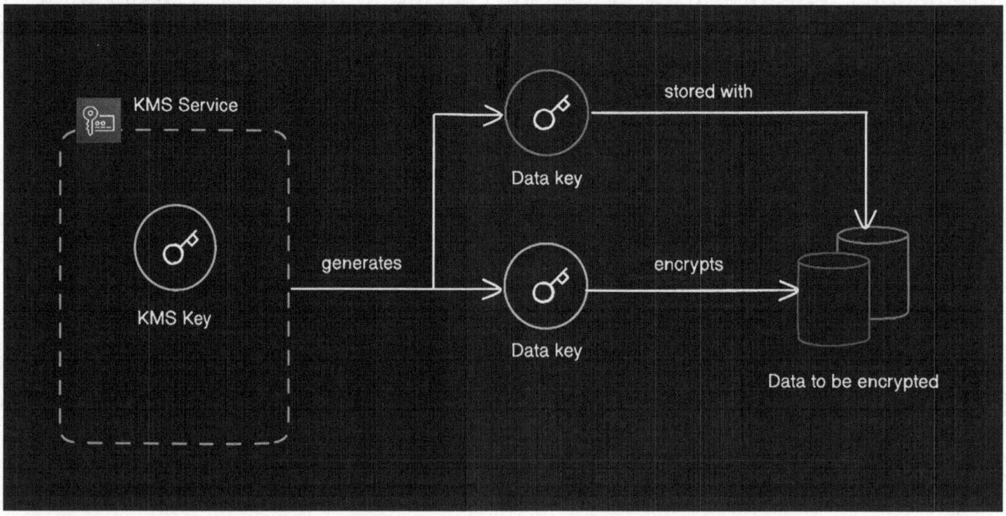

Figure 3.1: *Envelope encryption process where AWS KMS generates a data key to encrypt data and stores the encrypted data key alongside the data*

KMS Core Components

KMS consists of several core components that work together to provide robust encryption capabilities:

Customer Master Keys (CMKs)

Customer Master Keys (CMKs) are the primary resources in KMS. Each CMK contains a key material that is used to encrypt and decrypt data. There are three types of CMKs:

- **AWS-Managed CMKs**: Created, managed, and used on the customer's behalf by AWS. These keys are automatically available in services that are integrated with KMS (for example, `aws/s3`, `aws/ebs`, `aws/rds`)

- **Customer-Managed CMKs**: Created, managed, and used by customers. These provide more control, allowing you to establish and maintain key policies, enable/disable keys, rotate key material, and add tags
- **AWS-Owned CMKs**: Owned and managed by AWS for use in multiple accounts. Customers cannot view, manage, or audit these keys

Example: When enabling encryption for an RDS database, you can choose either the AWS-managed CMK for RDS (**`aws/rds`**) or a customer-managed CMK that you have created specifically for database encryption.

Key Policies

Key policies are resource policies attached to CMKs that control access to the key. Every CMK has exactly one key policy, which contains statements that determine who can use the key and how they can do it.

Key policies are crucial for the shared responsibility model as they:

- Define administrators who can manage the key
- Define users who can use the key for cryptographic operations
- Enable IAM policies to allow access to the key
- Grant access to AWS services to use the key on your behalf

json

```
{
    "Version": "2012-10-17",
    "Statement": [
        {
            "Sid": "Enable IAM User Permissions",
            "Effect": "Allow",
            "Principal": {"AWS": "arn:aws:iam::111122223333:-
root"},
            "Action": "kms:*",
            "Resource": "*"
        },
        {
            "Sid": "Allow access for Key Administrators",
            "Effect": "Allow",
            "Principal": {"AWS": "arn:aws:iam::111122223333:user/
admin"},
            "Action": [
                "kms:Create*",
                "kms:Describe*",
                "kms:Enable*",
                "kms:List*",
```

```
                "kms:Put*",
                "kms:Update*",
                "kms:Revoke*",
                "kms:Disable*",
                "kms:Get*",
                "kms:Delete*"
            ],
            "Resource": "*"
        },
        {
            "Sid": "Allow use of the key",
            "Effect": "Allow",
            "Principal": {"AWS": "arn:aws:iam::111122223333:user/
developer"},
            "Action": [
                "kms:Encrypt",
                "kms:Decrypt",
                "kms:ReEncrypt*",
                "kms:GenerateDataKey*",
                "kms:DescribeKey"
            ],
            "Resource": "*"
        }
    ]
}
```

Default AWS KMS Key Policy

The default key policy in AWS KMS grants full access to the root user of the AWS account (**`arn:aws:iam::<account-id>:root`**). It allows the account owner to manage the key and delegate further access using IAM policies.

By default, no other users, roles, or services are granted access unless explicitly added. For more granular control, it is recommended to define a custom key policy with specific permissions.

Grants

Grants are another mechanism to control access to CMKs. They allow you to delegate permissions to AWS services or other principals without modifying the key policy. Grants are commonly used to allow AWS services to use a CMK on behalf of a user.

Example: When enabling S3 bucket encryption with a customer managed CMK, S3 needs permission to use that CMK to encrypt and decrypt objects as they are uploaded and downloaded. Rather than modifying the key policy, you can create a grant that allows S3-specific permissions.

Data Keys

Data keys are encryption keys that KMS generates using a CMK. Unlike CMKs, which never leave KMS unencrypted, data keys are returned to your application to use for local encryption operations.

When you request a data key, KMS returns two versions:

- A plaintext version that you use for encryption
- An encrypted version (encrypted under the CMK) that you store alongside your encrypted data

This pattern, known as **envelope encryption**, is an efficient way to encrypt large amounts of data or data that must be encrypted outside of AWS.

How KMS Works: Envelope Encryption

KMS uses envelope encryption to provide efficient and secure encryption for your data. Here is how it works:

1. **Request a Data Key**: Your application requests a data key from KMS, specifying which CMK to use to generate and encrypt the data key
2. **Receive Two Versions**: KMS returns both a plaintext version and an encrypted version of the data key
3. **Encrypt Your Data**: Use the plaintext data key to encrypt your data. Then immediately remove the plaintext data key from memory
4. **Store Encrypted Data and Encrypted Key**: Store the encrypted data along with the encrypted data key
5. **Decryption Process**: When you need to decrypt the data, provide the encrypted data key to KMS and specify the CMK used to encrypt it. KMS decrypts the data key and returns the plaintext data key, which you can then use to decrypt your data

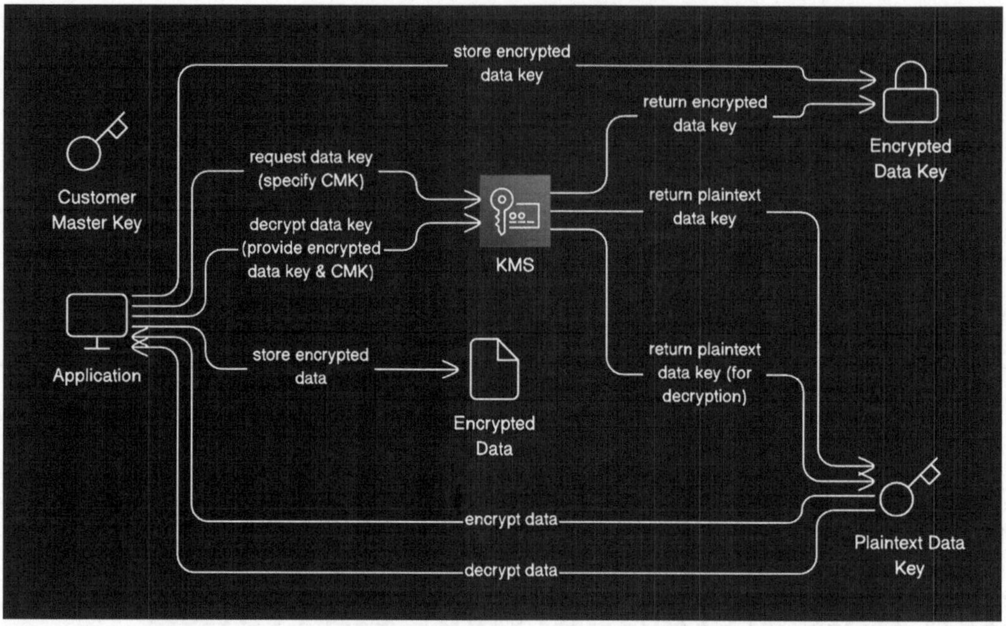

***Figure 3.2**: Envelope encryption workflow with AWS KMS*

Envelope encryption has several advantages:

- Minimizes the amount of data sent to KMS (only encrypting/decrypting the data key)
- Reduces latency by performing encryption operations locally
- Allows encryption of data larger than the KMS API limits
- Provides an additional layer of protection for your data

KMS Key Rotation

Key rotation is a security best practice that involves replacing the key material periodically in a CMK with new key material. This limits the amount of data encrypted under a single key and reduces the impact if the key is compromised.

AWS provides two options for key rotation:

- **Automatic Key Rotation**: For customer managed CMKs, you can enable automatic key rotation, which rotates the key material once per year
- **Manual Key Rotation**: Create a new CMK and change your applications to use the new CMK. This approach grants you control over the timing of the rotation and the key material

When a CMK is rotated, KMS maintains the old key material indefinitely to decrypt data that was encrypted before rotation. Any new data is encrypted with the newest key material.

Exam Tip: *Remember that automatic key rotation is only available for customer managed CMKs with key material generated by KMS. Imported key material cannot be automatically rotated.*

KMS Integration with CloudTrail

AWS CloudTrail logs all KMS API calls, while providing an audit trail of key usage. This integration is critical for monitoring key usage, detecting unauthorized access attempts, and meeting compliance requirements.

Every API call to KMS is recorded in CloudTrail logs, including:

- Who made the request
- When was the request made
- Which service was used
- What actions were performed
- Which resources were acted upon

Here is a sample CloudTrail log entry for a KMS Decrypt operation:

json

```
{
    "eventVersion": "1.05",
    "userIdentity": {
        "type": "IAMUser",
        "principalId": "AIDACKCEVSQ6C2EXAMPLE",
        "arn": "arn:aws:iam::111122223333:user/developer",
        "accountId": "111122223333",
        "accessKeyId": "AKIAIOSFODNN7EXAMPLE",
        "userName": "developer"
    },
    "eventTime": "2020-07-25T23:41:52Z",
    "eventSource": "kms.amazonaws.com",
    "eventName": "Decrypt",
    "awsRegion": "us-west-2",
    "sourceIPAddress": "192.0.2.0",
    "userAgent": "aws-cli/1.18.97 Python/3.6.10 Linux-
/4.9.217-0.1.ac.205.84.332.metal1.x86_64 botocore/1.17.20",
    "requestParameters": {
        "encryptionContext": {
```

```
            "aws:s3:arn": "arn:aws:s3:::example-bucket/example
-object"
        },
        "keyId": "arn:aws:kms:us-west-2:111122223333:key/1234ab-
cd-12ab-34cd-56ef-1234567890ab"
    },
    "responseElements": null,
    "requestID": "a9d9fcf1-2eca-4ab8-a5a9-EXAMPLE",
    "eventID": "38b9a3f2-26d4-417e-9aca-EXAMPLE",
    "readOnly": true,
    "resources": [
        {
            "accountId": "111122223333",
            "type": "AWS::KMS::Key",
            "ARN": "arn:aws:kms:us-west-
2:111122223333:key/1234abcd-12ab-34cd-56ef-1234567890ab"
        }
    ],
    "eventType": "AwsApiCall",
    "managementEvent": true,
    "recipientAccountId": "111122223333"
}
```


Creating and Managing KMS Keys

It is time to review the process of creating and managing a customer managed CMK in KMS:

Creating a CMK

Steps to Create a Customer Managed Key (CMK):

1. **Navigate to the KMS Console**: Go to the AWS Management Console and open the KMS service
2. **Create Key**: Choose **`"Create key"`** to begin the process
3. **Configure Key**: Select the key type (symmetric or asymmetric), key usage (encrypt/decrypt or sign/verify), and key material origin (KMS, external, or AWS CloudHSM)
4. **Add Labels**: Provide an alias and description for the key
5. **Define Administrative Permissions**: Select the IAM users and roles that can administer (but not use) the key
6. **Define Usage Permissions**: Select the IAM users and roles that can use the key for cryptographic operations

7. **Review and Finish**: Review the key policy and create the key

Managing CMK Permissions

After creating a CMK, you can manage permissions using:

- **Key Policies**: Edit the key policy to add or remove permissions
- **IAM Policies**: Use IAM policies in conjunction with key policies to control access
- **Grants**: Create, retire, and revoke grants to delegate permissions for specific operations

Example IAM Policy for KMS Access

json

```
{
    "Version": "2012-10-17",
    "Statement": [
        {
            "Effect": "Allow",
            "Action": [
                "kms:Encrypt",
                "kms:Decrypt",
                "kms:ReEncrypt*",
                "kms:GenerateDataKey*",
                "kms:DescribeKey"
            ],
            "Resource": "arn:aws:kms:us-west-
2:111122223333:key/1234abcd-12ab-34cd-56ef-1234567890ab"
        }
    ]
}
```

Monitoring CMK Usage

KMS integrates with AWS CloudWatch to provide metrics on key usage. Key metrics to monitor include:

- **`ServiceCountExceeded`:** The number of times requests were throttled because they exceeded the request quota
- **`5MinuteRequestCount`:** The number of requests processed by KMS in a 5-minute period

Setting up CloudWatch alarms on these metrics can allow you to detect unusual patterns that might indicate unauthorized access or misconfigured applications.

KMS Pricing Considerations

When using KMS, consider the following pricing factors:

- **Monthly Fee:** Every customer-managed CMK incurs a monthly fee
- **API Requests:** Each API request to KMS incurs a fee, which depends on the type of request
- **AWS Managed CMKs:** There is no monthly fee for AWS managed CMKs, but you will still incur charges for processing API requests

For cost optimization, consider:

- Using AWS managed CMKs when appropriate
- Implementing client-side caching for data keys to reduce API calls
- Using envelope encryption to minimize interactions with KMS

Encryption for AWS Services

AWS provides integrated encryption capabilities across its service portfolio. We will now learn how encryption works with three key services: Amazon S3, Amazon RDS, and Amazon EBS.

S3 Encryption Mechanisms

Amazon S3 (Simple Storage Service) is one of the most widely used AWS services, storing objects ranging from public web assets to highly sensitive data. S3 offers multiple ways to encrypt data, which gives you flexibility to meet your security and compliance requirements.

Server-Side Encryption Options

S3 provides three options for server-side encryption:

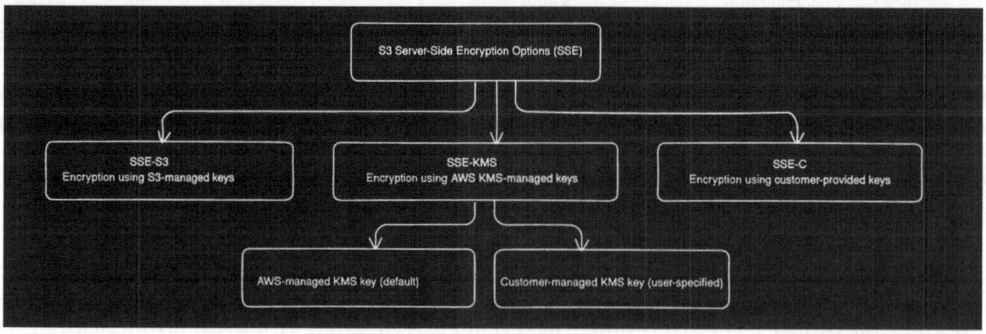

Figure 3.3: *S3 Encryption Options*

- **Server-Side Encryption with Amazon S3-Managed Keys (SSE-S3)**

  SSE-S3 is the simplest encryption option, where S3 handles both the encryption and the encryption keys.

  - S3 encrypts each object with a unique key
  - The object key itself is encrypted with a master key that S3 regularly rotates
  - S3 uses AES-256 encryption algorithm
  - Simply add the header **`x-amz-server-side-encryption: AES256`** to your PUT request

Example S3 API call with SSE-S3:

bash

```
aws s3api put-object \
  --bucket my-bucket \
  --key my-file.txt \
  --body my-file.txt \
  --server-side-encryption AES256
```

When to use SSE-S3: This is suitable when you wish to encrypt data but don't need to manage the encryption keys. It is the easiest option to implement and use.

- **Server-Side Encryption with AWS KMS Keys (SSE-KMS)**

  SSE-KMS offers additional benefits beyond SSE-S3 by using AWS KMS to manage your encryption keys.

  - Provides an additional layer of protection and control over your keys
  - Enables audit trails via CloudTrail to see who used which keys to access particular objects
  - Offers user control over key permissions
  - Supports automatic key rotation

Example S3 API call with SSE-KMS:

bash

```
aws s3api put-object \
  --bucket my-bucket \
  --key my-file.txt \
  --body my-file.txt \
  --server-side-encryption aws:kms \
  --ssekms-key-id 1234abcd-12ab-34cd-56ef-1234567890ab
```

When to use SSE-KMS: Use this option when you need additional control over your encryption keys, or when you need to track who accessed encrypted objects.

- **Server-Side Encryption with Customer-Provided Keys (SSE-C)**

  SSE-C allows you to provide your own encryption keys that you manage outside of AWS.

  - You start by providing the encryption key as part of your request to S3
  - S3 performs the encryption/decryption operations
  - AWS does not store your encryption key
  - You must provide the same key for retrieval

Example S3 API call with SSE-C:

bash

```
aws s3api put-object \
  --bucket my-bucket \
  --key my-file.txt \
  --body my-file.txt \
  --sse-customer-algorithm AES256 \
  --sse-customer-key $(echo -n "your-secret-key-in-base64" |
base64)
```

When to use SSE-C: This is appropriate when you need to maintain control of your encryption keys but want to leverage S3's server-side encryption capabilities.

Client-Side Encryption for S3

If you prefer to encrypt your data before it leaves your client, you can implement client-side encryption:

- **Client-Side Encryption with AWS KMS-Managed Keys (CSE-KMS)**
  - You use KMS to generate a data key
  - The client encrypts the data with the data key
  - The encrypted data key is stored alongside the encrypted data
  - AWS S3 Encryption Client can simplify this process
- **Client-Side Encryption with Client-Side Master Keys (CSE-C)**
  - You manage and protect your master keys
  - The client encrypts the data before sending to S3
  - The keys never leave your control or get sent to AWS
  - You are responsible for key protection and management

When to use client-side encryption: You may use this approach when you need end-to-end control of the encryption process, or have compliance requirements that mandate data encryption before leaving your environment.

Default Encryption for S3 Buckets

To ensure all objects are encrypted when stored in S3, you can enable default encryption at the bucket level via the following steps:

1. **Navigate to S3 Console**: Select your bucket and go to the "**Properties**" tab
2. **Default Encryption**: Choose either SSE-S3 or SSE-KMS
3. **Select KMS Key (if applicable)**: If using SSE-KMS, specify which KMS key to use

Alternatively, you can use a bucket policy to enforce encryption:

json

```
{
    "Version": "2012-10-17",
    "Statement": [
        {
            "Effect": "Deny",
            "Principal": "*",
            "Action": "s3:PutObject",
            "Resource": "arn:aws:s3:::my-bucket/*",
            "Condition": {
                "StringNotEquals": {
                    "s3:x-amz-server-side-encryption": "AES256"
                }
            }
        }
    ]
}
```

This policy denies **PutObject** requests that don't include the SSE-S3 encryption header.

RDS Encryption Options

Amazon Relational Database Service (RDS) stores some of the most sensitive data in many organizations. Encryption for RDS helps protect this data, providing security for databases containing personal information, financial data, or intellectual property.

RDS Encryption at Rest

When you enable encryption for an RDS instance, AWS automatically encrypts:

- The underlying storage for the DB instance

- Automated backups
- Read replicas
- Snapshots

RDS encryption at rest uses the AWS KMS service and can only be enabled during instance creation. The encryption process is transparent to the application, meaning:

- No modifications to your database clients are required
- There is minimal impact on database performance
- AWS handles all the encryption/decryption processes automatically

Steps to enable encryption for a new RDS instance

1. **Navigate to RDS Console**: Start the DB instance creation process
2. **Configure Advanced Settings**: Find the "`Encryption`" section
3. **Enable Encryption**: Check "`Enable Encryption`"
4. **Select KMS Key**: Choose an AWS managed key or a customer-managed key

Important Limitations

- You cannot enable encryption on an existing unencrypted RDS instance
- You cannot change the KMS key once the instance is created
- You cannot convert an encrypted instance to an unencrypted one

Migrating from Unencrypted to Encrypted RDS Instances

If you have an existing unencrypted RDS instance that you want to encrypt, you can use the following process:

1. **Create a Snapshot:** Take a snapshot of your unencrypted DB instance
2. **Copy the Snapshot:** Create an encrypted copy of the snapshot (you can enable encryption while copying)
3. **Restore from Snapshot:** Create a new DB instance from the encrypted snapshot
4. **Update Application:** Point your application to the new encrypted DB instance
5. **Verify and Decommission:** Verify that everything works, and then decommission the old instance

   bash

   ```
   # Create a snapshot
   aws rds create-db-snapshot \
   ```

```
    --db-instance-identifier myinstance \
    --db-snapshot-identifier mydbsnapshot

  # Copy and encrypt the snapshot
  aws rds copy-db-snapshot \
    --source-db-snapshot-identifier mydbsnapshot \
    --target-db-snapshot-identifier myencryptedsnapshot \
    --kms-key-id arn:aws:kms:us-west-2:111122223333:key/1234abcd-
  12ab-34cd-56ef-1234567890ab

  # Restore from the encrypted snapshot
  aws rds restore-db-instance-from-db-snapshot \
    --db-instance-identifier mynewencryptedinstance \
    --db-snapshot-identifier myencryptedsnapshot
```

RDS Encryption in Transit

To secure data in transit to and from your RDS instances, AWS supports SSL/TLS encryption for all database engines. The configuration varies by engine:

MySQL and MariaDB

sql

```
-- Connect using SSL
mysql -h myinstance.rds.amazonaws.com --ssl-ca=rds-ca-2019-root.pem

-- Require SSL for all connections (run on the DB)
GRANT USAGE ON *.* TO 'mysqluser'@'%' REQUIRE SSL;
```

PostgreSQL

sql

```
-- Enable SSL requirement in PostgreSQL
ALTER USER postgres PASSWORD 'new-password' CONNECTION LIMIT 10 VALID
UNTIL '2023-01-01' CONNECTION SECURITY SSL;

-- Configure pg_hba.conf to require SSL
host all all 0.0.0.0/0 require ssl
```

Oracle

sql

```
-- Force SSL for Oracle connections
ALTER SYSTEM SET SQLNET.ENCRYPTION_SERVER=REQUIRED SCOPE=BOTH;
ALTER SYSTEM SET SQLNET.ENCRYPTION_TYPES_SERVER='AES256' SCOPE=BOTH;
```

SQL Server

sql

```
-- For SQL Server, enable encryption in the connection string
"Server=myinstance.rds.amazonaws.com;Encrypt=True;"
```

RDS and Transparent Data Encryption (TDE)

For SQL Server Enterprise Edition and Oracle Enterprise Edition, RDS supports Transparent Data Encryption (TDE):

- **Oracle TDE**: Encrypts data before it is written to storage
- **SQL Server TDE**: Performs real-time I/O encryption and decryption of data and log files

Best Practices for RDS Encryption

Implementing encryption best practices for Amazon RDS ensures that sensitive data remains secure throughout its lifecycle. Following these guidelines helps maintain compliance, minimize risks, and strengthen overall database security in AWS environments.

- **Enable encryption for all production RDS instances** to protect sensitive data
- **Use customer managed KMS keys** for greater control over key rotation and access
- **Audit access to encrypted databases** using CloudTrail
- **Implement encryption in transit** using SSL/TLS connections
- **Rotate database credentials regularly** to limit exposure
- **Consider using Parameter Groups** to enforce SSL connections

EBS Volume Encryption

Amazon Elastic Block Store (EBS) provides persistent block storage volumes for use with Amazon EC2 instances. EBS encryption offers a straightforward way to encrypt data at rest on these volumes.

Working of EBS Encryption

When you create an encrypted EBS volume, AWS performs the following steps:

1. AWS generates a data key from your specified KMS key.
2. AWS stores the encrypted data key with the volume metadata.
3. When the volume is attached to an EC2 instance, AWS calls KMS to decrypt the data key.

4. AWS uses the decrypted data key in the hypervisor memory to encrypt disk I/O.
5. The decrypted data key never leaves the host and is removed from memory whenever the instance is stopped or terminated.

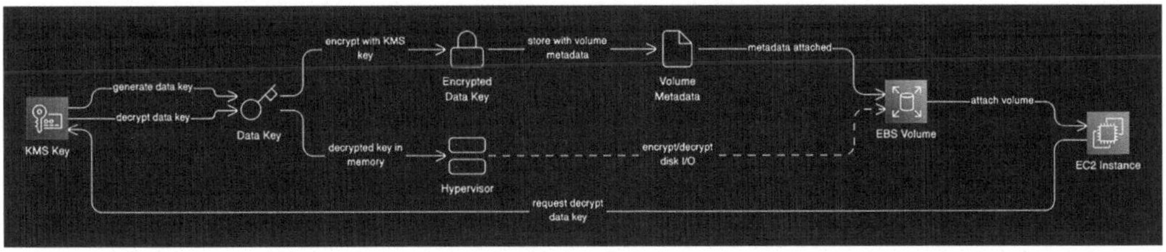

Figure 3.4: *How AWS KMS encrypts and decrypts EBS volumes by generating a data key, storing its encrypted form in volume metadata, and using the decrypted key in memory for disk I/O*

This process is fully managed by AWS, with no action required from you or your applications.

Key benefits of EBS encryption include:

- Data at rest is encrypted inside the volume.
- All data moving between the volume and the instance is encrypted.
- All snapshots created from the volume are encrypted.
- All volumes created from those snapshots are encrypted.

Enabling EBS Encryption

You can enable encryption for new EBS volumes in two ways:

- **Enable encryption for individual volumes**

  Use this when you are creating a new EBS volume:

  bash

  ```
  aws ec2 create-volume \
    --availability-zone us-west-2a \
    --size 100 \
    --volume-type gp2 \
    --encrypted \
    --kms-key-id arn:aws:kms:us-west-2:111122223333:key/1234abcd-
  12ab-34cd-56ef-1234567890ab
  ```

- **Enable encryption by default**

  You can configure your AWS account to encrypt all new EBS volumes automatically in the following manner:

bash

```
aws ec2 enable-ebs-encryption-by-default

# Verify the setting
aws ec2 get-ebs-encryption-by-default
```

When you enable encryption by default, you can specify which KMS key to use:

bash

```
aws ec2 modify-ebs-default-kms-key-id \
  --kms-key-id arn:aws:kms:us-west-2:111122223333:key/1234abcd-
12ab-34cd-56ef-1234567890ab
```

Converting Unencrypted Volumes to Encrypted

Like RDS, you cannot directly encrypt an existing unencrypted EBS volume. Instead, you must:

- **Create a snapshot** of the unencrypted volume
- **Create an encrypted copy** of the snapshot
- **Create a new encrypted volume** from the encrypted snapshot
- **Attach the new volume** to your instance
- **Transfer data** from the old volume to the new encrypted volume (if required)

bash

```
# Create a snapshot
aws ec2 create-snapshot \
  --volume-id vol-1234567890abcdef0 \
  --description "Snapshot of unencrypted volume"

# Create an encrypted copy
aws ec2 copy-snapshot \
  --source-region us-west-2 \
  --source-snapshot-id snap-1234567890abcdef0 \
  --description "Encrypted copy of snapshot" \
  --encrypted \
  --kms-key-id arn:aws:kms:us-west-2:111122223333:key/1234abcd-
12ab-34cd-56ef-1234567890ab

# Create a new volume from the encrypted snapshot
aws ec2 create-volume \
  --availability-zone us-west-2a \
  --snapshot-id snap-0987654321fedcba0 \
  --volume-type gp2
```

EBS Encryption and EC2 Instances

The encryption state of an EBS volume affects how it can be used with EC2 instances:

- **Unencrypted volumes**: Can be attached to any supported instance type
- **Encrypted volumes**: Can only be attached to instance types that support EBS encryption

When you create an Amazon Machine Image (AMI) from an instance with encrypted EBS volumes:

- The AMI includes block device mapping information for the encrypted volumes.
- Instances launched from this AMI use the same KMS key to encrypt their volumes.
- The volumes remain encrypted with the same key.

Monitoring EBS Encryption

You can monitor your EBS encryption usage through:

1. **AWS Config**: Track compliance with rules like ensuring all EBS volumes are encrypted
2. **CloudTrail**: Monitor API calls to KMS for decrypting EBS volume keys
3. **AWS Trusted Advisor**: Check for unencrypted EBS volumes

Setting up AWS Config rule for EBS encryption:

json

```
{
    "ConfigRuleName": "encrypted-volumes",
    "Description": "Checks whether EBS volumes are encrypted",
    "Source": {
        "Owner": "AWS",
        "SourceIdentifier": "ENCRYPTED_VOLUMES"
    },
    "Scope": {
        "ComplianceResourceTypes": [
            "AWS::EC2::Volume"
        ]
    }
}
```

Securing Data in Transit

While encrypting data at rest is crucial, securing data as it travels between services is equally important. AWS provides multiple ways to encrypt data in transit.

Transport Layer Security (TLS)

TLS (and its predecessor, SSL) is a cryptographic protocol that provides communications security over a computer network. AWS services support TLS for securing connections:

- **API Calls**: All AWS API endpoints support HTTPS/TLS.
- **Service-to-Service Communication**: Internal AWS service communications use TLS.
- **Application-Level Communication**: Your applications can use TLS to communicate with AWS services.

To enforce TLS for API calls, you can use IAM policy conditions:

json

```
{
    "Version": "2012-10-17",
    "Statement": [
        {
            "Effect": "Deny",
            "Action": "*",
            "Resource": "*",
            "Condition": {
                "Bool": {
                    "aws:SecureTransport": "false"
                }
            }
        }
    ]
}
```

This policy denies all actions when the request is not using TLS.

AWS Certificate Manager (ACM)

AWS Certificate Manager simplifies managing and deploying TLS certificates:

- **Provision Certificates**: Request and obtain free public certificates for your domains.
- **Certificate Renewal**: ACM handles automatic renewal of your certificates.

- **Integration with AWS Services**: ACM integrates with services such as CloudFront, API Gateway, and Elastic Load Balancing.

Using ACM to secure a public-facing application:

- **Request a certificate** in ACM for your domain
- **Validate ownership** via DNS validation or email validation
- **Deploy the certificate** to a supported AWS service, such as an Application Load Balancer
- **Configure listeners** to use HTTPS with your certificate

VPN Connections

For secure communication between your on-premises network and your AWS VPC, you can use:

AWS Site-to-Site VPN

- Creates an encrypted tunnel between your network and your VPC
- Uses IPsec to protect the connection
- Requires a virtual private gateway on the AWS side and a customer gateway on your end

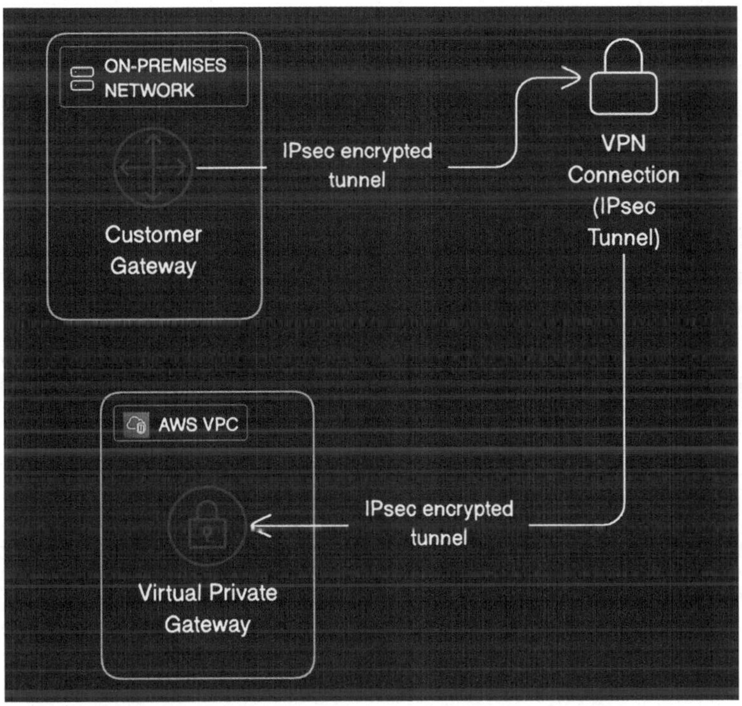

Figure 3.5: *AWS Site-to-Site VPN Architecture*

AWS Client VPN

- Enables secure connections from remote clients to your VPC
- Uses OpenVPN protocol
- Supports certificate-based authentication, Active Directory, and federated authentication

AWS Direct Connect with VPN

- Combines a private, dedicated network connection with an encrypted VPN tunnel
- Provides both privacy and encryption
- Offers higher bandwidth and more consistent performance than internet-based connections

AWS PrivateLink

PrivateLink provides private connectivity between VPCs, AWS services, and on-premises networks:

- Traffic does not traverse the public internet.
- Services appear as if they were in your own VPC.
- No need for VPN, NAT, or internet gateways.

Common use cases include:

- **Secure Inter-VPC Communication**: Connect services across VPCs without exposing them to the internet
- **Private SaaS Access**: Access partner services without exposing your VPC to the internet
- **Hybrid Cloud Connections**: Connect on-premises applications to AWS services securely

API Gateway with Custom Domain Names and TLS

For securing APIs, AWS API Gateway supports:

- **HTTPS Endpoints**: All API Gateway endpoints use HTTPS by default
- **Custom Domain Names**: Associate your APIs with custom domain names
- **TLS Certificates:** Use certificates from ACM to secure your custom domains
- **TLS Version Requirements**: Enforce minimum TLS versions for API clients

To configure minimum TLS version:

bash

```
aws apigateway update-domain-name \
  --domain-name api.example.com \
  --security-policy TLS_1_2
```

Compliance and Regulatory Considerations

Data protection measures must align with legal and regulatory requirements. AWS services are designed to help you meet various compliance obligations, but it is essential to understand your responsibilities.

Key Regulatory Frameworks

Understanding key regulatory frameworks is essential for implementing compliant data protection strategies in AWS. These frameworks define the standards and legal obligations organizations must follow when managing and securing sensitive data in the cloud.

General Data Protection Regulation (GDPR)

GDPR regulates the processing of personal data of EU citizens and residents:

- **Data Encryption**: GDPR encourages, though does not explicitly require, encryption.
- **AWS Services**: KMS, CloudHSM, and encryption features in services such as S3, RDS, and EBS help meet GDPR requirements.
- **Data Subject Rights**: S3 Object Lock and Glacier Vault Lock can help implement retention policies.

Health Insurance Portability and Accountability Act (HIPAA)

HIPAA regulates protected health information (PHI) in the United States:

- **Required Encryption**: HIPAA requires encryption for PHI at rest and in transit
- **Business Associate Agreement (BAA)**: Required for using AWS with PHI
- **Eligible Services**: Not all AWS services are eligible for use with PHI; check AWS's HIPAA eligible services list

Payment Card Industry Data Security Standard (PCI DSS)

PCI DSS applies to organizations handling credit card data:

- **Encryption Requirements**: PCI DSS requires encryption of cardholder data at rest and in transit.
- **Key Management**: Strict requirements for cryptographic key management.
- **AWS Compliance**: Many AWS services are PCI DSS compliant, but you must configure them correctly.

Federal Risk and Authorization Management Program (FedRAMP)

FedRAMP standardizes security assessment and authorization for cloud services used by US federal agencies:

- **Impact Levels**: Different requirements based on information sensitivity
- **Encryption Requirements**: Varies by impact level but generally requires encryption at rest and in transit
- **AWS GovCloud**: Specialized region designed to meet FedRAMP High requirements

AWS Compliance Programs

AWS maintains compliance certifications and attestations, which you can leverage, such as:

- **AWS Artifact**: Portal for on-demand access to AWS compliance documentation.
- **Shared Responsibility**: AWS secures the cloud infrastructure, but you must secure what you put in the cloud.
- **Compliance-Ready Features**: Services such as AWS Config, CloudTrail, and Security Hub help demonstrate compliance.

Implementing Compliance Controls

To meet compliance requirements, consider the following data protection strategies:

- **Data Classification**: Identify and categorize sensitive data based on compliance requirements
- **Encryption Policies**: Define and enforce encryption standards aligned with regulations

- **Access Controls**: Implement least privilege access to sensitive data
- **Audit Logging**: Configure CloudTrail and service-specific logs to track data access
- **Key Management**: Establish processes for secure key management and rotation
- **Monitoring and Alerting**: Set up automated detection of compliance violations

Key Management Best Practices

Effective key management is important to maintain the security of your encrypted data. Follow these best practices to protect your encryption keys:

Key Lifecycle Management

- **Key Generation**: Use proper entropy sources for key generation, or leverage AWS KMS for this purpose
- **Key Storage**: Store keys securely, preferably using a dedicated key management system like AWS KMS
- **Key Usage**: Limit the scope and permissions for each key
- **Key Rotation**: Rotate keys regularly to limit the risk of compromise
- **Key Retirement**: Properly archive keys that are no longer being used actively
- **Key Deletion**: Have a process for securely deleting keys when they are no longer needed

Implementing Key Rotation

Regular key rotation is a security best practice that helps in:

- Limiting the amount of data protected by a single key
- Reducing the impact of a compromised key
- Meeting compliance requirements

For AWS KMS keys, implement rotation in one of the two ways:

Automatic Rotation: Enable automatic annual rotation for KMS-generated CMKs

bash

```
aws kms enable-key-rotation \
1.  --key-id 1234abcd-12ab-34cd-56ef-1234567890ab
```

Manual Rotation: Create a new CMK and update applications to use it.

bash

```
# Create new CMK
aws kms create-key --description "New key for rotation"

# Update alias to point to new key
aws kms update-alias \
  --alias-name alias/my-key \
2.  --target-key-id 9876dcba-98fe-76dc-54ba-1234567890ab
```

Multi-Region Keys

For applications that operate across multiple AWS regions, consider using KMS multi-region keys:

- **Primary Key**: Create a primary key in one region
- **Replica Keys**: Create replica keys in other regions with the same key ID and material
- **Benefits**: Encrypt in one region and decrypt in another without having to re-encrypt

bash

```
# Create a multi-region primary key
aws kms create-key \
  --multi-region \
  --description "Multi-region primary key"

# Create a replica in another region
aws kms replicate-key \
  --key-id 1234abcd-12ab-34cd-56ef-1234567890ab \
  --replica-region eu-west-1
```

Using AWS CloudHSM with KMS

For the highest level of key control, consider integrating AWS CloudHSM with KMS:

1. **Create a CloudHSM Cluster**: Deploy a dedicated hardware security module
2. **Configure a Custom Key Store**: Connect KMS to your CloudHSM cluster
3. **Create CMKs in the Custom Key Store**: Generate keys that are protected by the HSM

Benefits of this approach include:

- Keys are generated and used exclusively within HSMs.
- Keys never leave the HSM unencrypted.
- FIPS 140-2 Level 3 validated hardware.
- Single-tenant HSM access.

Monitoring Key Usage

Implement comprehensive monitoring of your encryption keys:

1. **CloudTrail Logs**: Review all KMS API calls to detect unauthorized access
2. **CloudWatch Alarms**: Set alerts to detect unusual key usage patterns
3. **AWS Config Rules**: Check for proper key configuration and compliance
4. **Key Tags**: Use tags to organize keys and control access based on tags

Example CloudWatch alarm for detecting unusual key usage:

bash

```
aws cloudwatch put-metric-alarm \
  --alarm-name KMS-UnusualUsage \
  --metric-name NumberOfOperationsPerformed \
  --namespace AWS/KMS \
  --statistic Sum \
  --period 300 \
  --threshold 100 \
  --comparison-operator GreaterThanThreshold \
  --dimensions Name=KeyId,Value=1234abcd-12ab-34cd-56ef-
1234567890ab \
  --evaluation-periods 1 \
  --alarm-actions arn:aws:sns:us-west-2:111122223333:Security
Alerts
```

Backup and Recovery of Keys

Plan for key backup and recovery:

- **Document Key Metadata**: Maintain extensive records of key IDs, aliases, and usage
- **Export Asymmetric Key Pairs**: For asymmetric CMKs, export the public key for verification

- **Consider Key Material Import**: For critical keys, consider importing your own key material to maintain a backup
- **Test Recovery Procedures**: Regularly practice key recovery scenarios

Conclusion

So far, this chapter has provided you a comprehensive overview of data protection and encryption in AWS. We have explored the fundamental concepts of encryption, the capabilities of AWS Key Management Service, and detailed encryption options for key AWS services including S3, RDS, and EBS.

The sections above have also examined how to secure data in-transit using technologies like TLS, discussed regulatory compliance considerations, and shared key management best practices. The hands-on lab demonstrated how to implement a comprehensive encryption solution for a financial application, with encryption at-rest and in-transit.

By implementing the encryption strategies discussed in this chapter, you can enhance the security posture of your AWS environment significantly and protect sensitive data from unauthorized access. Remember that encryption is just one aspect of a defence-in-depth strategy, and should be combined with proper access controls, network security, and monitoring to create a comprehensive security solution.

In the next chapter, we will build on these foundational aspects to explore network security in AWS, including VPC configuration, security groups, network ACLs, and AWS firewall services that protect your resources from network-based threats.

Points to Remember

- AWS KMS is the central service for encryption key management in AWS, supporting both AWS-managed and customer-managed keys.
- Envelope encryption is used to secure data while minimizing the amount of data sent to KMS, improving performance and reducing cost.
- S3 offers multiple encryption options: SSE-S3 (AWS managed), SSE-KMS (KMS managed), and SSE-C (customer provided keys).
- RDS encryption must be enabled at the time of creating an instance. It encrypts the database, backups, and snapshots, and also reads replicas.
- EBS encryption can be enabled by default in your account and encrypts both volumes and snapshots.
- Use AWS Certificate Manager and TLS to secure data in transit between services and clients.

- Implement key rotation to limit the amount of data encrypted with a single key version and reduce the impact of key compromise.
- Regulatory frameworks like GDPR, HIPAA, and PCI DSS often require encryption of sensitive data both at rest and in-transit.
- Monitoring KMS usage through CloudTrail and CloudWatch is essential for detecting unauthorized access and ensuring compliance.

Multiple Choice Questions

1. Which AWS service provides centralized management of encryption keys?
    a. AWS IAM
    b. AWS KMS
    c. AWS CloudHSM
    d. AWS Inspector
2. Which encryption technique does AWS KMS use to avoid sending large amounts of data to the KMS service?
    a. Asymmetric encryption
    b. Hardware security modules
    c. Envelope encryption
    d. Client-side encryption
3. Which S3 encryption option allows customers to provide their own keys but lets AWS perform the encryption?
    a. SSE-S3
    b. SSE-KMS
    c. SSE-C
    d. CSE-KMS
4. Once an RDS instance is launched without encryption, how can you encrypt its data?
    a. Enable encryption directly on the instance
    b. Create a snapshot, copy it with encryption enabled, and restore from the encrypted snapshot

   c. Use AWS DMS to migrate data to an encrypted instance
   d. Both b and c are correct

5. Which service should you use to simplify the provisioning and management of SSL/TLS certificates?
   a. AWS IAM
   b. AWS KMS
   c. AWS Certificate Manager
   d. AWS Secrets Manager

6. When using KMS customer managed keys, what is the default key rotation period when automatic rotation is enabled?
   a. 30 days
   b. 90 days
   c. 1 year
   d. 3 years

7. Which of the following is NOT a valid encryption option for Amazon S3?
   a. Server-Side Encryption with S3-Managed Keys (SSE-S3)
   b. Server-Side Encryption with KMS-Managed Keys (SSE-KMS)
   c. Server-Side Encryption with EC2-Managed Keys (SSE-EC2)
   d. Server-Side Encryption with Customer-Provided Keys (SSE-C)

8. Which IAM policy condition can be used to enforce TLS for all AWS API calls?
   a. `aws`
   b. `aws: SecureTransport`
   c. `ats`
   d. `ams`

9. What happens to your data if you delete a KMS key that was used to encrypt it?
   a. The data is automatically decrypted before the key is deleted.
   b. The data remains encrypted but can no longer be decrypted.
   c. AWS automatically re-encrypts the data with a new key.
   d. AWS prevents the key deletion if it is still in use.

10. Which AWS service is designed for workloads that require FIPS 140-2 Level 3 validated hardware for key management?
    a. AWS KMS
    b. AWS CloudHSM
    c. AWS Secrets Manager
    d. AWS Certificate Manager

Answers

1. b
2. c
3. c
4. d
5. c
6. c
7. c
8. b
9. b
10. b

References

- AWS Key Management Service Developer Guide: https://docs.aws.amazon.com/kms/latest/developerguide/
- Amazon S3 Encryption: https://docs.aws.amazon.com/AmazonS3/latest/dev/UsingEncryption.html
- Amazon RDS Encryption: https://docs.aws.amazon.com/AmazonRDS/latest/UserGuide/Overview.Encryption.html
- Amazon EBS Encryption: https://docs.aws.amazon.com/AWSEC2/latest/UserGuide/EBSEncryption.html
- AWS Certificate Manager User Guide: https://docs.aws.amazon.com/acm/latest/userguide/
- AWS CloudHSM User Guide: https://docs.aws.amazon.com/cloudhsm/latest/userguide/
- AWS Compliance Programs: https://aws.amazon.com/compliance/programs/

CHAPTER 4
Network Security in AWS

Introduction

This chapter will address network security, which is one of the most critical aspects of AWS security. Today, it is imperative to protect your network infrastructure, as it is the cornerstone of a robust security strategy. Following this line of thought, you may think of your AWS network as a fortress–if the perimeter is compromised, all the resources within it become vulnerable to threats and malicious attacks.

In this chapter, you will walk through the key components of AWS network security, including VPC configuration, security groups, network ACLs, firewalls, traffic monitoring, and protecting hybrid environments. After mastering these concepts, you'll be able to design and implement secure network architectures that protect your AWS workloads from external threats, while enabling secure communication between your resources.

Whether you are building a new environment in AWS or securing an existing deployment, developing a thorough understanding of network security principles and AWS-specific tools will ensure your success in the AWS Security Specialty exam and will also help you protect your organization's critical assets and data in the cloud.

Structure

This chapter will tackle the following topics:

- VPC Fundamentals and Secure Design
    - What is a VPC
    - Key Attributes and Components
    - Secure VPC Design Principles
    - Subnets: Public vs. Private
    - Internet Gateway (IGW)

    - Types of DDoS Attacks
    - Security Best Practices for DDoS Protection
    - DDoS Incident Response with Shield Advanced
- Securing Hybrid Cloud Environments
    - AWS Site-to-Site VPN
    - Components of a Site-to-Site VPN
    - VPN Connection Options and Security Best Practices
    - AWS Direct Connect and Its Benefits
    - Direct Connect Components and Resiliency Models
    - Security Best Practices for Direct Connect
    - Securing Hybrid Architecture with AWS Transit Gateway
    - Example: Segmented Transit Gateway Architecture
    - Security Best Practices for Transit Gateway
- VPC Endpoints and Private Connections
    - What are VPC Endpoints
    - Types of VPC Endpoints (Gateway, Interface, Gateway Load Balancer)
    - Benefits of Using Private Connections
- Hands-on Lab: Configuring a Secure VPC
    - Setting Up a Multi-Tier VPC
    - Implementing Security Groups and NACLs
    - Enabling VPC Flow Logs for Network Monitoring
    - Testing Network Security Controls

VPC Fundamentals and Secure Design

Your journey into AWS network security begins with the Amazon Virtual Private Cloud (VPC), which is the fundamental building block that enables you to provision a logically isolated section of the AWS Cloud.

Thus, let us explore the core components and best practices for designing secure VPCs.

Overview of VPC Flow Logs

A VPC is your private network in the AWS cloud. It allows you to define your network topology, including IP address ranges, subnets, route tables, and network gateways.

Think of it as your own data centre in the cloud, which gives you complete control over network configuration and security.

Key attributes of a VPC

A Virtual Private Cloud (VPC) consists of several key attributes that define its structure, connectivity, and security controls. Understanding these components is essential for designing and managing a secure and scalable AWS network environment.

- **IP Address Range**: Defined using CIDR notation (for example, 10.0.0.0/16)
- **Regions and Availability Zones**: VPCs exist within a specific region but can span multiple Availability Zones for high availability
- **Subnets**: Subdivisions of your VPC's IP address range that can be public or privatc
- **Route Tables**: Control traffic routing between subnets and gateways
- **Network Access Control**: Implemented through security groups and network ACLs

Secure VPC Design Principles

Consider the following principles when designing a VPC to strengthen security:

- **Implement Network Segmentation**: Divide your network into security zones with different levels of trust
- **Follow the Principle of Least Privilege**: Only allow necessary traffic between segments
- **Plan for Scalability**: Design your CIDR blocks to accommodate future growth
- **Design for High Availability**: Deploy resources across multiple Availability Zones
- **Maintain a Defense-in-Depth Approach**: Implement multiple security controls at various layers

VPC Components for Secure Networking

To build a secure and well-structured VPC, it is important to understand how its components interact to control traffic and protect resources. Each element plays a specific role in maintaining network segmentation, accessibility, and defense against external threats.

Subnets: Public vs. Private

Subnets are segments of a VPC's IP address range, where you place AWS resources. A critical security decision is to determine which subnets should be public (accessible from the internet) and which should be private (isolated from the internet).

Public Subnets:

- Contain resources that need direct internet access (for example, load balancers, bastion hosts)
- Have a route to an Internet Gateway
- Should only host resources that need to be publicly accessible

Private Subnets:

- Contain resources that cannot not be directly accessed from the internet (for example, databases, application servers)
- Access the internet via a NAT Gateway or NAT Instance (if needed)
- Provide an additional layer of security for the most sensitive resources

Security Best Practice: It is recommended to place sensitive workloads and data in private subnets, and only necessary frontend components in public subnets.

Internet Gateway (IGW)

An Internet Gateway connects the VPC to the internet, allowing instances with public IPs to communicate with the internet. While it is necessary for public-facing applications, an IGW is also a potential entry point for attackers.

Security Best Practice: Use an IGW only for subnets that require public internet access and implement additional security controls, such as security groups and NACLs to protect resources in public subnets.

NAT Gateway

A Network Address Translation (NAT) Gateway enables instances in private subnets to initiate outbound traffic to the internet while preventing inbound traffic from it.

Security Best Practice: Deploy NAT Gateways in multiple Availability Zones for high availability. Use them instead of directly exposing instances to the internet whenever possible.

VPC Peering

VPC Peering allows direct network routing between two VPCs, enabling resources to communicate as if they are on the same network.

Security Best Practice: Limit peering connections to only what is necessary and use security groups to control traffic between peered VPCs. Regularly audit peering connections as they can create unexpected network paths.

Transit Gateway

AWS Transit Gateway is a network transit hub that simplifies network architecture by allowing you to connect multiple VPCs and on-premises networks.

Security Best Practice: Implement route table controls at the Transit Gateway to segment traffic and prevent unwanted communication between connected networks.

Example: Multi-Tier VPC Architecture

A secure VPC design typically includes multiple tiers, each with its own security controls. Consider this example of a three-tier web application:

- **Web Tier (Public Subnets):**
  - Hosts load balancers and web servers
  - Deployed across multiple Availability Zones
  - Protected by security groups allowing only HTTP/HTTPS traffic
- **Application Tier (Private Subnets):**
  - Contains application servers
  - No direct internet access
  - Security groups allow traffic only from the web tier
- **Database Tier (Private Subnets):**
  - Houses database servers
  - Most restrictive security controls
  - Security groups allow traffic only from the application tier

This architecture implements defense-in-depth by ensuring that:

- Internet traffic can only reach the web tier
- The application tier can only be accessed by the web tier
- The database tier can only be accessed by the application tier

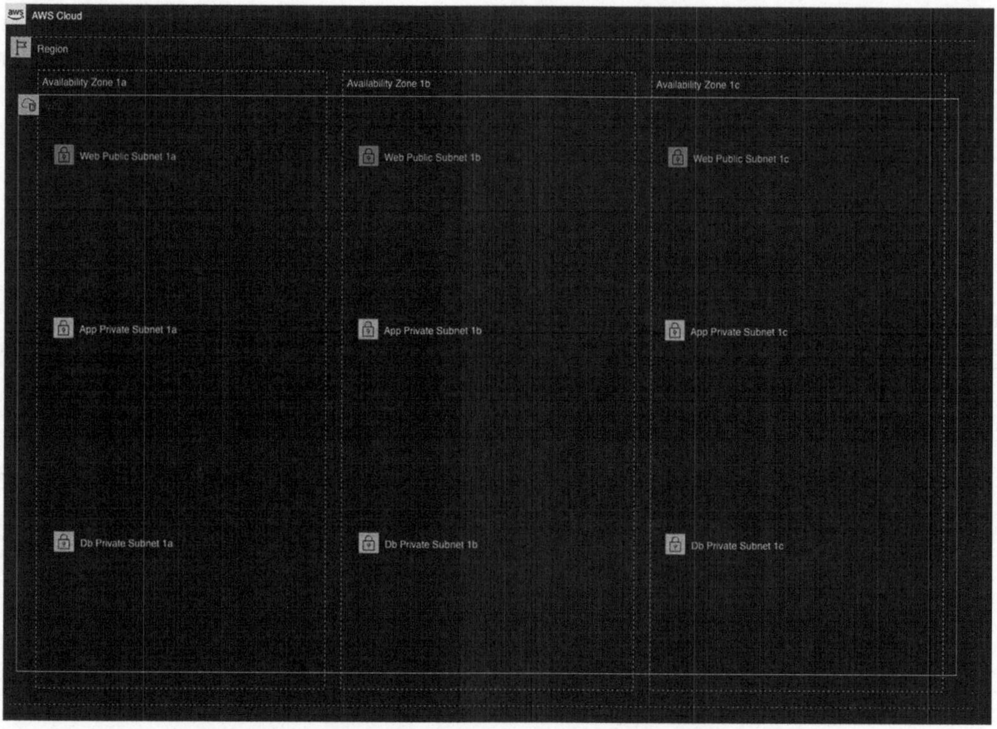

Figure 4.1: *Three-tier VPC Architecture*

CIDR Block Planning

Proper CIDR block planning is essential for network segmentation and future scalability. Consider the following factors when planning your VPC's CIDR blocks:

- **Size of Address Space Needed**: Account for current and future resources
- **Subnet Sizing**: Ensure subnets have enough IP addresses for your needs
- **Overlap Avoidance**: Prevent overlapping with the existing networks or potential VPC peers
- **Reserved Addresses**: Remember that AWS reserves the first four and last addresses in each subnet

Security Best Practice: Plan your CIDR allocations to enable clear network segmentation and maintain adequate space for growth. Use consistent CIDR patterns across environments to simplify management.

VPC Flow Logs for Network Visibility

While we will explore VPC Flow Logs in more detail later in this chapter, it is important to note that enabling flow logs is a critical component of secure VPC design as they provide visibility into network traffic patterns and potential security issues.

Security Best Practice: Enable VPC Flow Logs at the VPC, subnet or network interface level to capture metadata about IP traffic flowing to and from network interfaces. This data is invaluable for security monitoring and incident response.

Security Groups and Network ACLs

Security Groups and Network ACLs are primary tools for controlling traffic to and from resources within your VPC. While they serve similar purposes, they operate differently and are the most effective when used together as complementary controls.

Security Groups: Instance-Level Firewalls

Security Groups act as virtual firewalls for your EC2 instances and other AWS resources. They control inbound and outbound traffic at the instance level.

Key Characteristics of Security Groups

Security groups act as virtual firewalls at the instance level, controlling inbound and outbound traffic. The following characteristics define how they function and differentiate them from other network security mechanisms in AWS.

- **Stateful Filtering**: If you allow an inbound connection, the response traffic is automatically allowed regardless of outbound rules
- **Allow Rules Only**: You can only specify allow rules, not deny rules
- **Instance-Level Application**: Applied to instances rather than subnets
- **Evaluated as a Collective**: All rules are evaluated before deciding whether to allow traffic

Example Security Group Configuration for a Web Server

The following example illustrates a typical security group configuration for a web server. It allows public access to web traffic while restricting administrative access to trusted network ranges within the VPC.

Type	Protocol	Port Range	Source	Description
HTTP	TCP	80	0.0.0.0/0	Allow HTTP from anywhere

HTTPS	TCP	443	0.0.0.0/0	Allow HTTPS from anywhere
SSH	TCP	22	10.0.0.0/16	Allow SSH only from within VPC

Table 4.1: *Security group rules allowing HTTP and HTTPS access from anywhere, and restricting SSH access to the VPC range 10.0.0.0/16*

Security Best Practices for Security Groups:

- **Follow the Principle of Least Privilege**: Only open ports that are absolutely necessary
- **Use Specific Source IPs or CIDR Ranges**: Avoid using 0.0.0.0/0 (all IPs) except for public-facing services
- **Reference Other Security Groups**: Use security group IDs as sources rather than IP ranges when possible
- **Implement a Naming Convention**: Use clear, consistent names that indicate purpose and environment
- **Regularly Audit Security Groups**: Remove unused rules and verify that the existing rules are still necessary
- **Avoid Opening Large Port Ranges**: Be specific about the required ports rather than using wide ranges
- **Document the Purpose of Each Rule**: Use description fields effectively

Network ACLs: Subnet-Level Firewalls

Network Access Control Lists (NACLs) are an additional layer of security that act as a firewall and control traffic that enters and exits subnets within your VPC.

Key Characteristics of Network ACLs

Network Access Control Lists (NACLs) provide an additional layer of security at the subnet level. The following characteristics describe how NACLs operate and how they differ from security groups in managing network traffic.

- **Stateless Filtering**: You must specify both inbound and outbound rules
- **Allow and Deny Rules**: You can explicitly allow or deny traffic
- **Subnet-Level Application**: Applied to the subnet, affecting all instances
- **Rule Number Precedence**: Rules are evaluated in numerical order, with lower numbers taking precedence
- **Default Behavior**: Allows all traffic by default but also permits modifications

Example Network ACL Configuration for a Private Subnet

The following example demonstrates a secure Network ACL configuration for a private subnet. It allows only necessary inbound traffic while denying all other connections to maintain strict access control within the VPC.

Inbound Rules:

Rule #	Type	Protocol	Port Range	Source	Allow/Deny	Description
100	All TCP	TCP	1024-65535	0.0.0.0/0	ALLOW	Allow return traffic
200	SSH	TCP	22	10.0.0.0/16	ALLOW	Allow SSH from VPC
300	MYSQL	TCP	3306	10.0.10.0/24	ALLOW	Allow MySQL from App Subnet
*	All Traffic	All	All	0.0.0.0/0	DENY	Deny all other traffic

Table 4.2: *Network ACL rules allowing return traffic, restricted SSH and MySQL access within the VPC, and denying all other traffic*

Outbound Rules:

Rule #	Type	Protocol	Port Range	Destination	Allow/Deny	Description
100	All TCP	TCP	1024-65535	0.0.0.0/0	ALLOW	Allow outbound response traffic
200	HTTPS	TCP	443	0.0.0.0/0	ALLOW	Allow outbound HTTPS
*	All Traffic	All	All	0.0.0.0/0	DENY	Deny all other traffic

Table 4.3. *Outbound network ACL rules allowing HTTPS and return traffic, while denying all other outbound traffic*

Security Best Practices for Network ACLs

Network ACLs (NACLs) act as an additional layer of defense at the subnet level. The following best practices help you configure them effectively to enhance network protection and maintain operational flexibility.

- **Use NACLs as a Secondary Defense:** Implement them alongside security groups for defense-in-depth
- **Implement Explicit Deny Rules**: Block known malicious IP ranges or ports

- **Leave Room between Rule Numbers:** Use increments of 100 to allow for future insertion of rules
- **Remember Ephemeral Ports:** Include rules for ephemeral ports (1024-65535) for return traffic
- **Keep It Simple:** Overly complex NACL rules can be difficult to maintain and troubleshoot
- **Test Thoroughly:** Verify the impact of NACL changes before implementing in production

Security Groups vs. Network ACLs: When to Use Each

Understanding the differences between security groups and NACLs helps you determine when to use each of the following controls:

Feature	Security Groups	Network ACLs
Scope	Instance level	Subnet level
State	Stateful	Stateless
Rule Types	Allow rules only	Allow and deny rules
Rule Evaluation	All rules evaluated	Rules evaluated in numbered order
Default Action	Deny all inbound, allow all outbound	Depends on default NACL configuration

Table 4.4: *Comparison of Security Groups and Network ACLs by scope, state, rule types, evaluation method, and default actions*

Use Security Groups When

Security groups are ideal for controlling inbound and outbound traffic at the instance level. Use them in the following scenarios to simplify management and enforce fine-grained access control.

- You need stateful filtering.
- You want to allow traffic between specific instances.
- You are managing access for a specific application or service.
- You want to simplify management with security group references.

Use Network ACLs When

Network ACLs provide stateless, subnet-level controls for managing network traffic. Apply them in these situations to complement security groups and strengthen perimeter defenses.

- You need subnet-wide controls.
- You want to explicitly block specific traffic (deny rules).
- You need a backup defense mechanism at the subnet level.
- You want to block specific IP addresses or CIDR blocks.

Example: Complementary Use of Security Groups and NACLs

Consider a database server in a private subnet:

- **Network ACL (Subnet Level):**
  - Block well-known malicious IP ranges
  - Restrict access to specific ports from authorized subnets only
  - Implement broad subnet-level protection
- **Security Group (Instance Level):**
  - Allow database connections only from specific application security groups
  - Permit management access only from bastion hosts
  - Implement fine-grained, instance-specific controls

This layered approach provides defense-in-depth by using NACLs as a broad filter and security groups for precise control.

Common Security Group and NACL Misconfigurations

Be aware of these common security pitfalls:

- **Overly Permissive Rules**: Using 0.0.0.0/0 unnecessarily or opening all ports
- **Unused Rules**: Leaving rules that no longer serve a purpose
- **Improper Rule Ordering in NACLs**: Placing deny rules after allow rules, negating their effect
- **Missing Ephemeral Port Rules in NACLs**: Forgetting to allow return traffic
- **Inconsistent Inbound/Outbound Rules in NACLs**: Creating conflicting rules that block legitimate traffic

- **Security Group Sprawl**: Creating too many security groups, making management difficult
- **Insufficient Documentation**: Not documenting the purpose of security groups or rules

Security Best Practice: Regularly audit your security groups and NACLs using AWS Config Rules or third-party tools to identify and remediate misconfigurations.

VPC Flow Logs and Traffic Monitoring

Visibility into network traffic is crucial for identifying suspicious activities, troubleshooting connectivity issues, and demonstrating compliance. VPC Flow Logs provide valuable insights into the traffic flowing through your VPC.

Understanding VPC Flow Logs

VPC Flow Logs capture information about the IP traffic going to and from network interfaces in your VPC. They allow you to monitor traffic patterns, detect anomalies, and gain insights into network behavior.

Flow logs can be created at three levels:

1. **VPC Level:** Captures traffic for all network interfaces in the VPC
2. **Subnet Level**: Captures traffic for all network interfaces in the subnet
3. **Network Interface Level**: Captures traffic for a specific network interface

Understanding Flow Log Records

Each flow log record represents a network flow and includes the following information:

- Source and Destination IP addresses
- Source and Destination ports
- Protocols
- Number of packets and bytes transferred
- Start and End time of the flow
- Action (ACCEPT or REJECT)
- Log Status

Example Flow Log Record

```
2 123456789010 eni-1234567890abcdef 172.31.16.139 172.31.16.21
20641 22 6 20 4249 1418530010 1418530070 ACCEPT OK
```

Here is what each field represents in the above example:

- Version
- Account ID
- Network Interface ID
- Source IP
- Destination IP
- Source Port
- Destination Port
- Protocol (6 = TCP)
- Packets
- Bytes
- Start Time
- End Time
- Action (ACCEPT)
- Log Status

Security Insights from VPC Flow Logs

Flow logs provide valuable information for security analysis:

- **Detecting Unauthorized Access Attempts**: Identify rejected connection attempts to restricted ports
- **Identifying Abnormal Traffic Patterns**: Spot unexpected increases in traffic or connections to unusual destinations
- **Investigating Security Incidents**: Trace the path of potential attackers through your network
- **Demonstrating Compliance**: Show evidence of network security controls for auditors

Best Practices for VPC Flow Logs

To maximize the value of VPC Flow Logs for monitoring and security analysis, apply the following practices that ensure accuracy, efficiency, and compliance.

- **Enable Flow Logs on All Production VPCs**: Comprehensive visibility is essential for security
- **Establish Baselines**: Understand normal traffic patterns to identify anomalies

- **Implement Automated Alerting**: Set up CloudWatch Alarms for unexpected traffic patterns
- **Retain Logs Appropriately**: Configure retention periods based on compliance requirements
- **Use Custom Formats**: Include only the fields you need to reduce storage costs
- **Integrate with SIEM Tools**: Forward logs to security information and event management systems for correlation with other security data
- **Analyze Traffic Regularly**: Schedule routine reviews of traffic patterns to identify potential security issues

Security Best Practice: Combine VPC Flow Logs with AWS GuardDuty, which uses flow logs data along with other sources to detect potential security threats.

Limitations of VPC Flow Logs

While flow logs are powerful, understand their limitations:

- **Not Real-Time**: There is a delay before flow data becomes available for analysis.
- **No Packet Content**: Flow logs capture metadata only, not actual packet contents.
- **No Support for All Traffic**: Some traffic is not monitored, including DNS traffic to AWS resolvers, Windows license activation, and traffic to the instance metadata service.
- **Limited Retention**: Default retention in CloudWatch Logs is limited unless configured otherwise.
- **No Packet-Level Detail**: Flow logs do not provide deep packet inspection capabilities.

Despite these limitations, VPC Flow Logs remain a vital component of your AWS network security strategy, offering valuable insights into traffic patterns and potential security issues.

AWS Network Firewall and Web Application Firewall (WAF)

As your AWS network security matures, you'll need more sophisticated tools for traffic filtering and protection. AWS offers powerful managed firewall services that provide enhanced protection beyond security groups and NACLs.

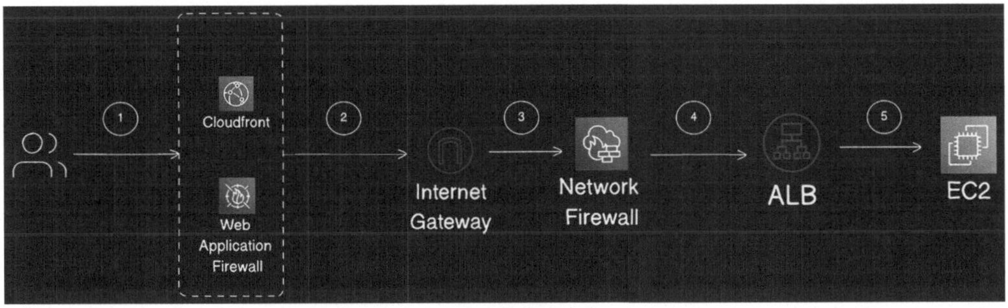

Figure 4.2: *A multi-layer AWS defense-in-depth architecture filtering traffic through CloudFront+WAF, Internet Gateway, Network Firewall, ALB, and finally to secured EC2 instances*

AWS Network Firewall: Advanced Network Protection

AWS Network Firewall is a managed service that makes it easy to deploy essential network protections for all of your Amazon VPCs. It provides stateful inspection, intrusion prevention, and web filtering capabilities to help protect your virtual networks.

Key Features of AWS Network Firewall

- **Stateful Inspection**: Deep packet inspection to detect and block threats
- **Intrusion Prevention**: Built-in protections against common network threats
- **Web Filtering**: Control outbound access to domains and websites
- **Traffic Monitoring**: Visibility into network traffic patterns
- **Custom Rule Development**: Create custom rules to address specific threats

Network Firewall Architecture

AWS Network Firewall is deployed in a dedicated subnet within your VPC. Traffic is routed through the firewall endpoint, allowing inspection before it reaches your protected resources.

Typical Deployment Patterns:

- **Ingress Inspection**: Inspect traffic coming into your VPC from the internet
- **Egress Inspection**: Monitor and control traffic leaving your VPC
- **East-West Inspection**: Examine traffic moving between VPCs or subnets

Network Firewall Rule Groups

Network Firewall uses two types of rule groups:

- **Stateless Rule Groups**: Simple pattern matching without tracking connection state
  - Protocol identification
  - Source/destination filtering
  - Efficiently process traffic that doesn't need state tracking
- **Stateful Rule Groups**: Context-aware inspection that maintains connection state
  - Deep packet inspection
  - Application layer filtering
  - Support for Suricata-compatible intrusion prevention rules

Implementing AWS Network Firewall

To deploy Network Firewall effectively:

1. **Plan Your Architecture**: Determine traffic flow and inspection points
2. **Create Rule Groups**: Define stateless and stateful rules
3. **Configure a Firewall Policy**: Associate rule groups with your policy
4. **Deploy the Firewall**: Create a firewall endpoint in a dedicated subnet
5. **Update Routing**: Modify route tables to direct traffic through the firewall

Security Best Practices for Network Firewall

AWS Network Firewall strengthens perimeter security and enforces traffic inspection across your VPCs. The practices below outline how to design and operate firewall rules for maximum protection and performance.

- **Defense-in-Depth**: Use Network Firewall alongside security groups and NACLs
- **Least Privilege**: Only allow necessary traffic patterns
- **Consistent Policies**: Apply similar protections across all environments
- **Regular Updates**: Keep rules updated to protect against emerging threats
- **Logging and Monitoring**: Enable and analyze firewall logs
- **Redundancy**: Deploy across multiple Availability Zones

AWS Web Application Firewall (WAF): Protecting Web Applications

While Network Firewall focuses on network-layer protection, AWS WAF specializes in protecting web applications from common web exploits that could affect availability, compromise security, or consume excessive resources.

Key Features of AWS WAF

- **Application Layer (Layer 7) Protection**: Filter HTTP/HTTPS traffic
- **Web Attack Protection**: Defend against common vulnerabilities such as SQL injection and cross-site scripting
- **Bot Control**: Identify and manage bot traffic
- **Rate-Based Rules**: Automatically block IP addresses that make too many requests
- **IP Reputation Lists**: Block requests from known malicious IP addresses
- **Geolocation Restrictions**: Control access based on country of origin

AWS WAF Integration Points

AWS WAF can be deployed to protect:

- **Amazon CloudFront Distributions**
- **Application Load Balancers**
- **Amazon API Gateway REST APIs**
- **AWS AppSync GraphQL APIs**
- **Amazon Cognito User Pools**

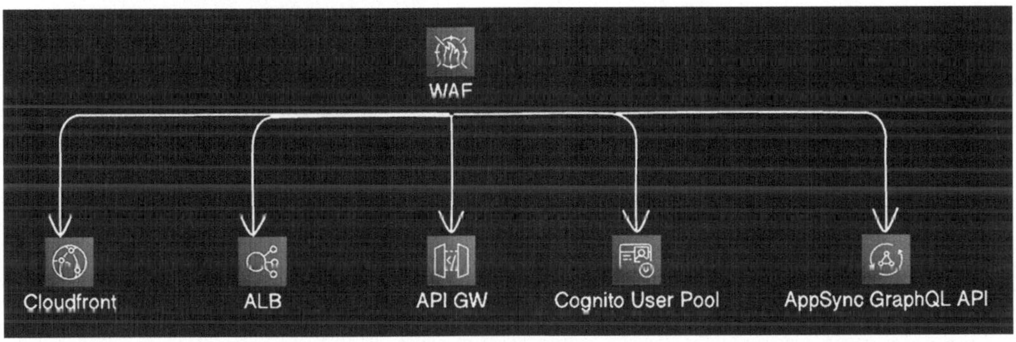

***Figure 4.3**: A centralized AWS WAF protecting multiple entry points including CloudFront, ALB, API Gateway, Cognito User Pool, and AppSync GraphQL API*

WAF Components

AWS WAF is built around modular components that define how web traffic is filtered and inspected. The following key elements describe how these components work together to protect web applications:

- **Web ACLs (Access Control Lists)**: The primary container for WAF rules
- **Rules**: Conditions that inspect web requests
- **Rule Groups**: Reusable collections of rules
- **IP Sets**: Reusable collections of IP addresses and ranges
- **Regex Pattern Sets**: Reusable collections of regular expressions

Types of WAF Rules

AWS WAF supports several rule types to provide comprehensive protection:

- **Managed Rules**: Pre-configured rule groups maintained by AWS or AWS Marketplace sellers
- **Rate-Based Rules**: Block IPs that exceed a specified request threshold
- **IP Set Rules**: Allow or block based on source IP addresses
- **Geographic Rules**: Control access based on country
- **String Match Rules**: Inspect various parts of the request for specific strings
- **Regex Pattern Rules**: Use regular expressions to identify patterns in requests
- **Size Constraint Rules**: Enforce limits on request components
- **SQL Injection Rules**: Detect and block SQL injection attempts
- **Cross-Site Scripting (XSS) Rules**: Identify and block XSS attacks

AWS Managed Rules for WAF

AWS provides a set of managed rule groups that address common threats:

- **Core Rule Set (CRS)**: Basic protection against common web threats
- **Admin Protection**: Protects admin pages from unauthorized access
- **Known Bad Inputs**: Blocks request patterns associated with exploitation
- **SQL Database**: Protects against SQL injection attacks
- **Linux Operating System**: Defends against Linux-specific exploits
- **POSIX Operating System**: Protects against POSIX OS vulnerabilities
- **Windows Operating System**: Defends against Windows-specific exploits
- **PHP Application**: Protects PHP applications

- **WordPress Application**: Secures WordPress installations

Security Best Practices for AWS WAF

Implementing AWS WAF effectively requires thoughtful rule configuration and continuous monitoring. Follow these best practices to improve resilience against common web exploits.

- **Layer Defenses**: Use WAF alongside other security controls
- **Start in Monitoring Mode**: Test rules before enforcing them
- **Enable Logging**: Capture detailed logs for analysis
- **Use Rate-Limiting**: Implement rate-based rules to prevent abuse
- **Implement Bot Control**: Use AWS WAF Bot Control to manage bot traffic
- **Regular Reviews**: Analyze traffic patterns and adjust rules
- **Stay Current**: Keep managed rules updated

AWS Shield and DDoS Protection

Distributed Denial of Service (DDoS) attacks attempt to make your website or application unavailable by overwhelming it with traffic from multiple sources. AWS Shield provides protection against these attacks.

AWS Shield Standard vs. Advanced

AWS offers two tiers of DDoS protection:

AWS Shield Standard

AWS Shield Standard automatically safeguards all AWS customers against common, frequently occurring DDoS attacks. The key features below highlight how it integrates seamlessly with other AWS services for baseline protection.

- **Included at no additional cost** for all AWS customers
- **Automatic protection** against common, frequently occurring network and transport layer DDoS attacks
- **Integrated with CloudFront and Route 53** for edge location protection

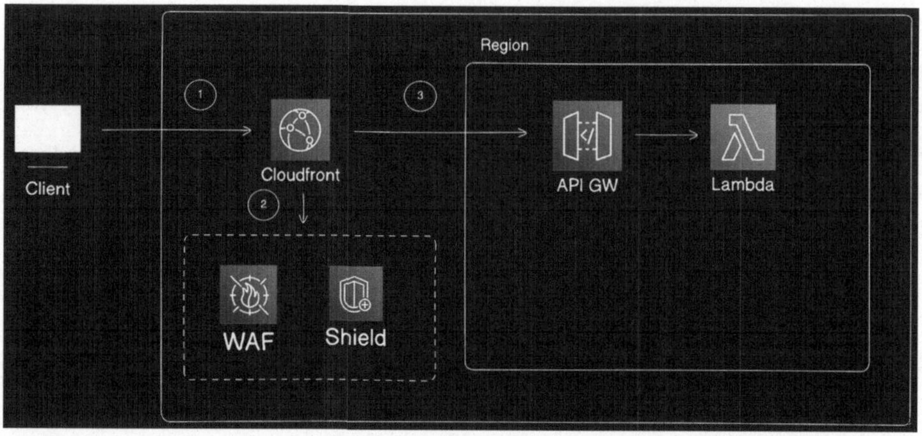

Figure 4.4: *Client requests pass through CloudFront, protected by AWS WAF and Shield, before reaching API Gateway and triggering Lambda functions in the AWS region*

AWS Shield Advanced

AWS Shield Advanced provides enhanced, subscription-based DDoS protection with real-time visibility and expert support. The following points summarize its advanced features and benefits for mission-critical workloads.

- **Subscription-based service** for enhanced DDoS protection
- **24/7 access to the AWS DDoS Response Team (DRT)**
- **Real-time attack visibility**
- **Protection for EC2, ELB, CloudFront, Global Accelerator, and Route 53**
- **Cost protection** for scaling during DDoS attacks
- **Integrates with AWS WAF** at no additional cost

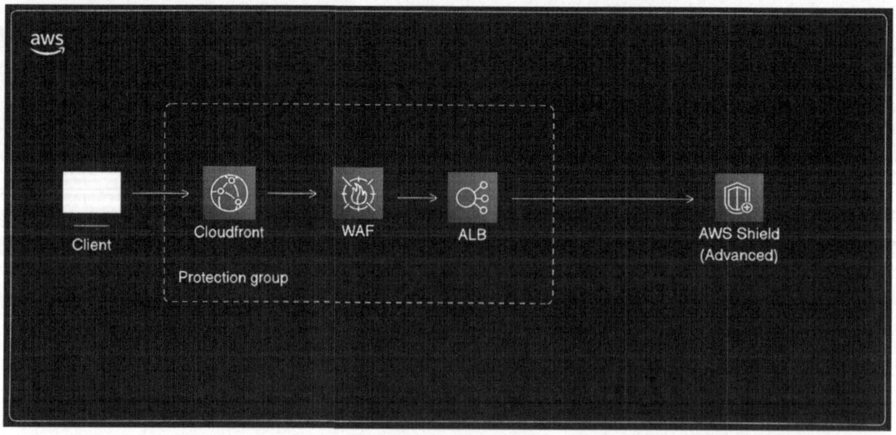

Figure 4.5: *Client traffic flows through CloudFront, WAF, and ALB as part of a protection group, with AWS Shield Advanced providing enhanced DDoS protection*

Feature	Shield Standard	Shield Advanced
Protection Level	Network & Transport (Layer 3 & 4)	Network, Transport & Application (Layer 3, 4 & 7)
24/7 DDoS Response Team	No	Yes
Real-time metrics and reports	No	Yes
Cost protection	No	Yes (up to $3,000/month)
WAF integration	No	Yes (included)
Proactive engagement	No	Yes (optional)
Price	Free	Subscription ($3,000/month)

Table 4.5: *Comparison of AWS Shield Standard and Shield Advanced features, protection levels, and pricing*

Types of DDoS Attacks

Understanding the attacks Shield protects against is essential:

- **Volumetric Attacks**: Consume bandwidth with massive traffic volume
    - **UDP Floods**: Send large numbers of UDP packets to random ports
    - **Amplification Attacks**: Exploit protocols like NTP, DNS, or SSDP
- **Protocol Attacks**: Exploit server resources with malformed packets
    - **SYN Floods**: Send SYN packets but never complete the handshake
    - **Fragmented Packet Attacks**: Send malformed or fragmented packets
- **Application Layer Attacks**: Target application vulnerabilities
    - **HTTP Floods**: Overwhelm web servers with seemingly legitimate requests
    - **Slow Loris Attacks**: Establish connections and keep them open as long as possible

Security Best Practices for DDoS Protection

Defending against Distributed Denial of Service (DDoS) attacks requires a proactive, multi-layered approach. The following best practices will help you build resilient architectures capable of withstanding large-scale attacks.

- **Understand Your Traffic Patterns**: Establish baselines to identify anomalies
- **Architect for Resilience**: Design systems to withstand traffic surges
- **Enable Shield Advanced** for business-critical applications
- **Implement WAF rules** to protect application endpoints
- **Configure automated response** to scale during attacks

- **Regularly test DDoS readiness** with simulated events
- **Develop a DDoS response playbook** for incident response

DDoS Incident Response with Shield Advanced

When facing an active DDoS attack, Shield Advanced provides both automated and guided response capabilities. The following steps outline what happens during an attack and how AWS assists in mitigation and recovery.

1. **Detection**: AWS Shield identifies attack signatures
2. **Notification**: You receive alerts via CloudWatch and Health Dashboard
3. **Analysis**: Review attack metrics in the Shield console
4. **Response**: Shield automatically mitigates the attack
5. **Engagement**: Contact the DDoS Response Team for complex attacks
6. **Post-incident**: Review the attack and refine defenses

Securing Hybrid Cloud Environments

Many organizations operate in hybrid environments, with resources stored both in AWS and on-premises data centers. Securing these hybrid architectures requires special consideration to ensure consistent protection across environments.

AWS Site-to-Site VPN: Secure Connection to AWS

AWS Site-to-Site VPN creates an encrypted tunnel between your on-premises network and your AWS VPC, allowing secure communication between environments.

Components of Site-to-Site VPN

A Site-to-Site VPN consists of several key components that work together to establish secure, encrypted connectivity between your on-premises network and your AWS environment.

- **Customer Gateway (CGW)**: Represents your on-premises VPN device
- **Virtual Private Gateway (VGW)**: The VPN endpoint on the AWS side
- **Transit Gateway**: Optional component for connecting multiple VPCs and networks
- **VPN Connection**: The encrypted tunnel between your network and AWS

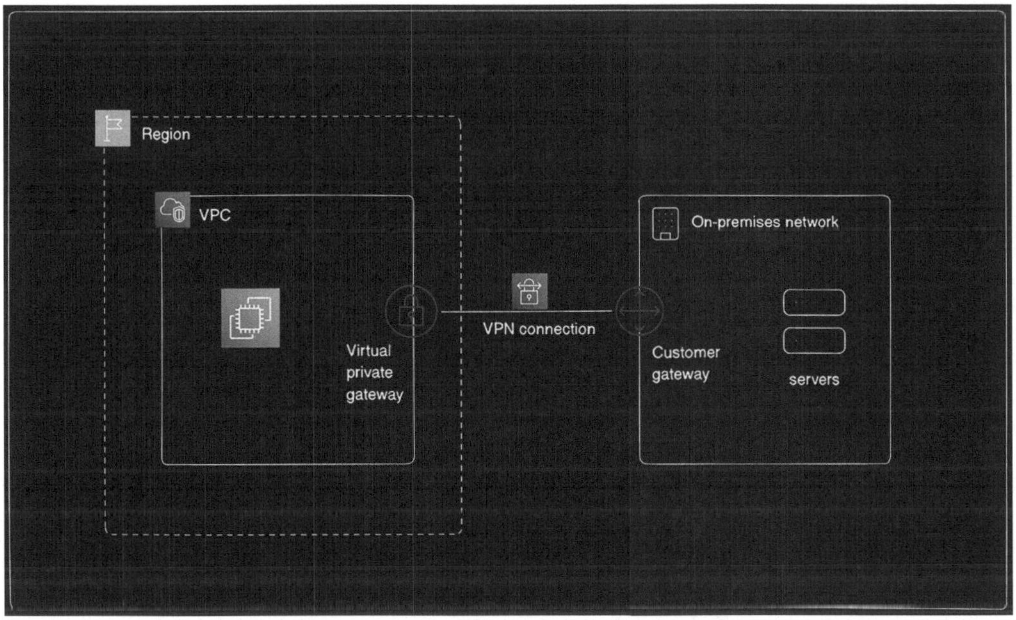

***Figure 4.6:** A Site-to-Site VPN connection linking an on-premises network (via a customer gateway) to an AWS VPC (via a virtual private gateway) for secure, encrypted communication*

VPN Connection Options

AWS offers two types of VPN connections:

- **AWS Site-to-Site VPN**: Connect your on-premises network to AWS
  - IPsec encrypted tunnels
  - Supports static routes or dynamic routing (BGP)
  - Up to 1.25 Gbps per tunnel
- **AWS Client VPN**: Secure access for remote users
  - OpenVPN-based service
  - SSL/TLS encrypted connections
  - Integrates with existing identity providers

Security Best Practices for VPN

Implementing these VPN best practices helps ensure secure, resilient, and well-monitored connectivity between your on-premises and AWS environments.

- **Use Strong Encryption**: Configure VPN with AES-256 encryption
- **Implement Redundant Tunnels**: Create multiple tunnels for high availability
- **Enable Tunnel Logging**: Monitor VPN connection activity

- **Use BGP for Dynamic Routing**: Enables automatic failover
- **Monitor Connectivity**: Set up alarms for tunnel status
- **Regularly Update VPN Devices**: Keep on-premises equipment current
- **Consider AWS Direct Connect** for high bandwidth or sensitive workloads

AWS Direct Connect: Dedicated Network Connection

While VPN provides secure connectivity over the internet, AWS Direct Connect offers a dedicated private connection between your on-premises network and AWS, with benefits including:

- **Consistent Network Performance**: Private connection avoids internet congestion
- **Reduced Bandwidth Costs**: Lower data transfer rates compared to internet
- **Increased Throughput**: Up to 100 Gbps connections available
- **Enhanced Security**: Traffic does not traverse the public internet

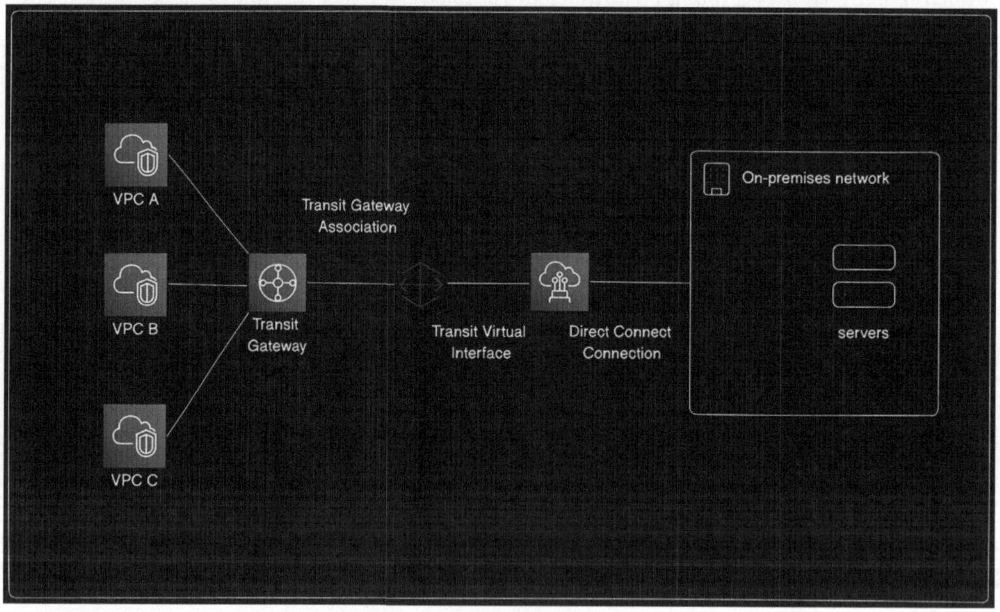

Figure 4.7: *A Site-to-Site VPN securely connecting an on-premises network to an AWS VPC through a customer gateway and a virtual private gateway*

Direct Connect Components

AWS Direct Connect includes several core components that together enable private, high-bandwidth network connectivity between your data center and AWS.

- **Connections**: Physical connections to AWS
- **Virtual Interfaces (VIFs)**: Logical connections over Direct Connect
    - **Public VIF**: Connect to AWS public services
    - **Private VIF**: Connect to resources in a VPC
    - **Transit VIF**: Connect to a Transit Gateway
- **Direct Connect Gateways**: Connect to multiple VPCs across regions

Direct Connect Resiliency Models

To ensure high availability, AWS recommends implementing one of these resiliency models:

- **Maximum Resiliency**: Multiple connections at multiple locations
- **High Resiliency**: Multiple connections at multiple locations with one connection active
- **Development and Test**: Single connection for non-critical workloads
- **Classic**: Paired connections at separate locations

Security Best Practices for Direct Connect

To maintain confidentiality and availability when using AWS Direct Connect, follow these best practices focused on encryption, redundancy, and connection monitoring.

- **Layer Encryption on Top**: Use MACsec for layer 2 or VPN for layer 3 encryption
- **Implement Resiliency**: Use multiple connections
- **Control Routing**: Use BGP prefix filtering
- **Monitor Connections**: Set up CloudWatch alarms
- **Consider Using a Direct Connect Partner** for expertise
- **Complement with VPN** for complete resiliency

Securing Hybrid Architecture with AWS Transit Gateway

AWS Transit Gateway serves as a central hub for connecting VPCs, on-premises networks, and third-party services. It simplifies network architecture while providing enhanced security controls.

Key Features of Transit Gateway

AWS Transit Gateway simplifies complex network topologies by acting as a central hub. The following features illustrate how it enhances connectivity and security across multiple networks:

- **Centralized Connectivity**: Connect multiple VPCs and on-premises networks
- **Simplified Routing**: Single routing configuration
- **Enhanced Security Controls**: Control traffic between networks
- **Monitoring and Visibility**: Insights into cross-network traffic
- **Support for Multiple Connection Types**: VPN, Direct Connect, peering

Security Controls in Transit Gateway

Transit Gateway offers several integrated security mechanisms that help you manage routing, visibility, and access across interconnected VPCs and on-premises systems.

- **Route Tables**: Control which networks can communicate
- **Network ACLs and Security Groups**: Additional protection for VPC resources
- **VPC Attachment Approvals**: Require explicit approval for new connections
- **Network Manager**: Visibility into global network
- **Flow Logs**: Monitor traffic across the network

Example: Segmented Transit Gateway Architecture

In a hybrid environment, you can use Transit Gateway to create isolated network segments listed here:

- **Production Segment**: Production VPCs and resources
- **Development Segment**: Development and testing environments
- **Shared Services Segment**: Common services like Active Directory
- **On-Premises Segment**: Connections to your data centers

Each segment has its own route table, controlling which networks can communicate with each other.

Security Best Practices for Transit Gateway

Adhering to these best practices will help you strengthen the security of your Transit

Gateway deployments by improving segmentation, visibility, and control over inter-VPC traffic.

- **Implement Network Segmentation**: Use multiple route tables
- **Control Inter-VPC Traffic**: Only allow necessary communication
- **Enable Monitoring**: Use Flow Logs and CloudWatch
- **Secure Attachments**: Use appropriate security controls for each VPC
- **Regularly Audit Routes**: Ensure routes reflect current requirements
- **Consider Encryption**: Use VPN or encryption services for sensitive traffic

VPC Endpoints and Private Connections

VPC Endpoints allow you to privately connect your VPC to supported AWS services and VPC endpoint services without requiring an internet gateway, NAT device, VPN connection, or Direct Connect connection. This enhances security by keeping traffic within the AWS network and avoiding exposure to the public internet.

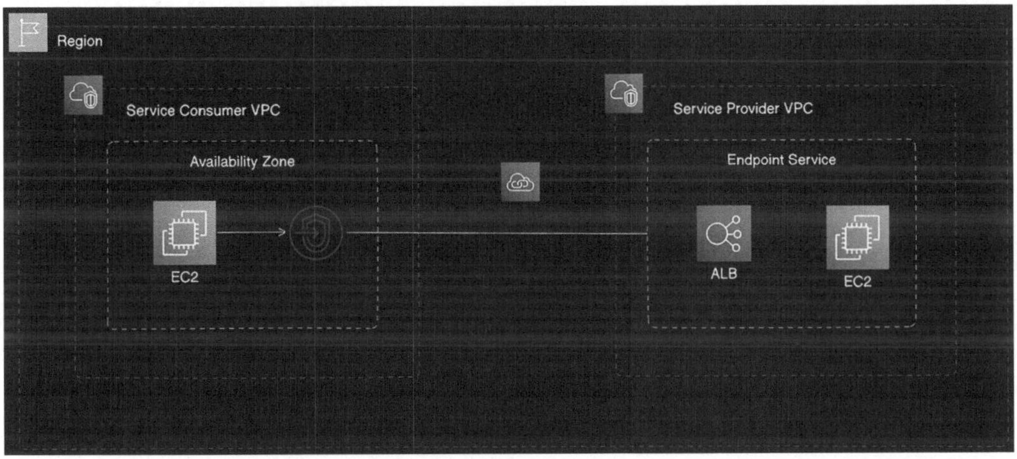

***Figure 4.8**: An AWS PrivateLink setup where a service consumer VPC connects to a service provider VPC's endpoint service, routing EC2 traffic through AWS Shield to an ALB and EC2 in the provider VPC*

Types of VPC Endpoints

AWS offers three types of VPC endpoints:

- **Gateway Endpoints**: For Amazon S3 and DynamoDB
  - Uses route tables to direct traffic
  - No additional cost

- **Interface Endpoints (Powered by AWS PrivateLink)**: Most AWS services
    - Use Elastic Network Interfaces (ENIs) with private IPs
    - Accessible from on-premises via Direct Connect or VPN
    - Charges apply per endpoint per hour and for data processed
- **Gateway Load Balancer Endpoints**: For third-party appliances
    - Routes traffic to security appliances
    - Allows inspection and processing of traffic

Advanced Network Security Controls

In this section, we will explore advanced network security controls and configurations that build on the foundational concepts we have covered earlier. These advanced controls help security engineers address complex scenarios and create robust, defense-in-depth architectures.

Traffic Mirroring for Network Monitoring and Threat Detection

AWS Traffic Mirroring is a powerful feature that allows you to copy network traffic from an elastic network interface attached to your EC2 instances, and send that traffic to out-of-band security and monitoring appliances for deep packet inspection.

Key Benefits of Traffic Mirroring

Traffic Mirroring enables deep network visibility by allowing you to inspect live traffic for analysis and threat detection. The following benefits explain how it supports monitoring and compliance.

- **Deep Packet Inspection**: Analyze actual packets rather than just connection metadata
- **Intrusion Detection**: Identify malicious activity through packet analysis
- **Network Forensics**: Capture traffic for post-incident investigation
- **Compliance Monitoring**: Ensure that traffic patterns conform to regulatory requirements
- **Transparent Deployment**: Mirror traffic without affecting application performance

Traffic Mirroring Components

Traffic Mirroring is built on key components that define how traffic is captured, filtered, and delivered for analysis. Understanding these components ensures accurate and efficient deployment.

- **Mirror Source**: The Elastic Network Interface (ENI) from which to copy traffic
- **Mirror Target**: The destination for mirrored traffic (another ENI, Network Load Balancer, or Gateway Load Balancer endpoint)
- **Mirror Filter**: Rules defining which traffic to mirror (by protocol, port, direction, and so on)
- **Mirror Session**: Configuration linking the source, target, and filter

Implementation Considerations

When implementing Traffic Mirroring, consider the following:

- **Bandwidth Requirements**: Mirroring creates a copy of traffic, potentially doubling bandwidth
- **Storage Needs**: Packet capture solutions need sufficient storage for retained traffic
- **Analysis Capacity**: Ensure that security tools can handle the volume of mirrored traffic
- **Filtering Strategy**: Mirror only the traffic necessary for your security objectives
- **Legal and Privacy Concerns**: Ensure compliance with applicable regulations regarding traffic monitoring

Security Best Practices for Traffic Mirroring

To use Traffic Mirroring securely and responsibly, apply these best practices focused on access control, encryption, and effective monitoring management.

- **Mirror Selectively**: Only mirror traffic relevant to your security needs
- **Secure the Monitoring Systems**: Apply strict access controls to systems receiving mirrored traffic
- **Encrypt Sensitive Data**: Consider application-level encryption for sensitive data
- **Implement Monitoring Rotation**: Periodically change which instances are monitored
- **Document Monitoring Activities**: Maintain records of what traffic is mirrored and why

Advanced VPC Designs for Security

Security-focused VPC designs implement multiple layers of control to protect resources while maintaining necessary connectivity. Let us explore some advanced VPC designs that enhance security.

Multi-VPC Hub and Spoke Architecture

A hub and spoke architecture centralizes security controls while allowing business units to maintain separation:

- **Hub VPC** (Security VPC)
    - Houses security infrastructure (firewalls, IDS/IPS, monitoring)
    - Contains shared services (directory services, logging)
    - Serves as the central connection point for all traffic
- **Spoke VPCs** (Workload VPCs)
    - Contain application-specific resources
    - Connect to the hub for security services and external connectivity
    - Maintain isolation between different applications or environments
- **Connectivity**
    - Transit Gateway connects all VPCs
    - Route tables control traffic flow through security services
    - Gateway Load Balancer endpoints facilitate traffic inspection

This architecture enables:

- Centralized security monitoring and management
- Consistent policy enforcement across all workloads
- Simplified compliance through standardized controls
- Cost-effective deployment of security services

VPC Ingress Routing

VPC Ingress Routing allows you to route all incoming traffic through security appliances before it reaches your applications:

- Configure an Internet Gateway for external connectivity
- Create Gateway Route Tables to direct incoming traffic
- Route traffic through network security appliances (firewalls, IDS/IPS)
- After inspection, forward traffic to its destination

Example Routing Configuration

```
# Internet Gateway Route Table (IGW-RT)
Destination: 10.0.0.0/16 | Target: eni-securityappliance

# Security Appliance Subnet Route Table
Destination: 0.0.0.0/0 | Target: local
Destination: 10.0.0.0/16 | Target: local

# Application Subnet Route Table
Destination: 0.0.0.0/0 | Target: nat-gateway
Destination: 10.0.0.0/16 | Target: local
```

VPC-to-VPC Security Controls

For environments requiring strict controls between VPCs, consider these approaches:

- **Transit Gateway Network Manager**
  - Creates separate route tables for different security domains
  - Controls which VPCs can communicate with each other
  - Applies network access control rules at the Transit Gateway level
- **VPC Peering with Security Groups**
  - Establish VPC peering only between VPCs that need to communicate
  - Use security group references to allow precise access control
  - Implement least privilege access patterns
- **Private NAT Gateway Architecture**
  - Deploy private NAT gateways in shared services VPCs
  - Force traffic through centralized inspection points
  - Maintain source IP information for audit purposes

Security Best Practices for Multi-VPC Designs

When managing complex, multi-VPC architectures, following these best practices ensures consistent configuration, visibility, and governance across all environments.

- **Document Network Flows**: Maintain diagrams and documentation of intended traffic patterns
- **Standardize Naming and Tagging**: Use consistent naming conventions and resource tags
- **Implement Infrastructure as Code**: Manage network configuration through tools like AWS CloudFormation

- **Regularly Audit Connectivity**: Use VPC Reachability Analyzer to verify isolation
- **Establish Guardrails**: Use Service Control Policies in AWS Organizations to prevent unauthorized changes

Network Protection against Emerging Threats

As network attacks evolve, AWS continuously enhances its security services to address emerging threats. Here, we will explore advanced protection measures against some of the most common attack vectors.

Protection against Reflective DDoS Attacks

Reflective DDoS attacks exploit legitimate services to amplify malicious traffic. AWS Shield provides protection against these attacks, but instituting additional measures like the following can enhance your security posture:

- **Block Unnecessary Protocols**: Use Network ACLs to block common reflection vectors:
    - UDP port 19 (CharGen)
    - UDP port 53 (DNS) from unauthorized sources
    - UDP port 123 (NTP)
    - UDP port 389 (LDAP)
    - UDP port 1900 (SSDP)
    - UDP port 11211 (Memcached)
- **Implement Rate-Based Rules**: Use AWS WAF rate-based rules to block IP addresses sending excessive requests
- **Configure Shield Advanced with Proactive Engagement**: Allow the DDoS Response Team (DRT) to access your WAF and Shield configurations

Mitigating Sophisticated Layer 7 Attacks

Layer 7 (application layer) attacks are becoming more sophisticated, targeting specific application vulnerabilities. It is advisable to take the following steps to mitigate them:

1. **Implement Advanced AWS WAF Rules**
    a. Deploy AWS Managed Rules for known threats
    b. Create custom rules for application-specific vulnerabilities
    c. Use rate-based rules to limit requests per IP
    d. Implement bot control to filter automated traffic

2. **Use Origin Protection**
    a. Hide application servers behind CloudFront
    b. Use origin access identity to prevent direct access
    c. Implement custom headers for origin verification
3. **Deploy Application-Specific Protection**
    a. Configure parameter validation in API Gateway
    b. Implement request throttling for APIs
    c. Use AWS WAF Fraud Control Account Takeover Prevention (ATP) rules

Detecting and Preventing Network Reconnaissance

Attackers often conduct reconnaissance before launching targeted attacks. To detect and prevent them on time, make sure to do the following:

- **Monitor and Block Port Scanning**
    - Configure GuardDuty to detect port scanning activity
    - Use NACLs to block excessive connection attempts
    - Implement VPC Flow Logs analysis to identify patterns
- **Protect Network Information**
    - Disable ICMP where not required
    - Use private DNS to hide internal naming
    - Implement strict egress filtering to prevent information leakage
- **Deploy Deception Techniques**
    - Consider honeypot instances to detect reconnaissance
    - Set up canary tokens to alert on unauthorized access attempts
    - Use decoy DNS records and services

Protecting against DNS-Based Attacks

DNS is a critical service that can be targeted by attackers. To protect it against such threats, you must take the following steps:

1. **Mitigate DNS Hijacking**
    a. Enable DNSSEC for public domains
    b. Implement strict access controls for DNS management

   c. Use Route 53 with its built-in DDoS protection

2. **Prevent DNS Data Exfiltration**
   a. Deploy Route 53 DNS Firewall to block unauthorized domains
   b. Monitor DNS query logs for suspicious patterns
   c. Limit recursive DNS queries to trusted resolvers

3. **Defend against DNS Reflection Attacks**
   a. Restrict access to public DNS resolvers
   b. Configure rate limits for DNS queries
   c. Implement response rate limiting on DNS servers

Network Encryption and Private Communication

Encryption is a critical component of network security, protecting data as it travels across networks. AWS provides multiple options for implementing network encryption.

VPN Encryption Options

AWS offers the following VPN solutions with different encryption capabilities:

- **AWS Site-to-Site VPN**
  - IPsec encryption with AES-128 or AES-256
  - SHA-1 or SHA-2 hashing algorithms
  - Perfect Forward Secrecy with Diffie-Hellman key exchange
  - NAT traversal support
- **AWS Client VPN**
  - TLS 1.2 encryption
  - Certificate-based authentication
  - SAML 2.0 integration for identity federation
  - Split-tunnel configuration options
- **AWS Accelerated Site-to-Site VPN**
  - Combines Global Accelerator with Site-to-Site VPN
  - Improved performance for global connections

- Same encryption options as standard Site-to-Site VPN

Encryption for Direct Connect

AWS Direct Connect provides dedicated network connections to AWS, but does not encrypt traffic by default. To add encryption:

- **MACsec Encryption**
  - Layer 2 encryption for Direct Connect dedicated connections
  - Available on connections of 10 Gbps or higher
  - AES-256 encryption with GCM authentication
  - Key rotation every 24 hours
- **IPsec over Direct Connect**
  - Establish VPN tunnels over Direct Connect
  - Combines private connectivity with encryption
  - Requires virtual private gateway or transit gateway
  - Can reduce effective throughput due to encryption overhead
- **VPN CloudHub with Direct Connect**
  - Connect multiple sites through Direct Connect and VPN
  - Encrypted hub-and-spoke topology
  - Centralized routing and security policies

Encryption between EC2 Instances

Encrypting communication between EC2 instances helps safeguard data in transit within your AWS environment. The following methods describe the main options for implementing secure instance-to-instance communication.

- **Nitro Enclaves**
  - Isolated compute environments for sensitive processing
  - Secure local communications with parent instance
  - Attestation for verifying enclave identity
- **Application-Layer Encryption**
  - Implement TLS for service-to-service communication
  - Use mutual TLS (mTLS) for authentication and encryption
  - Deploy service mesh solutions like AWS App Mesh with TLS

- **WireGuard or Similar VPN Solutions**
  - Deploy lightweight VPN between instances
  - Create encrypted overlay networks
  - Suitable for cross-region communication

Best Practices for Network Encryption

Effective network encryption requires strong cryptographic standards and secure key management. The following practices ensure your encrypted communication channels remain robust and compliant.

- **Use Modern Cryptographic Standards**
  - Implement AES-256 when possible
  - Avoid deprecated algorithms like 3DES or MD5
  - Use Perfect Forward Secrecy (PFS) where available
- **Manage Encryption Keys Securely**
  - Rotate keys and certificates regularly
  - Use AWS Certificate Manager for TLS certificate management
  - Consider AWS KMS for centralized key management
- **Document Encryption Architecture**
  - Maintain inventory of encrypted communications
  - Document encryption standards and protocols
  - Regularly review for compliance with security requirements

Micro Segmentation Strategies in AWS

Micro segmentation is a security approach that divides the network into small, isolated segments, restricting communication between segments to reduce attack surface. AWS provides several tools for implementing micro segmentation.

Security Group-Based Micro segmentation

Security groups provide the most granular network controls in AWS:

- **Instance-Level Segmentation**
  - Create security groups based on function and risk level
  - Reference security groups rather than IP ranges
  - Apply multiple security groups to achieve precise control

- **Service-Oriented Grouping**
  - Align security groups with specific services
  - Create tiered access patterns (for example, `web → app → data`)
  - Implement security group reference chains

Network ACL-Based Segmentation

Network ACLs provide subnet-level controls:

- **Zone-Based Segmentation**
  - Create distinct network zones (such as DMZ, application, data)
  - Apply specific NACLs to each zone
  - Control traffic between zones with explicit rules
- **Risk-Based NACL Configurations**
  - Apply stricter NACLs to high-risk or regulated subnets
  - Implement default-deny policies with explicit allows
  - Create NACL tiers based on security requirements

Transit Gateway-Based Segmentation

Transit Gateway enables VPC-level segmentation:

- **Security Domain Isolation**
  - Create separate Transit Gateway route tables for each domain
  - Control routing between domains at a central point
  - Implement inspection for cross-domain traffic
- **Organizational Segmentation**
  - Align Transit Gateway routing with organizational structure
  - Create separate routing domains for different business units
  - Implement shared services with controlled access patterns

Network Security Monitoring Strategies

Effective network security requires comprehensive monitoring to detect potential threats. AWS provides multiple tools for monitoring network activity.

Centralized VPC Flow Log Analysis

VPC Flow Logs provide insights into network traffic patterns, but require proper analysis:

- **Centralized logging architecture**
  - Direct all VPC Flow Logs to a central S3 bucket
  - Implement Athena for SQL-based analysis
  - Use QuickSight for visualization of traffic patterns
- **Automated analysis patterns**
  - Create Lambda functions to process logs
  - Implement anomaly detection algorithms
  - Set up alerts for suspicious patterns

GuardDuty for Network Threat Detection

Amazon GuardDuty analyzes various data sources, including VPC Flow Logs, to detect threats:

- **Network-focused threat detection**
  - `UnauthorizedAccess /SSHBruteForce`
  - `Recon /PortProbeUnprotectedPort`
  - `Impact /PortSweep`
  - `Impact /DenialOfService`
- **Custom threat detection with GuardDuty Detector**
  - Create custom finding types
  - Set severity levels based on your environment
  - Implement automated responses

Network-Focused CloudWatch Alarms

CloudWatch can monitor network metrics and trigger alarms:

- **VPC-level monitoring**
  - NetworkIn and NetworkOut metrics

  - NetworkPacketsIn and NetworkPacketsOut metrics
  - Alert on unusual traffic volumes
- **Security group and NACL monitoring**
  - Track rejected connection attempts
  - Monitor for unusual protocol usage
  - Alert on traffic to unusual ports

Security Information and Event Management (SIEM) Integration

For comprehensive security monitoring, integrate network logs with a SIEM solution:

- **AWS-Native SIEM with Security Hub**
  - Aggregate security findings from multiple services
  - Implement custom insights for network-focused detection
  - Create automated workflows for response
- **Third-Party SIEM Integration**
  - Forward VPC Flow Logs to external SIEM
  - Implement Kinesis Data Firehose for real-time delivery
  - Correlate network events with other security data

Best Practices for Network Security Monitoring

Comprehensive network monitoring enables early detection of anomalies and threats. Use these best practices to maintain continuous visibility and ensure timely response to potential security issues.

- **Establish Baselines**: Document normal traffic patterns
- **Implement Automated Detection**: Create alerts for deviations from baseline
- **Develop Escalation Procedures**: Define response actions for different alert types
- **Test Detection Capabilities**: Conduct regular detection exercises
- **Regular Review and Tuning**: Adjust monitoring based on changing threat landscape

Automating Network Security Controls

Automation is the key to maintaining consistent security controls across complex

AWS environments. Infrastructure as Code (IaC) and AWS native automation tools can help you implement and maintain network security.

CloudFormation for Network Security

AWS CloudFormation enables you to define network security infrastructure as code. It also has different types of automation features, that are defined with their respective functions:

- **Security Group Automation**
  - Define security groups with least privilege access
  - Use parameters for flexible deployment
  - Implement conditions for environment-specific controls
- **NACL Automation**
  - Define strict NACLs for different subnet tiers
  - Use CloudFormation macros for complex rule generation
  - Implement environment-specific rule sets
- **VPC Deployment Automation**
  - Create standardized VPC designs with security built-in
  - Use nested stacks for modular network components
  - Implement service catalog for self-service deployment

AWS Config for Compliance Monitoring

AWS Config can continuously monitor and enforce network security compliance. Therefore, let us have a look at the following rules for each of these functions:

- **Network Security Rules**
  - `vpc-sg-open-only-to-authorized-ports`
  - `vpc-default-security-group-closed`
  - `subnet-auto-assign-public-ip-disabled`
  - `vpc-flow-logs-enabled`
- **Custom AWS Config Rules**
  - Create Lambda-based rules for organization-specific requirements
  - Implement rules for security group reference chains
  - Create compliance checks for encryption requirements

Automated Remediation with Lambda

AWS Lambda can automatically remediate network security issues via the following features:

- **Security Group Cleanup**
  - Detect and remove overly permissive rules
  - Identify and close unused security groups
  - Fix non-compliant configurations
- **Automated VPC Flow Log Enablement**
  - Detect VPCs without flow logs
  - Automatically enable logging with standardized settings
  - Send notifications for manual review

Event-Driven Security Automation

Event-driven security automation allows AWS services to respond automatically to specific network or security events. Using Amazon EventBridge, you can detect changes, trigger predefined responses, and maintain continuous protection without manual intervention. The following examples show common automation use cases.

- **Automated Threat Response**
  - Block IP addresses identified in GuardDuty findings
  - Isolate compromised instances via security group changes
  - Implement temporary NACLs for active attacks
- **Configuration Drift Detection**
  - Monitor for unauthorized security group changes
  - Alert on new route table entries
  - Detect modifications to VPC peering arrangements

Best Practices for Security Automation

Security automation should be implemented thoughtfully to maintain reliability and avoid unintended impacts. The following best practices ensure that your automated systems remain secure, auditable, and aligned with operational standards:

- **Implement Change Management**: Track and approve automated changes
- **Start with Monitoring before Remediation**: Begin with alerts, and then add remediation
- **Test Automation Thoroughly**: Verify automated actions work as expected

- **Document Automated Processes**: Maintain documentation of all automated workflows
- **Implement Circuit Breakers**: Create limits on automated actions to prevent cascading failures

Preparing for the AWS Security Specialty Exam: Network Security Focus

The AWS Security Specialty exam includes significant coverage of network security topics. Here are some key areas to focus on while preparing for it:

VPC Security Knowledge Areas

Make sure that you understand the following:

- **Security group vs. NACL Behavior**
  - Stateful vs. stateless filtering
  - Rule evaluation order
  - Default behaviours
- **VPC Design for Security**
  - Public vs. private subnets
  - NAT gateway configurations
  - Traffic flow patterns
- **VPC Endpoints and PrivateLink**
  - Different endpoint types and use cases
  - Security considerations for each endpoint type
  - Endpoint policies

Advanced Network Protection Services

Make sure that you are familiar with the listed components of the following services:

- **AWS WAF Capabilities**
  - Managed rule sets
  - Custom rules and rule groups
  - Rate-based rules and Bot Control
- **AWS Shield Standard vs. Advanced**
  - Protection coverage for each tier

  - DDoS Response Team engagement
  - Cost protection features
- **AWS Network Firewall**
  - Stateful vs. stateless rule groups
  - Deployment architectures
  - Integration with other AWS services

Hybrid Connectivity Scenarios

Understand how to secure:

- **Site-to-Site VPN Connection**
  - Tunnel options and security
  - Route propagation
  - High availability configurations
- **Direct Connect Security**
  - Encryption options
  - Public vs. private virtual interfaces
  - Integration with Transit Gateway
- **Transit Gateway Implementations**
  - Route table configurations
  - Security domain isolation
  - Centralized inspection architectures

Common Exam Scenarios

Prepare for questions involving:

- **Identifying the most secure architecture** for a given requirement
- **Troubleshooting connectivity issues** related to security controls
- **Choosing appropriate security services** for specific threats
- **Implementing defense-in-depth** across network layers
- **Securing specific AWS services** at the network level

Exam Tips for Network Security Topics

Before attempting the AWS Certified Security – Specialty Exam, it is crucial to understand how AWS network security services work together in real-world contexts.

The following tips will help you approach related exam questions with confidence and clarity:

- **Understand the "Why" behind Security Controls**: Do not just memorize services, understand their purpose and how they fit together
- **Focus on Defense-in-Depth Approaches**: Exam questions often revolve around multiple layers of controls
- **Know When to Use Each Service**: Understand which AWS security service is appropriate for specific threats
- **Be Familiar with Security Best Practices**: Many questions test the knowledge of AWS security best practices
- **Practice Explaining Architecture Decisions**: Should be able to justify why one approach is more secure than another

Conclusion

In this chapter, we explored the comprehensive network security controls available in AWS. We began with foundational components like Virtual Private Clouds (VPCs), security groups, and network ACLs, and went on to learn about advanced services such as AWS Network Firewall, Web Application Firewall (WAF), and Shield for DDoS protection.

In the next chapter, we will focus on **data protection and encryption strategies**, exploring how AWS services such as KMS, CloudHSM, and Secrets Manager safeguard sensitive information across storage and transit layers.

Multiple Choice Questions

1. Which AWS service allows you to monitor network traffic at the packet level by copying traffic from elastic network interfaces?

    a. VPC Flow Logs

    b. Traffic Mirroring

    c. CloudWatch Logs

    d. AWS Network Firewall

2. Your company needs to implement a centralized firewall solution that can perform deep packet inspection for traffic between VPCs. Which AWS service should you use?
    a. Security Groups
    b. Network ACLs
    c. AWS Network Firewall
    d. AWS WAF
3. You want to prevent data exfiltration via DNS queries from your VPC. Which AWS service is best suited for this requirement?
    a. AWS Shield
    b. Route 53 Resolver DNS Firewall
    c. Network ACLs
    d. AWS Systems Manager
4. Which AWS service allows you to connect multiple VPCs and on-premises networks while maintaining isolated routing domains for different security zones?
    a. VPC Peering
    b. AWS Transit Gateway
    c. AWS Direct Connect
    d. Site-to-Site VPN
5. You need to securely access Amazon S3 from instances in a private subnet without going through the internet. Which solution should you implement?
    a. NAT Gateway
    b. S3 Gateway Endpoint
    c. S3 Interface Endpoint
    d. Internet Gateway
6. Which AWS service can help you determine if there is a path through your network configuration that allows one resource to access another?
    a. VPC Flow Logs
    b. IAM Access Analyzer

   c. VPC Reachability Analyzer
   d. AWS Config

7. A security audit has identified that some of your EC2 instances have security groups that allow unrestricted SSH access from the internet. Which AWS service can automatically remediate this issue?
   a. AWS Config with remediation actions
   b. AWS Firewall Manager
   c. AWS Shield
   d. VPC Flow Logs

8. Your organization has implemented a Zero Trust security model. Which of the following is NOT a principle of Zero Trust architecture?
   a. Verify explicitly
   b. Assume breach
   c. Trust but verify
   d. Use least privilege access

Answers

1. b
2. c
3. b
4. b
5. b
6. c
7. a
8. c

References

- AWS Documentation: https://docs.aws.amazon.com/vpc/latest/userguide/what-is-amazon-vpc.html
- AWS Documentation: https://docs.aws.amazon.com/vpc/latest/userguide/vpc-security-groups.html
- AWS Documentation: https://docs.aws.amazon.com/vpc/latest/userguide/vpc-network-acls.html
- AWS Documentation: https://docs.aws.amazon.com/vpc/latest/userguide/flow-logs.html
- AWS Documentation: https://docs.aws.amazon.com/network-firewall/latest/developerguide/what-is-aws-network-firewall.html
- AWS Documentation: https://docs.aws.amazon.com/waf/latest/developerguide/what-is-aws-waf.html
- AWS Documentation: https://docs.aws.amazon.com/waf/latest/developerguide/shield-chapter.html
- AWS Documentation: https://docs.aws.amazon.com/vpc/latest/privatelink/vpc-endpoints.html
- AWS Documentation: https://docs.aws.amazon.com/vpc/latest/tgw/what-is-transit-gateway.html
- AWS Documentation: https://docs.aws.amazon.com/vpc/latest/mirroring/what-is-traffic-mirroring.html
- AWS Documentation: https://docs.aws.amazon.com/Route53/latest/DeveloperGuide/resolver-dns-firewall.html
- AWS Whitepaper: https://d1.awsstatic.com/whitepapers/building-a-scalable-and-secure-multi-vpc-aws-network-infrastructure.pdf
- AWS Whitepaper: https://docs.aws.amazon.com/pdfs/whitepapers/latest/aws-security-best-practices/aws-security-best-practices.pdf

Chapter 5
Logging, Monitoring, and Incident Response

Introduction

In today's cloud environments, security is no longer just about building strong walls–it's about knowing when those walls have been tested or breached, and responding appropriately. This chapter focuses on some critical aspects of AWS security: establishing comprehensive logging and monitoring systems to detect security events, and implementing effective incident response strategies when those events occur.

Consider this scenario: A financial services company migrates its payment processing system to AWS. Despite implementing strong security controls, they experience a data breach. The post-incident investigation reveals that unusual API calls were made to their S3 buckets weeks before the breach, but without proper logging and monitoring, these warning signs went unnoticed. If the company had instituted effective logging, monitoring, and incident response procedures in place before, this breach could have been detected and mitigated early.

In this chapter, we will explore AWS services like CloudTrail and CloudWatch that provide visibility into your AWS environment. We will also examine how to set up monitoring and alerting systems to detect unusual activity, develop effective incident response strategies, and create security dashboards to visualize your security posture. By the end of this chapter, you will be equipped to implement a comprehensive security monitoring and incident response framework on AWS.

Structure

In this chapter, we will cover the following topics:

- Understanding AWS Logging Services
    - AWS CloudTrail
    - AWS CloudWatch Logs

    - VPC Flow Logs
    - S3 Access Logs
    - Load Balancer Access Logs
- Monitoring and Alerting for Security Events
    - AWS CloudWatch Metrics and Alarms
    - AWS EventBridge
    - AWS Security Hub
    - Amazon GuardDuty
- Developing an Incident Response Strategy
    - The Incident Response Lifecycle
    - AWS Incident Response Best Practices
    - Automated Response with AWS Services
- Creating Security Dashboards and Metrics
    - AWS CloudWatch Dashboards
    - Amazon QuickSight for Security Visualization
    - Key Security Metrics to Track

Understanding AWS Logging Services

Logging is the foundation of a robust security monitoring system. AWS provides several logging services that capture different aspects of a cloud environment.

Let us explore these services and understand their security implications.

AWS CloudTrail

AWS CloudTrail enables governance, compliance, operational auditing, and risk auditing of your AWS account. CloudTrail logs, continuously monitors, and retains account activity about actions across your AWS infrastructure, giving you more control over storage, analysis, and remediation actions.

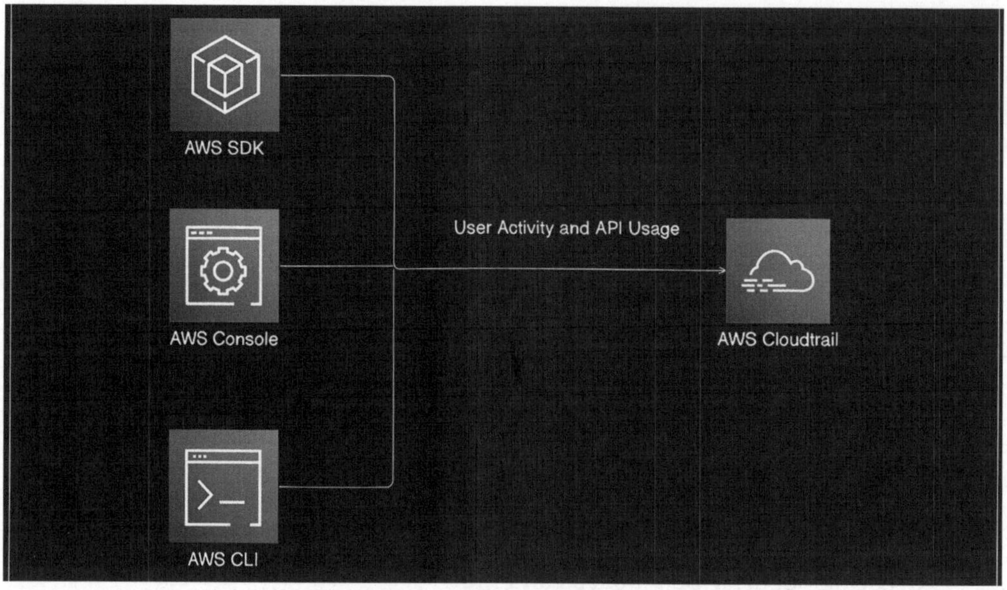

Figure 5.1: *AWS CloudTrail captures user activity and API usage from AWS SDK, Console, and CLI for auditing and monitoring*

Key Security Features of CloudTrail

Before exploring CloudTrail configuration in depth, it is important to understand the key security capabilities that make it a cornerstone for auditing and compliance within AWS environments.

- **API Activity Tracking**: CloudTrail records API calls made within your AWS account, including the identity of the caller, the time of the call, the source IP address, the request parameters, and the response elements.
- **Management and Data Events**: CloudTrail can log management events (operations performed on resources in your AWS account) and data events (resource operations performed on or within a resource).
- **Log File Integrity Validation**: This feature helps you determine whether a CloudTrail log file was modified, deleted, or unchanged after CloudTrail delivered it.
- **Multi-Region and Multi-Account Logging**: CloudTrail can aggregate logs from multiple regions and accounts into a single S3 bucket, providing centralized visibility.
- **Integration with EventBridge**: CloudTrail integrates with Amazon EventBridge to trigger automated responses to specific API activities.

Best Practices for CloudTrail

Implementing CloudTrail effectively requires more than simply enabling it. The following best practices ensure complete visibility, integrity, and protection of your audit logs.

- **Enable CloudTrail across all regions**: This ensures comprehensive coverage of your AWS environment
- **Configure log file integrity validation**: This helps detect tampering with log files
- **Store logs in a dedicated, access-restricted S3 bucket**: This protects the integrity of your logs
- **Enable log file encryption**: This adds an additional layer of protection to your log data
- **Implement lifecycle policies for log retention**: This helps meet compliance requirements while managing storage costs
- **Monitor CloudTrail logs in near real-time**: Integrate with CloudWatch Logs for alerts on suspicious activity

AWS CloudWatch Logs

While CloudTrail focuses on API activity, AWS CloudWatch Logs provides a centralized service for monitoring, storing, and accessing log files from various AWS resources, applications, and services.

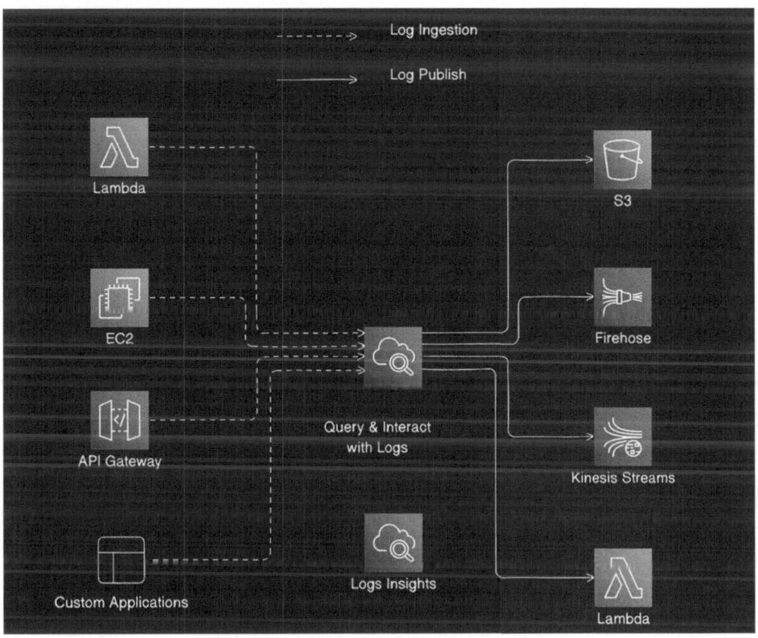

Figure 5.2: Applications and services like Lambda, EC2, and API Gateway ingest logs into CloudWatch, which then enables querying via Logs Insights and publishing to destinations like S3, Firehose, Kinesis Streams, and Lambda

Key Security Features of CloudWatch Logs

CloudWatch Logs provides essential monitoring and analysis capabilities that enhance operational visibility and security insight across your AWS resources. The following key features highlight its importance in centralized logging.

- **Centralized Log Management**: CloudWatch Logs aggregates logs from multiple sources, providing a unified view of your environment.
- **Real-time Monitoring**: CloudWatch Logs allows you to monitor logs in real-time, helping you detect security issues as they occur.
- **Metric Filters and Alarms**: You can create metric filters to extract values from logs and set alarms to notify you when specific patterns are detected.
- **Log Retention and Archiving**: CloudWatch Logs supports customizable retention periods and can archive logs to Amazon S3 for long-term storage.
- **Log Groups and Log Streams**: CloudWatch Logs organizes log data into log groups and log streams, making it easier to manage and analyze logs.

Best Practices for CloudWatch Logs

To maximize the security value of CloudWatch Logs, these practices help you retain, protect, and organize log data efficiently while meeting compliance requirements.

- **Define Appropriate Log Retention Periods**: Balance operational needs with compliance requirements
- **Create Metric Filters for Important Security Events**: This allows you to set alarms for specific security incidents
- **Configure Log Exports to S3 for Long-Term Storage**: This provides an immutable record of log data
- **Use Resource Tags to Categorize and Filter Logs**: This helps manage logs in complex environments
- **Implement Access Controls to Protect Log Data**: This prevents unauthorized access to sensitive log information

VPC Flow Logs

VPC Flow Logs give you a detailed visibility into network traffic patterns. The following features outline how this service enhances your ability to detect anomalies and maintain secure connectivity.

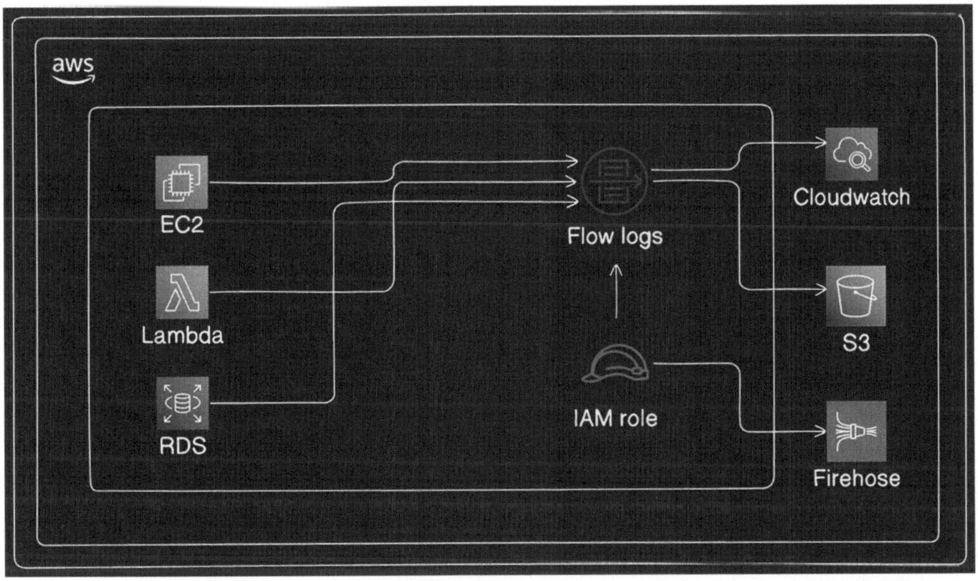

Figure 5.3: *Flow logs capture network traffic from EC2, Lambda, and RDS, and publish it to CloudWatch, S3, or Firehose using IAM roles for access control*

Key Security Features of VPC Flow Logs

Applying these best practices will help ensure that your VPC Flow Logs deliver accurate, actionable insights for both network security monitoring and troubleshooting.

- **Network Traffic Analysis**: VPC Flow Logs provide visibility into network traffic patterns, helping identify potential security issues.
- **Granular Logging Options**: You can create flow logs for VPCs, subnets, or individual network interfaces.
- **Custom Traffic Filtering**: You can specify whether to log accepted or rejected traffic, or both.
- **Integration with CloudWatch Logs and S3**: Flow logs can be published to CloudWatch Logs for real-time monitoring or to S3 for long-term storage.

Best Practices for VPC Flow Logs

To ensure VPC Flow Logs provide maximum visibility and actionable insights, follow these best practices that focus on comprehensive data collection, analysis, and proactive threat detection.

- **Enable Flow Logs for All VPCs**: This ensures comprehensive network traffic visibility

- **Log Both Accepted and Rejected Traffic**: This provides a complete picture of network activity
- **Create Metric Filters for Specific Network Threats**: This helps detect potential network-based attacks
- **Analyze Flow Logs Regularly**: Look for unusual patterns or unexpected connections
- **Implement Automated Analysis Tools**: Consider using Amazon Athena or third-party tools to analyze flow logs at scale

S3 Access Logs

S3 Access Logs provide detailed records of requests made to an S3 bucket and are particularly important for monitoring access to sensitive data stored in S3.

Key Security Features of S3 Access Logs

S3 Access Logs provide critical transparency into who is accessing your data and how. The following features explain how this service supports accountability and security auditing:

- **Detailed Request Logging**: S3 Access Logs capture details about requests made to your bucket, such as the requester, bucket name, request time, action, response status, and error code.
- **Independent Logging Destination**: Logs are stored in a separate bucket, ensuring that logs are preserved even if the source bucket is compromised.
- **No Additional Charges**: There is no extra charge for enabling S3 Access Logs, although standard S3 storage and data transfer rates apply.

Best Practices for S3 Access Logs

The following recommendations help you implement S3 Access Logs in a way that maintains data integrity, reduces risks, and supports ongoing security analysis.

- **Enable Access Logging for All Sensitive Buckets**: This ensures you have visibility into who is accessing your data
- **Store Logs in a Separate Account**: This provides an additional layer of separation between your data and your logs
- **Implement Automated Log Analysis**: Use tools like Amazon Athena to query and analyze access logs
- **Set Up Alerts for Unauthorized Access Attempts**: Monitor for failed access attempts or unusual access patterns

- **Include Log Analysis in Your Security Review Process**: Regularly review access logs as part of your security program

Load Balancer Access Logs

In AWS architecture, enabling load balancer access logs is crucial for security monitoring as they provide detailed information about requests sent to your load balancer.

Key Security Features of Load Balancer Access Logs

Access logs from AWS load balancers capture detailed request information vital for performance analysis and threat detection. The following points summarize the primary security benefits.

- **Comprehensive Request Details**: Logs include information such as the client's IP address, request path, backend server response, and request processing time.
- **Support for Different Load Balancer Types**: Access logs are available for Application Load Balancers, Network Load Balancers, and Classic Load Balancers.
- **Integration with S3**: Logs are stored in an S3 bucket, allowing for long-term retention and analysis.

Best Practices for Load Balancer Access Logs

To fully leverage load balancer access logs, adopt these practices to secure log data, detect threats early, and ensure compliance with monitoring standards.

- **Enable Access Logs for All Load Balancers**: This provides visibility into all incoming traffic
- **Analyze Logs for Suspicious Patterns**: Look for unusual request patterns or attempted exploits
- **Set Up Automated Alerts for Potential Attacks**: Monitor for indicators of SQL injection, XSS, or other web application attacks
- **Correlate Load Balancer Logs with Other Security Telemetry**: Combine with application logs and WAF logs for a complete picture
- **Implement Log Retention Policies**: Balance operational needs with compliance requirements

Monitoring and Alerting for Security Events

While logging services capture data about events in your AWS environment, monitoring and alerting systems help you identify security issues and respond to them proactively.

AWS CloudWatch Metrics and Alarms

AWS CloudWatch Metrics collect data about the performance of your AWS resources and applications. CloudWatch Alarms monitor metrics and trigger actions when thresholds are exceeded.

Key Security Applications of CloudWatch Metrics and Alarms

CloudWatch Metrics and Alarms play a crucial role in proactive security monitoring. The following examples show how these tools can detect, alert, and respond to security-related events.

- **Resource Utilization Monitoring**: Unusual spikes in CPU, memory, or network usage can indicate security issues such as cryptojacking or DDoS attacks.
- **API Call Volume Monitoring**: Sudden increases in API call volume might indicate credential compromise or unauthorized access.
- **Authentication Failure Tracking**: A high number of authentication failures could signal brute force attack attempts.
- **Custom Security Metrics**: You can create custom metrics based on log data to track specific security events.

Best Practices for CloudWatch Metrics and Alarms

Applying these practices ensures your alarms are properly tuned, actionable, and integrated into automated response workflows.

- **Create Alarms for Critical Security Events**: Focus on high-impact events like root account usage or changes to security groups
- **Set Appropriate Thresholds**: Balance between detecting real issues and avoiding alert fatigue
- **Implement Automated Remediation Wherever Appropriate**: Use EventBridge and Lambda to automatically respond to certain security events

- **Test Your Alarms Regularly**: Ensure your monitoring system works as expected
- **Document Your Alerting Strategy**: Maintain clear documentation on what metrics are being monitored and how alerts are handled

AWS EventBridge

Amazon EventBridge (formerly CloudWatch Events) is a serverless event bus service that makes it easy to connect your applications with data from various sources, including AWS services, SaaS applications, and your own applications.

Key Security Applications of EventBridge

EventBridge enables security automation by connecting AWS services and custom workflows. The following use cases demonstrate how it can streamline event handling and threat response.

- **Automated Security Response**: EventBridge can trigger automated responses to security events, such as isolating compromised instances or revoking access keys.
- **Security Event Routing**: EventBridge can route security events from various sources to appropriate targets for processing and analysis.
- **Cross-Account Event Sharing**: EventBridge supports sharing events across AWS accounts, enabling centralized security monitoring in multi-account environments.
- **Custom Security Event Processing**: EventBridge allows you to filter and transform events before sending them to targets, enabling sophisticated security event processing.

Best Practices for EventBridge

To ensure EventBridge contributes effectively to your security posture, follow these best practices for rule design, documentation, and response automation.

- **Create Rules for Critical Security Events**: Focus on events that require immediate attention or automated response
- **Implement a Defense-in-Depth Approach**: Use multiple rules to detect different aspects of security incidents
- **Test Your Event Rules and Response Processes**: Ensure that they work as expected in different scenarios
- **Document Your EventBridge Rules**: Maintain clear documentation on what events are being monitored and how they are handled

- **Use Event Patterns to Filter Events**: Target only relevant events to reduce noise and improve efficiency

AWS Security Hub

AWS Security Hub provides a comprehensive view of your security state in AWS and helps you check your environment against security industry standards and best practices.

Key Security Features of Security Hub

AWS Security Hub provides a centralized view of your security state across multiple services and accounts. The following features outline its core functionality for continuous compliance and threat management.

- **Centralized Security Findings**: Security Hub aggregates and prioritizes findings from multiple AWS services and third-party products.
- **Automated Security Checks**: Security Hub performs automated, continuous security checks based on AWS best practices and industry standards.
- **Compliance Monitoring**: Security Hub helps you assess your environment for compliance with standards such as PCI DSS, CIS AWS Foundations Benchmark, and AWS Foundational Security Best Practices.
- **Integration with AWS Services**: Security Hub integrates with services like GuardDuty, Inspector, and Macie to provide a unified view of security findings.
- **Custom Actions and Automated Response**: Security Hub enables you to create custom actions and automate responses to security findings.

Best Practices for Security Hub

Implementing these best practices helps you maintain consistent compliance, automate remediation, and get the most actionable insights from Security Hub findings.

- **Enable All Relevant Standards**: Implement the security standards that align with your compliance requirements
- **Configure Integrations with Other Security Services**: Ensure that Security Hub receives findings from all relevant sources
- **Regularly Review and Remediate Findings**: Establish a process for addressing security issues identified by Security Hub
- **Use Custom Actions for Common Remediation Tasks**: Automate responses to frequently occurring security findings

- **Implement Cross-Account Aggregation**: In multi-account environments, aggregate findings into a central security account

Amazon GuardDuty

Amazon GuardDuty is a threat detection service that continuously monitors for malicious activity and unauthorized behavior in your AWS accounts and workloads.

Key Security Features of GuardDuty

Amazon GuardDuty offers intelligent threat detection by analyzing AWS data sources. The following features describe how it continuously identifies and prioritizes potential risks.

- **Intelligent Threat Detection**: GuardDuty uses machine learning, anomaly detection, and integrated threat intelligence to identify potential security threats
- **Comprehensive Coverage**: GuardDuty analyzes multiple data sources, including AWS CloudTrail events, VPC Flow Logs, and DNS logs
- **Minimal Operational Overhead**: GuardDuty is fully managed and requires no additional infrastructure, agents, or sensors
- **Continuous Monitoring**: GuardDuty continuously monitors your AWS environment, providing near real-time detection of potential security issues
- **Detailed Findings**: GuardDuty generates detailed security findings with evidence and recommended remediation steps

Best Practices for GuardDuty

To optimize GuardDuty's effectiveness, apply the following best practices to ensure comprehensive coverage, accurate detection, and automated remediation across all accounts and regions.

- **Enable GuardDuty Across All Accounts and Regions**: Use AWS Organizations and GuardDuty delegated administrator to centrally manage GuardDuty
- **Customize Finding Severity Thresholds**: Adjust severity thresholds based on your organization's risk tolerance
- **Use Trusted IP Lists and Threat Lists**: Configure GuardDuty with trusted IP lists and threat intelligence lists
- **Implement Automated Responses**: Use EventBridge and Lambda to automatically respond to critical GuardDuty findings
- **Regularly Review and Tune Findings**: Analyze findings regularly to identify false positives and improve detection

Developing an Incident Response Strategy

An effective incident response strategy is critical for minimizing the impact of security incidents in your AWS environment. In this section, we will explore the incident response lifecycle, AWS best practices for incident response, and how to automate response using AWS services.

The Incident Response Lifecycle

The incident response lifecycle consists of several phases that guide organizations through the process of preparing for, detecting, and responding to security incidents. Let's examine each phase and how they apply to AWS environments.

Preparation

The preparation phase involves establishing processes, tools, and resources necessary to respond effectively to security incidents.

Key Preparation Activities

- **Develop Incident Response Plans**: Create detailed plans that outline roles, responsibilities, and procedures for handling different types of security incidents
- **Establish Communication Channels**: Define clear communication protocols for incident response teams, stakeholders, and external entities
- **Deploy Security Tools**: Implement logging, monitoring, and analysis tools to support incident detection and investigation
- **Train Response Teams**: Conduct regular training and simulation exercises to ensure response teams are ready to handle incidents
- **Create Forensic-Ready AMIs**: Prepare Amazon Machine Images (AMIs) with forensic tools pre-installed for quick deployment during investigations

AWS-Specific Preparation

- **Enable Comprehensive Logging**: Ensure CloudTrail, VPC Flow Logs, and other relevant logs are enabled across all accounts and regions
- **Set Up Security Automation**: Deploy AWS Config Rules, Security Hub, and GuardDuty to automate security checks and threat detection
- **Create Incident Response IAM Roles**: Configure IAM roles specifically for incident response activities with appropriate permissions
- **Establish a Secure S3 Bucket for Evidence**: Set up an S3 bucket with appropriate access controls and encryption for storing forensic evidence

- **Document AWS Environment**: Maintain up-to-date documentation of your AWS infrastructure, including network diagrams, security groups, and IAM policies

Detection and Analysis

The detection and analysis phase involves identifying potential security incidents and gathering information to understand their scope and impact.

Key Detection and Analysis Activities

- **Monitor Security Alerts**: Continuously monitor alerts from security tools and services to identify potential incidents
- **Perform Initial Triage**: Assess alerts to determine if they represent actual security incidents that require response
- **Collect and Analyze Evidence**: Gather logs, network traffic data, and other relevant information to understand the nature of the incident
- **Determine Scope and Impact**: Identify affected systems, data, and users to understand the extent of the incident
- **Establish Incident Timeline**: Create a chronological record of events related to the incident

AWS-Specific Detection and Analysis

- **Use GuardDuty Findings**: Review GuardDuty findings to identify potential threats and suspicious activities
- **Analyze CloudTrail Logs**: Examine CloudTrail logs to understand API activity related to the incident
- **Review VPC Flow Logs**: Analyze VPC Flow Logs to identify suspicious network traffic patterns
- **Leverage CloudWatch Insights**: Use CloudWatch Logs Insights to query and analyze log data related to the incident
- **Snapshot Affected Resources**: Create snapshots of affected EC2 instances and EBS volumes for forensic analysis

Containment, Eradication, and Recovery

These phases involve limiting the damage from an incident, eliminating the threat, and restoring affected systems to normal operation.

Key Containment, Eradication, and Recovery Activities

- **Isolate Affected Systems**: Separate compromised systems from the network to prevent further damage

- **Eliminate Threat Actors**: Remove unauthorized access and malicious code from affected systems
- **Patch Vulnerabilities**: Address security weaknesses that led to the incident
- **Restore from Clean Backups**: Rebuild compromised systems from known-good backups or images
- **Verify Security**: Conduct security checks to ensure threats have been eliminated and vulnerabilities addressed

AWS-Specific Containment, Eradication, and Recovery

- **Isolate EC2 Instances**: Modify security groups or subnet ACLs to isolate compromised instances
- **Revoke IAM Credentials**: Deactivate compromised IAM access keys and user credentials
- **Terminate Unauthorized Resources**: Shut down unauthorized EC2 instances, Lambda functions, or other resources
- **Restore from AWS Backups**: Use AWS Backup, AMIs, or snapshots to restore clean versions of compromised resources
- **Deploy CloudFormation Stacks**: Use CloudFormation to quickly rebuild clean environments

Post-Incident Activity

The post-incident phase involves reviewing the incident, documenting lessons learned, and implementing improvements to prevent similar incidents in the future.

Key Post-Incident Activities

- **Document the Incident**: Create a detailed record of the incident, including timeline, actions taken, and outcomes
- **Conduct Root Cause Analysis**: Identify the underlying causes that led to the incident
- **Hold Lessons Learned Meetings**: Discuss what worked well and what could be improved in the response process
- **Update Incident Response Plans**: Revise plans based on lessons learned and emerging threats
- **Implement Preventive Measures**: Enhance security controls to prevent similar incidents in the future

AWS-Specific Post-Incident Activities

- **Review AWS Security Posture**: Use AWS Security Hub or Trusted Advisor to assess and strengthen your security posture

- **Enhance Monitoring and Alerting**: Update CloudWatch Alarms and EventBridge rules based on lessons learned
- **Implement Additional Security Controls**: Deploy AWS Config Rules, WAF rules, or other controls to address identified vulnerabilities
- **Update IAM Policies**: Refine IAM policies to implement least privilege and limit potential damage from compromised credentials
- **Automate Remediation**: Develop Lambda functions to automate responses to similar incidents in the future

AWS Incident Response Best Practices

AWS provides a range of services and features that can enhance your incident response capabilities. Here are some best practices for incident response in AWS environments:

Adopt a Cloud-Native Approach

Traditional incident response processes often rely on direct access to physical hardware and network infrastructure. In AWS environments, a cloud-native approach leverages AWS services and APIs for more effective incident response.

Best Practices

- **API-Driven Response**: Use AWS APIs to gather information and take actions during incident response, rather than relying on host-based tools
- **Use AWS-Native Security Services**: Leverage services like GuardDuty, Security Hub, and Macie for detection and response
- **Automate Incident Response**: Implement automation using Lambda, EventBridge, and Step Functions to speed up response actions
- **Implement Infrastructure as Code**: Use CloudFormation or Terraform to create and manage resources consistently, making it easier to understand and respond to incidents

Prepare Your AWS Environment for Incident Response

Proper preparation can significantly improve the speed and effectiveness of incident response in AWS.

Best Practices

- **Enable MFA for All IAM Users**: Protect IAM users from credential compromise

- **Use AWS Organizations for Multi-Account Management**: Implement a structured multi-account strategy with dedicated security and logging accounts
- **Implement Service Control Policies (SCPs)**: Use SCPs to enforce security guardrails across your organization
- **Deploy AWS Config Rules**: Use AWS Config Rules to detect and automatically remediate misconfigurations
- **Establish a Forensic Environment**: Set up a separate AWS account or VPC for forensic analysis

Implement Effective Logging and Monitoring

Effective logging and monitoring are foundational to maintaining visibility, detecting anomalies, and ensuring compliance in AWS environments. The practices below outline how to design a proactive monitoring strategy that supports both security and operational goals.

Best Practices

- **Create Baselines**: Establish normal behavior patterns to help identify anomalies
- **Set Up Real-Time Alerting**: Configure CloudWatch Alarms and EventBridge rules for immediate notification of security events
- **Use Log Retention Policies**: Implement appropriate log retention periods to ensure logs are available when needed

Develop Incident Response Playbooks

Detailed playbooks provide step-by-step guidance for responding to specific types of incidents, helping ensure consistent and effective responses.

Here are some sample AWS Incident Response Playbooks:

Unauthorized Access Playbook

- **Identify Compromised Resources**: Use CloudTrail and GuardDuty to identify affected resources
- **Isolate Compromised Resources**: Modify security groups or move resources to an isolated subnet
- **Revoke Access**: Invalidate temporary credentials, revoke IAM access keys, or disable IAM users
- **Collect Evidence**: Take snapshots of affected EC2 instances and capture relevant logs.

- **Restore Clean Environment**: Terminate compromised instances and deploy clean replacements

Data Exfiltration Playbook

- **Identify Exfiltrated Data**: Use VPC Flow Logs and CloudTrail to identify data transfers
- **Block Exfiltration Channels**: Update security groups, NACLs, or S3 bucket policies to block unauthorized access
- **Assess Data Sensitivity**: Determine the nature and sensitivity of the exfiltrated data
- **Notify Stakeholders**: Communicate with legal, compliance, and public relations teams as needed
- **Implement Enhanced Monitoring**: Deploy additional controls to monitor and prevent future exfiltration

Automate Incident Response

Automation can significantly improve incident response speed and consistency.

Best Practices

- **Create Auto-Remediation Rules**: Use EventBridge and Lambda to automatically respond to common security events
- **Implement Security Information and Event Management (SIEM)**: Consider using Amazon Security Lake or third-party SIEM solutions for advanced analysis and automation
- **Deploy Chatbots for Incident Coordination**: Use AWS Chatbot to streamline incident communication and coordination
- **Build Incident Response Pipelines**: Use AWS Step Functions to orchestrate complex incident response workflows
- **Use Infrastructure as Code for Recovery**: Prepare CloudFormation templates for quickly rebuilding clean environments

Automated Response with AWS Services

Let us explore how different AWS services can be used to automate incident response-

AWS Lambda and EventBridge

AWS Lambda and EventBridge form the foundation of many automated response solutions, enabling you to detect and respond to security events programmatically.

AWS Step Functions for Complex Response Workflows

While Lambda functions are powerful, you can design more complex incident response workflows using AWS Step Functions, which allows you to coordinate multiple Lambda functions and AWS services.

Creating Security Dashboards and Metrics

Effective security monitoring requires comprehensive dashboards and metrics that provide visibility into your AWS environment's security posture. In this section, we will explore how to create security dashboards using AWS CloudWatch and Amazon QuickSight and identify key security metrics to track.

AWS CloudWatch Dashboards

CloudWatch Dashboards provide a customizable view of your AWS resources and can be particularly useful for security monitoring.

Key Benefits of CloudWatch Dashboards for Security

CloudWatch Dashboards provide a unified, visual interface for observing key security metrics across AWS services. The following benefits demonstrate how dashboards enhance situational awareness and support real-time decision-making:

- **Consolidated View**: Combine metrics, logs, and alarms from multiple AWS services in a single dashboard
- **Real-time Monitoring**: View security metrics in near real-time to quickly identify issues
- **Custom Widgets**: Create custom widgets to display specific security information
- **Cross-Region Visibility**: Monitor security metrics across multiple AWS regions
- **Sharing and Access Control**: Share dashboards with team members and control access with IAM

Best Practices for Security Dashboards

Following these best practices ensures that your dashboards communicate the right information clearly and help teams act quickly when anomalies occur.

- **Focus on Actionable Metrics**: Prioritize metrics that require attention when they deviate from normal patterns
- **Group Related Metrics**: Organize metrics logically to facilitate quick understanding
- **Use Appropriate Visualizations**: Choose the right visualization type for each metric (for example, line charts for trends, bar charts for comparisons)
- **Include Context**: Add reference lines or annotations to provide context for metric values
- **Set Appropriate Time Ranges**: Configure dashboard time ranges based on the typical timeframe for security analysis

Amazon QuickSight for Security Visualization

While CloudWatch Dashboards are excellent for real-time monitoring, Amazon QuickSight provides more advanced analytics and visualization capabilities for in-depth security analysis.

Key Benefits of QuickSight for Security Visualization

The following listed capabilities show how QuickSight enhances security analysis with powerful visualization and data integration features:

- **Advanced Analytics**: Apply machine learning and statistical algorithms to detect anomalies in security data
- **Interactive Dashboards**: Create interactive visualizations that allow security analysts to drill down into details
- **Data Integration**: Connect to multiple data sources, including S3, Athena, and RDS, to combine security information
- **Scheduled Reports**: Automate the delivery of security reports to stakeholders
- **Enterprise-Grade Sharing**: Share insights securely with fine-grained access controls

Example Security Analytics with QuickSight

QuickSight can be applied across multiple AWS data sources to uncover patterns and correlations in security events. The examples below highlight practical use cases for threat detection and compliance tracking.

- **VPC Flow Log Analysis**: Analyze network traffic patterns to identify suspicious communication

- **CloudTrail Activity Visualization**: Visualize API activity across accounts and regions to detect anomalies
- **IAM Usage Analysis**: Track IAM role and policy usage to identify potential privilege escalation
- **Security Finding Trends**: Analyze trends in GuardDuty and Security Hub findings over time
- **Compliance Dashboards**: Create visual representations of compliance status across your AWS environment

Key Security Metrics to Track

Effective security monitoring requires tracking the right metrics. Here are key security metrics that should be monitored in AWS environments:

Identity and Access Management Metrics

These metrics help evaluate how users, roles, and permissions are being utilized, providing insight into potential misuse, privilege escalation, or account compromise.

- **Root Account Usage**: Frequency and nature of root account usage
- **IAM User Activity**: Number of active IAM users and their actions
- **Permission Changes**: Frequency and nature of IAM policy modifications
- **Authentication Failures**: Number and patterns of failed login attempts
- **Role Assumption**: Frequency and patterns of role assumption across accounts

Network Security Metrics

Network metrics reveal how data flows within your AWS environment, helping detect anomalies such as unauthorized access attempts or misconfigured network controls.

- **Rejected VPC Flow Logs**: Count of rejected network connections
- **Public Resource Exposure**: Number of resources with public access
- **VPN/Direct Connect Usage**: Volume and patterns of traffic over private connections
- **Network ACL and Security Group Changes**: Frequency and nature of network control modifications
- **Cross-Region Traffic**: Volume and patterns of traffic between AWS regions

Data Protection Metrics

These metrics provide a window into active and emerging threats across your environment, helping you assess detection effectiveness and prioritize incident response.

- **Encryption Status**: Percentage of resources using encryption
- **Data Access Patterns**: Frequency and volume of data access operations
- **S3 Bucket Policy Changes**: Modifications to S3 bucket policies
- **Sensitive Data Access**: Access patterns for resources containing sensitive data
- **KMS Key Usage**: Patterns of encryption key usage

Threat Detection Metrics

These metrics provide a window into active and emerging threats across your environment, helping you assess detection effectiveness and prioritize incident response.

- **GuardDuty Findings**: Number and severity of GuardDuty findings
- **Security Hub Compliance**: Compliance status across security standards
- **Malware Detections**: Number of malware detections from antivirus tools
- **Unusual API Calls**: API calls that deviate from normal patterns
- **Geographic Anomalies**: Access from unusual geographic locations

Incident Response Metrics

Incident response metrics track the efficiency and effectiveness of your organization's reaction to security events, helping identify areas where processes can be optimized.

- **Mean Time to Detect (MTTD)**: Average time to detect security incidents
- **Mean Time to Respond (MTTR)**: Average time to respond to security incidents
- **Mean Time to Contain (MTTC)**: Average time to contain security incidents
- **Incident Resolution Rate**: Percentage of incidents successfully resolved
- **Recurrence Rate**: Percentage of incidents that recur after resolution

Conclusion

In this chapter, we have explored the essential components of logging, monitoring, and incident response in AWS. We have learned how to set up comprehensive logging using services like CloudTrail, CloudWatch Logs, and VPC Flow Logs. We have also explored how to establish effective monitoring and alerting mechanisms using CloudWatch Metrics, EventBridge, Security Hub, and GuardDuty.

The chapter also discussed the incident response lifecycle and how to develop an effective incident response strategy tailored to AWS environments. By leveraging automation through Lambda functions and Step Functions, we can respond to security incidents more quickly and consistently.

Finally, we also examined how to create security dashboards and track key security metrics, providing visibility into your AWS environment's security posture.

By implementing the logging, monitoring, and incident response practices described in this chapter, you will be well-equipped to detect and respond to security events in your AWS environment, minimizing their impact and protecting your organization's data and resources.

In the next chapter, we'll explore DevSecOps and security automation in AWS, focusing on how to integrate security into your development processes and automate security testing and remediation.

Points to Remember

- Enable comprehensive logging across your AWS environment using CloudTrail, CloudWatch Logs, VPC Flow Logs, and other logging services
- Implement effective monitoring and alerting using CloudWatch Metrics, EventBridge, Security Hub, and GuardDuty
- Develop an incident response strategy that covers preparation, detection, containment, eradication, recovery, and post-incident activities
- Leverage automation for incident response using Lambda, EventBridge, and Step Functions.
- Create security dashboards to track key security metrics and provide visibility into your security posture
- Regularly review and update your logging, monitoring, and incident response capabilities to address evolving threats

Multiple Choice Questions

1. Which AWS service records API calls made to AWS services in your account?

    a. AWS CloudWatch Logs

    b. AWS CloudTrail

   c. VPC Flow Logs

   d. AWS Config

2. Which AWS service provides threat detection capabilities using machine learning and threat intelligence?

   a. AWS Security Hub

   b. AWS Inspector

   c. AWS GuardDuty

   d. AWS Detective

3. What is the name of the AWS service that aggregates and prioritizes security findings from multiple sources?

   a. AWS CloudWatch

   b. AWS CloudTrail

   c. AWS Security Hub

   d. AWS Inspector

4. Which logging service captures information about IP traffic going to and from network interfaces in your VPC?

   a. AWS CloudTrail

   b. AWS CloudWatch Logs

   c. VPC Flow Logs

   d. S3 Access Logs

5. Which AWS service allows you to create rules that match events and route them to targets for processing?

   a. AWS EventBridge

   b. AWS CloudWatch

   c. AWS CloudTrail

   d. AWS Step Functions

Answers

1. b
2. c
3. c
4. c
5. a

References

- AWS CloudTrail Documentation: https://docs.aws.amazon.com/cloudtrail/
- AWS CloudWatch Documentation: https://docs.aws.amazon.com/cloudwatch/
- AWS Security Hub Documentation: https://docs.aws.amazon.com/securityhub/
- AWS GuardDuty Documentation: https://docs.aws.amazon.com/guardduty/
- AWS EventBridge Documentation: https://docs.aws.amazon.com/eventbridge/
- AWS VPC Flow Logs Documentation: https://docs.aws.amazon.com/vpc/latest/userguide/flow-logs.html
- AWS S3 Server Access Logging Documentation: https://docs.aws.amazon.com/AmazonS3/latest/userguide/ServerLogs.html
- AWS Lambda Documentation: https://docs.aws.amazon.com/lambda/
- AWS Step Functions Documentation: https://docs.aws.amazon.com/step-functions/
- AWS IAM Documentation: https://docs.aws.amazon.com/iam/
- AWS Security Best Practices: https://docs.aws.amazon.com/whitepapers/latest/aws-security-best-practices/
- AWS Security Incident Response Guide: https://docs.aws.amazon.com/whitepapers/latest/aws-security-incident-response-guide/
- AWS re:Inforce 2023 - SEC209: AWS Security & Incident Response: https://www.youtube.com/watch?v=8jyhsnh0ALQ
- AWS re:Invent 2022 - SEC404: Cloud threat detection and response: https://www.youtube.com/watch?v=mzdvjTpujHE
- NIST Special Publication 800-61 Revision 2, Computer Security Incident Handling Guide

CHAPTER 6
DevSecOps and Security Automation

Introduction

In today's rapidly evolving digital landscape, organizations are under increasing pressure to deliver secure applications quickly. Approaches to traditional security often viewed security as a final checkpoint before deployment, creating bottlenecks that slowed innovation. Enter DevSecOps—a revolutionary approach that integrates security throughout the software development lifecycle, making it everyone's responsibility rather than relegating it to a separate team.

AWS provides a comprehensive suite of tools and services that support DevSecOps practices, enabling organizations to automate security controls, continuously monitor compliance, and respond to threats rapidly. This chapter explores how to integrate security into DevOps workflows, focusing on their practical implementation using AWS services.

By the end of this chapter, you will understand how to automate security tasks, implement continuous compliance monitoring, and build security directly into your infrastructure as code. You will also gain hands-on experience with setting up automated security testing in CI/CD pipelines, which are skills that are increasingly valuable in today's security-conscious cloud environments.

Structure

In this chapter, we will cover the following topics:

- Fundamentals of DevSecOps
  - DevOps vs. DevSecOps
  - The DevSecOps lifecycle
  - Benefits of DevSecOps in AWS Environments

- Securing the CI/CD Pipeline
  - Security Tools for CI/CD
  - Secret Management
  - Infrastructure Validation
- Automating Compliance with AWS Config
  - Understanding AWS Config
  - Creating Custom Rules
  - Remediating Non-Compliant Resources
- Infrastructure as Code Security
  - AWS CloudFormation for Secure Deployments
  - Testing IaC Templates for Vulnerabilities
  - Implementing Guardrails
- Common Mistakes and How to Avoid Them
  - Relying Solely on Manual Security Checks
  - Hardcoding Secrets in Code Repositories
  - Ignoring Security During Early Development Phases
  - Lack of Automated Remediation for Non-Compliance
  - Overlooking Monitoring and Logging Configurations
  - Misconfigured IAM Roles and Excessive Permissions
- Benefits
  - Reduced Time to Detect and Remediate Vulnerabilities
  - Continuous Compliance Without Slowing Deployment
  - Improved Collaboration between Dev, Sec, and Ops Teams
  - Lower Security Incident Costs through Proactive Prevention
  - Scalability of Security Processes with Growing Workloads
  - Stronger Alignment with Regulatory Requirements
- Future of DevSecOps
  - Increased Use of AI/ML for Automated Threat Detection
  - Tighter Integration of Security Tools within Developer IDEs
  - Expansion of Security-As-Code Frameworks
  - Greater Emphasis on Supply Chain Security for Software Components
  - Serverless and Container Security Automation as Defaults
  - Industry-Specific Compliance Automation Blueprints

Fundamentals of DevSecOps

This section introduces the concept of DevSecOps, explaining how it extends traditional DevOps by embedding security practices throughout the development lifecycle rather than treating them as a final step.

DevOps vs. DevSecOps

DevOps is a methodology focused on breaking down barriers between development and operations teams to enable faster and more reliable software releases. While DevOps emphasizes collaboration, automation, and continuous feedback, security was often treated as an afterthought as it was considered a separate concern that would be addressed at the end of the development cycle.

DevSecOps evolved as a response to this gap and integrated security as a core component throughout the software development lifecycle. The difference between DevOps and DevSecOps lies in when and how security is addressed:

In traditional DevOps

- Security is often handled by a separate team.
- Security checks occur late in the development cycle.
- Security can become a bottleneck before deployment.

In DevSecOps

- Security is integrated into every phase of development.
- Security checks are automated and continuous.
- Everyone shares responsibility for security.

The transition to DevSecOps is not just about adding security tools to a DevOps pipeline; it requires a shift where security is a part of everyone's job rather than the responsibility of a separate team.

The DevSecOps Lifecycle

Before exploring each stage in detail, it's useful to understand how security fits seamlessly into every phase of software delivery, from planning and coding to testing, deployment, and continuous monitoring.

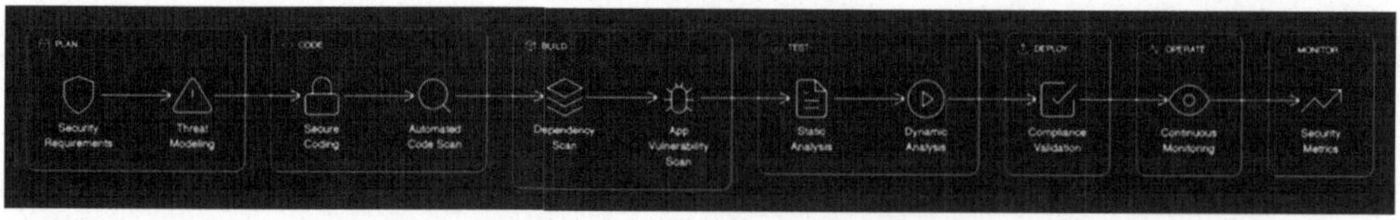

Figure 6.1: *End-to-end DevSecOps lifecycle integrating security from planning to monitoring*

The DevSecOps lifecycle integrates security at every phase of the software development process in the following ways:

- **Planning**: Security requirements and threat modeling are incorporated into planning sessions.
- **Coding**: Developers use secure coding practices and automated tools to check for security issues as they write code.
- **Building**: Automated security scans check dependencies and application code for vulnerabilities.
- **Testing**: Security testing is performed alongside functional testing, including dynamic and static analysis.
- **Deployment**: Infrastructure is validated for security compliance before deployment.
- **Operations**: Continuous monitoring allows one to detect security issues in production.
- **Monitoring**: Security metrics are collected and analyzed to improve the overall security posture.

Benefits of DevSecOps in AWS Environments

AWS provides the following advantages for implementing DevSecOps practices:

- **Comprehensive Security Services**: AWS offers integrated security services like Amazon GuardDuty, AWS Security Hub, and Amazon Inspector that can be automated as part of the DevSecOps pipeline.
- **Infrastructure as Code Support**: Services like AWS CloudFormation and AWS CDK enable security to be baked into infrastructure definitions and validated before deployment.
- **Native CI/CD Integration**: AWS Developer Tools such as CodePipeline, CodeBuild, and CodeDeploy, can incorporate security scanning and testing throughout the development process.
- **Compliance Automation**: AWS Config and AWS Security Hub provide automated compliance checks as per industry standards and best practices
- **Centralized Visibility**: Services like AWS Security Hub provide a unified view of security alerts and compliance status across AWS accounts.

Securing the CI/CD Pipeline

A Continuous Integration / Continuous Deployment (CI/CD) pipeline automates the process of building, testing, and deploying code. Securing this pipeline is critical, as it can become an attack vector if it is not protected properly.

Security Tools for CI/CD

The AWS services and integrated tools used in the illustrated CI/CD security pipeline are as follows:

- **Source Control (GitHub)**: An external repository where code changes are stored and managed; triggers the CI/CD process
- **Static Analysis**: AWS CodeBuild or integrated SAST tools, for example, SonarQube and Bandit, run in the build stage to detect insecure code patterns
- **Dependency Scanning**: CodeBuild or other integrated tools such as Safety and the OWASP Dependency-Check, check third-party packages for known vulnerabilities
- **Amazon Inspector**: Scans workloads for software vulnerabilities and unintended network exposure
- **Amazon ECR Image Scanning**: Analyzes container images stored in Amazon ECR for known CVEs before deployment
- **AWS Config**; Monitors deployed infrastructure to ensure compliance with security and configuration rules
- **AWS Security Hub**: Centralizes and prioritizes findings from Inspector, Config, and other security services
- **AWS CodeDeploy**: Deploys only the builds that pass all the security and compliance checks

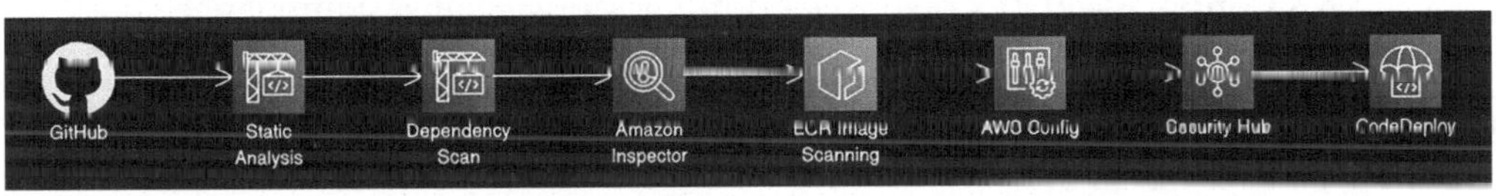

Figure 6.2: *CI/CD pipeline integrating GitHub with AWS security services for automated scanning and compliant deployments*

Secret Management

The secure management of credentials and secrets is critical for CI/CD pipelines. AWS provides several options to do so:

- **AWS Secrets Manager**: Centrally manages database credentials, API keys, and other secrets

- **AWS Systems Manager Parameter Store**: Stores configuration data including plain text and encrypted values
- **AWS KMS (Key Management Service)**: Manages encryption keys used throughout your applications and CI/CD process

Some best practices for secret management are as follows:

- Never store secrets in code repositories
- Rotate secrets regularly
- Limit access to secrets based on the principle of least privilege
- Audit secret access
- Implement Automated Secret Rotation

Infrastructure Validation

Infrastructure validation ensures that cloud resources are configured securely before deployment. The key approaches to this step include:

- **Defining Policy-as-Code**: Define security policies as code that can be automatically enforced
- **Performing Static Analysis**: Analyze infrastructure templates such as CloudFormation and Terraform for security issues before deployment
- **Dynamic Validation**: Verify deployed resources against security benchmarks

The AWS services that support infrastructure validation are:

- **AWS CloudFormation Guard**: Validates CloudFormation templates against policy rules
- `cfn-nag`: Identifies security issues in CloudFormation templates
- **AWS Config**: Evaluates resource configurations against compliance rules

Automating Compliance with AWS Config

AWS Config enables you to assess, audit, and evaluate the configurations of your AWS resources. It is a key component used to maintain continuous compliance in DevSecOps.

Understanding AWS Config

AWS Config continuously monitors and records AWS resource configurations, and also allows the user to do the following:

- **Track Resource Changes**: Maintain a historical record of configuration changes

- **Evaluate Compliance**: Assess resource configurations against desired configurations
- **Audit Security**: Verify that security controls are properly implemented
- **Visualize Relationships**: Understand how resources relate to each other

The core components of AWS Config include:

- **Configuration Items (CIs)**: Point-in-time snapshots of AWS resources
- **Configuration History**: Timeline of configuration changes for resources
- **Configuration Recorder**: Service that tracks changes to resource configurations
- **Config Rules**: Evaluations that check if resources comply with desired configurations

Creating Custom Rules

AWS Config provides many managed rules for common compliance checks, but you can also create custom rules for organization-specific requirements.

Custom rules are implemented as AWS Lambda functions that evaluate resource configurations. Here's a basic workflow with each of them:

1. **Identify the compliance requirement** you want to enforce
2. **Create a Lambda function** that evaluates resources against this requirement
3. **Register the Lambda function** as a custom AWS Config rule
4. **Define the scope** of the rule as in which resources does it apply to
5. **Set up notification** for non-compliant resources

Remediating Non-Compliant Resources

AWS Config can be integrated with AWS Systems Manager Automation or AWS Lambda to remediate non-compliant resources automatically.

The remediation process typically follows these steps:

1. AWS Config identifies a non-compliant resource.
2. A notification is sent (via Amazon SNS).
3. An automation workflow is triggered to remediate the issue.
4. The resource is re-evaluated to confirm compliance.

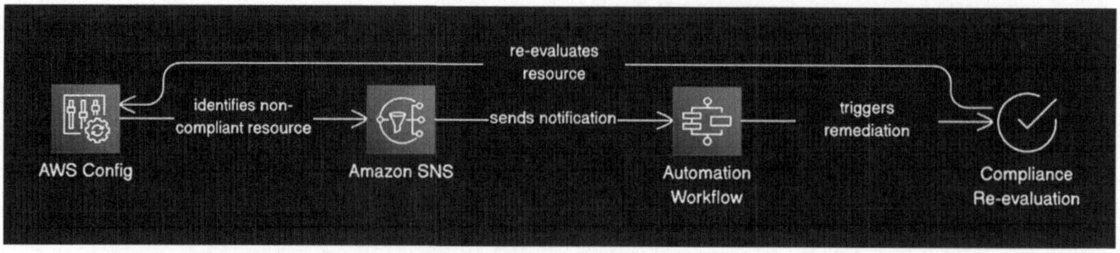

Figure 6.3: *Automated compliance remediation workflow using AWS Config, SNS, and Automation for continuous resource evaluation*

AWS Config Remediation can be configured via the following options:

- **Automatic Remediation**: Configure AWS Config rules with automatic remediation actions
- **Manual Remediation**: Review non-compliant resources and manually trigger remediation
- **Custom Remediation**: Implement custom remediation logic using Lambda functions

Infrastructure as Code Security

Infrastructure as Code (IaC) allows you to define your cloud infrastructure using code, while enabling consistent and repeatable deployments. AWS's native IaC service is called AWS CloudFormation, which allows one to define resources using YAML or JSON templates.

AWS CloudFormation for Secure Deployments

CloudFormation provides several security benefits that are as follows:

- **Consistency**: Ensures resources are deployed consistently with the same security configurations
- **Version Control**: Templates can be stored in version control systems, allowing tracking of security changes
- **Review Process**: Templates can be reviewed for security issues before deployment
- **Drift Detection**: Identifies when resources have been modified outside of CloudFormation

Best practices for secure CloudFormation deployments include:

- Use template parameters with constraints to enforce security requirements
- Apply the principle of least privilege to IAM roles
- Enable resource-level protections like deletion policies

- Use stack policies to prevent critical resource updates or deletions
- Implement a change management process for template updates

Testing IaC Templates for Vulnerabilities

Some tools that can identify security issues in CloudFormation templates are as follows:

- `cfn-nag`: An open-source tool that scans CloudFormation templates for security issues
- **CloudFormation Guard**: A Policy-as-Code evaluation tool for CloudFormation templates
- **AWS CloudFormation Linter**: Validates CloudFormation templates for syntax and best practices

These tools can be integrated into CI/CD pipelines to automatically check templates before deployment.

Implementing Guardrails

Guardrails are preventative controls that ensure infrastructure deployments meet security requirements. In AWS, guardrails can be implemented using:

- **AWS Organizations Service Control Policies (SCPs)**: To limit actions that can be performed in member accounts.
- **AWS CloudFormation Stack Policies**: To control which resources can be updated or deleted during stack updates.
- **AWS IAM Permission Boundaries**: To limit the maximum permissions an IAM entity can have.

These guardrails work together to enforce security standards across an AWS environment.

Common Mistakes and How to Avoid Them

Even mature DevSecOps implementations can suffer from recurring mistakes. The following subsections highlight typical missteps and provide clear, actionable guidance for preventing them.

Relying Solely on Manual Security Checks

In many development environments, manual security reviews remain the default approach for identifying vulnerabilities, but this reliance often creates inefficiencies and leaves gaps that automation could prevent.

Mistake

Many teams still depend on periodic, manual security reviews until later in the development process. This approach introduces bottlenecks, increases human error risk, and delays the detection of vulnerabilities.

How to Avoid

- Integrate automated security scans (static analysis, dependency scanning, container scanning) directly into the CI/CD pipeline
- Use AWS-native tools such as Amazon Inspector, ECR Image Scanning, and AWS Config Rules to run checks continuously
- Establish security gates so that code with critical vulnerabilities cannot be promoted to production

Example Scenario

A development team at a fintech startup used to performed security reviews only once every two weeks, which involved manually checking the code for vulnerabilities before it was deployed. This meant that if a high-severity flaw was introduced on day one of the sprint, it could remain undetected for up to 14 days, and might be potentially released to production if the review was rushed or incomplete.

To address this situation, the team integrated automated security scanning into their AWS CI/CD pipeline in the following manner:

1. **Static Code Analysis**: Every commit triggers a CodeBuild project that runs Bandit for Python code, scanning for insecure functions, weak cryptography, and injection risks.

2. **Dependency Vulnerability Check:** Safety scans the project's dependencies against a public CVE database, failing the build if critical vulnerabilities are found.

3. **Container Image Scanning**: If the application uses Docker, built images are pushed to Amazon ECR where ECR Image Scanning automatically checks them for known vulnerabilities.

4. **Infrastructure Compliance Validation:** AWS Config Rules evaluate the CloudFormation templates to ensure IAM roles don't have ***:*** permissions, S3 buckets aren't public, and encryption is enabled.

5. **Security Gate**: If any scan reports a High severity issue, CodePipeline stops the deployment automatically, preventing insecure code from reaching production.

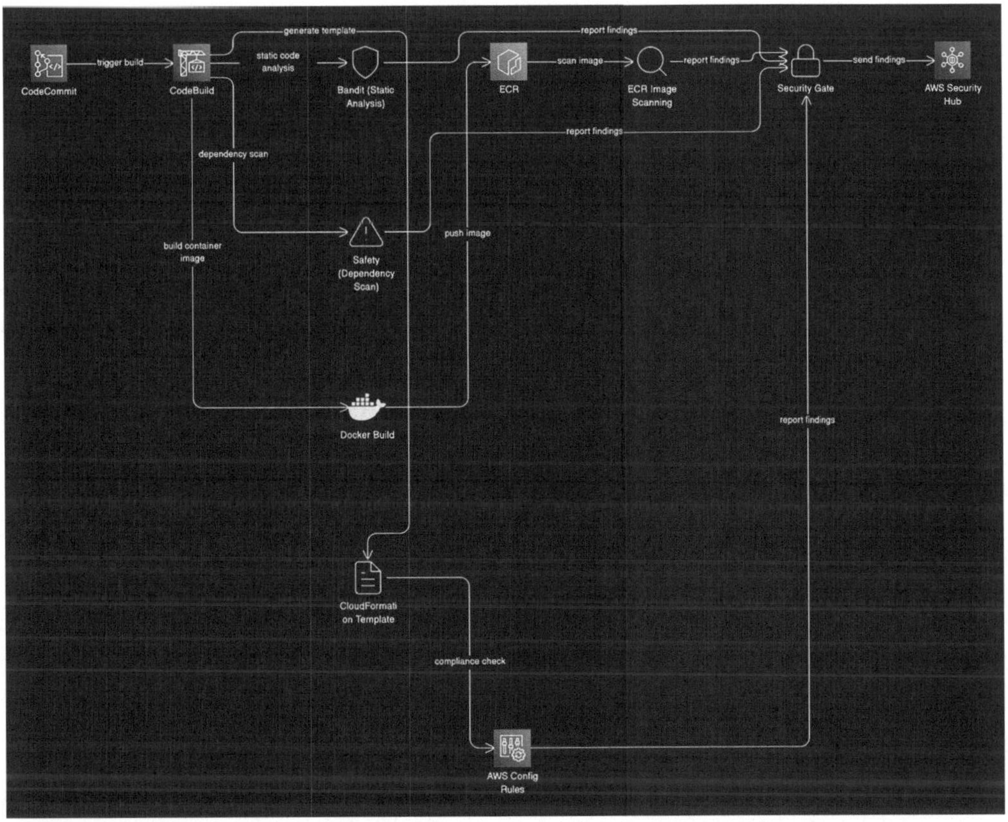

Figure 6.4: *End-to-end secure CI/CD pipeline with static analysis, dependency scanning, container image scanning, compliance checks, and centralized reporting in AWS Security Hub*

Outcome

By moving from manual reviews to automated scans, the team reduced vulnerability detection time from weeks to minutes, minimized human error, and ensured that critical security issues were caught before deployment.

Bad Practices

- Performing manual security reviews only at the end of the development cycle
- Relying solely on human review to detect vulnerabilities
- Ignoring low or medium vulnerabilities until "later"
- Allowing code with critical security flaws to progress to deployment
- Running vulnerability scans infrequently (for example, monthly or quarterly)
- Storing scan reports only on developer machines without centralized tracking
- Treating security checks as the responsibility of a single security team

Good Practices

- Integrating automated security scans at every stage of the CI/CD pipeline
- Using AWS-native tools like Amazon Inspector, ECR Image Scanning, and AWS Config Rules for continuous checks
- Prioritizing vulnerabilities by severity and remediating high-severity issues immediately
- Implementing security gates in CodePipeline that fail builds on critical findings
- Running scans on every commit and at scheduled intervals for deployed workloads
- Sending findings to AWS Security Hub for centralized, organization-wide visibility
- Fostering a shared responsibility model between Dev, Sec, and Ops teams

Hardcoding Secrets in Code Repositories

One of the most common and dangerous oversights in development security is embedding secrets directly in code. The following discussion explains why this practice is risky and how to manage credentials securely instead.

Mistake

Sometimes, developers store API keys, database passwords, or access tokens directly in the source code. Doing so exposes secret information to anyone with repository access and increases breach risks if the repository is public or compromised.

How to Avoid

- Store secrets in AWS Secrets Manager or AWS Systems Manager Parameter Store instead of the code
- Rotate secrets regularly using automated rotation policies

Example Scenario

A SaaS startup developing a customer analytics dashboard stores its database username and password directly in a Python configuration file:

```
# config.py
DB_USER = "admin"
DB_PASS = "SuperSecret123"
```

This file is committed to their private GitHub repository. One day, a junior developer accidentally forks the repository into a public space while testing a CI/CD workflow. Within hours, automated bots scan the public repository, find the hardcoded credentials, and try connecting to the production database.

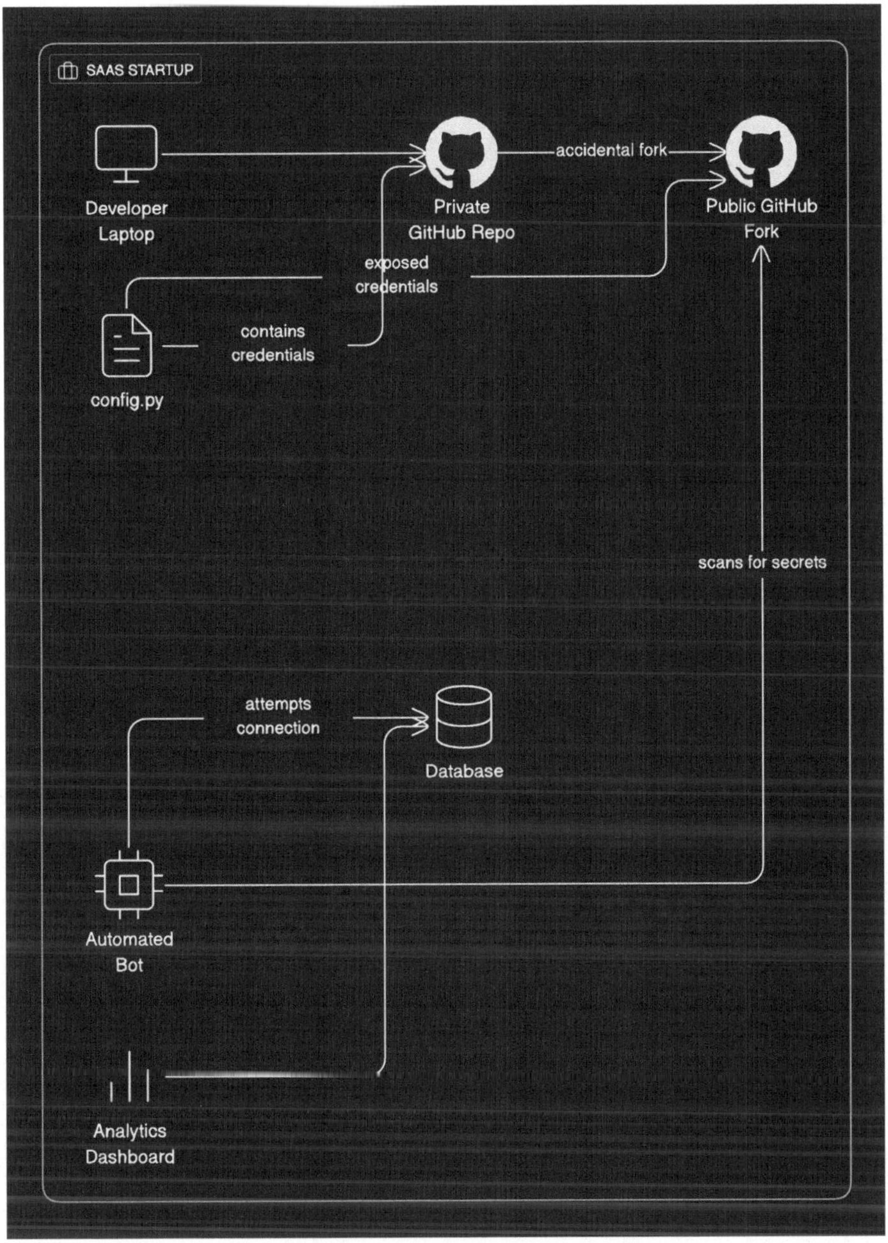

Figure 6.5: Credential exposure incident where hardcoded database secrets in a private GitHub repo are leaked via an accidental public fork and exploited by automated bots

Outcome

- Attackers gained read and write access to sensitive customer data.
- The company had to rotate database credentials immediately, patch the leak, and notify affected clients.

- Trust was damaged, and the team spent several days in incident response mode.
- By moving credentials into AWS Secrets Manager that was retrieved at runtime via the AWS SDK and enabling automated rotation, the company eliminated this risk entirely.

Bad Practices

- Storing credentials or API keys directly in code repositories
- Using hardcoded secrets for production systems
- Not rotating secrets regularly

Good Practices

- Using AWS Secrets Manager or AWS Systems Manager Parameter Store to store and manage secrets
- Retrieving secrets at runtime via SDK calls
- Enabling automatic rotation of secrets

Ignoring Security During Early Development Phases

Security must begin at the earliest stages of software design. This section explains the importance of integrating security requirements into planning and development, rather than treating them as a late-stage activity.

Mistake

Treating security as an afterthought means vulnerabilities are discovered late, making fixes costlier and disruptive.

How to Avoid

- Apply the `"Shift Left"` principle: include security requirements and threat modeling during the planning stage
- Educate developers on secure coding practices
- Run SAST and dependency checks as code is written, not after deployment

Example Scenario

A retail e-commerce company developed a new feature for processing returns without involving the security team until final testing. A last-minute review uncovered a SQL injection vulnerability in the API. Fixing it required major refactoring, delaying launch by three weeks and missing the holiday season.

Outcome

Implementing **`"Shift Left"`** security caught vulnerabilities within hours of introduction, reduced remediation costs, and avoided release delays.

Bad Practices

- Leaving security checks until final testing
- Skipping security planning during design
- Allowing developers to code without secure coding guidance

Good Practices

- Embedding security in planning and design
- Conducting threat modeling early
- Running SAST and dependency checks during development

Lack of Automated Remediation for Non-Compliance

Automation is central to maintaining continuous compliance in DevSecOps. The following section shows how relying on manual fixes can slow response times and how AWS tools can remediate issues automatically:

Mistake

Teams may detect non-compliant resources but rely on manual fixes, delaying remediation and increasing risk.

How to Avoid

- Use AWS Config with Lambda or Systems Manager Automation for instant remediation
- Apply policy-as-code frameworks like CloudFormation Guard
- Set and enforce SLAs for remediation timelines

Example Scenario

A financial services company found multiple public S3 buckets during a compliance scan, but manual remediation took 48 hours. By implementing AWS Config Managed Rules with Lambda auto-remediation, public access was removed within minutes.

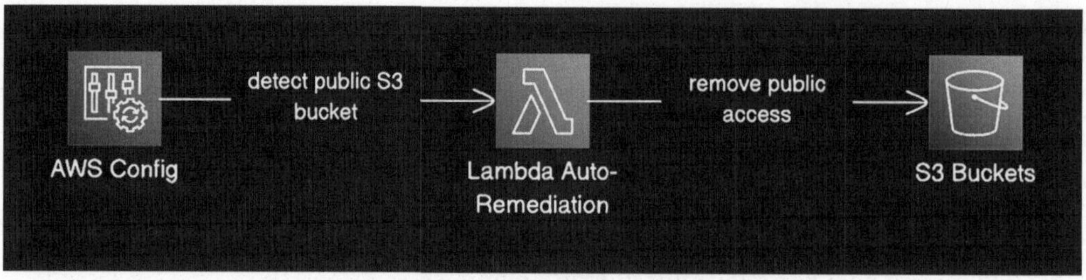

Figure 6.6: *Automated workflow where AWS Config detects public S3 buckets and triggers a Lambda function to remove public access*

Outcome

Reduced mean time to remediation from days to under five minutes, greatly limiting exposure.

Bad Practices

- Relying solely on manual fixes
- Allowing known non-compliance to remain in production

Good Practices

- Automating remediation with AWS Config and Lambda
- Blocking insecure deployments with policy-as-code

Overlooking Monitoring and Logging Configurations

Without comprehensive visibility, even well-secured systems remain vulnerable. The text below explains why monitoring and log management are critical for detecting threats and maintaining compliance.

Mistake

Without comprehensive monitoring, security teams lack visibility into incidents and configuration changes.

How to Avoid

- Enable CloudTrail in all regions with log validation
- Use GuardDuty for threat detection and Security Hub for central visibility
- Store logs in encrypted S3 buckets with strict access

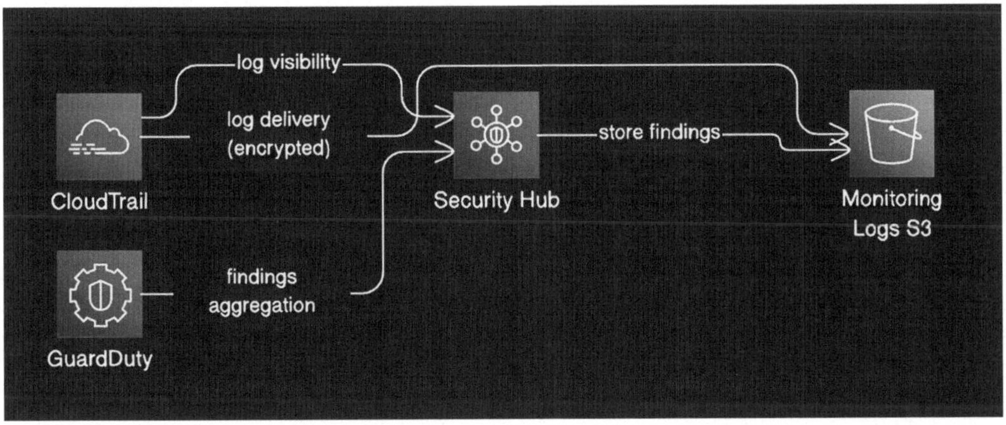

Figure 6.7: *Centralized security monitoring with CloudTrail and GuardDuty findings aggregated in Security Hub and stored securely in S3*

Example Scenario

A SaaS analytics firm detected unauthorized S3 data downloads only during a quarterly audit because CloudTrail wasn't fully enabled and no alerts were configured.

Outcome

By enabling CloudTrail in all regions, adding GuardDuty, and integrating SNS/Slack alerts, mean time to detect dropped from months to under five minutes.

Bad Practices

- Not enabling CloudTrail globally
- Storing logs insecurely

Good Practices

- Centralizing and securing logs
- Enabling real-time alerting

Misconfigured IAM Roles and Excessive Permissions

Improperly scoped permissions are a leading cause of security incidents in AWS. The following example illustrates the risks of over-privileged IAM roles and provides steps for enforcing least-privilege access.

Mistake

Overly broad IAM permissions increase the risk of privilege escalation and unauthorized access.

How to Avoid

- Apply least privilege to all IAM entities
- Use IAM Access Analyzer
- Apply permission boundaries and SCPs

Example Scenario

A healthcare SaaS provider attached an `Action":"*","Resource":"*"` policy to an EC2 role. When the instance was compromised, attackers accessed sensitive data, modified IAM policies, and launched cryptomining instances.

Outcome

Refining policies, enforcing SCPs, and enabling IAM Access Analyzer drastically reduced risk and limited credential abuse impact.

Bad Practices

- Granting wildcard permissions
- Using long-term credentials

Good Practices

- Defining narrow-scoped IAM policies
- Using temporary credentials and monitoring IAM changes

Benefits of DevSecOps in AWS Environments

Implementing DevSecOps principles in AWS brings measurable improvements in detection speed, compliance, and operational resilience. The following points outline key advantages with practical examples:

Reduced Time to Detect and Remediate Vulnerabilities

By embedding automated security scanning, compliance checks, and monitoring into every stage of the pipeline, vulnerabilities are detected within minutes rather than weeks. This significantly shortens the exposure window and reduces the risk of exploitation.

Example in AWS

- **Amazon Inspector** scans for CVEs in EC2 instances and containers right after build

- **Amazon GuardDuty** provides continuous threat detection for suspicious activities in real time
- **AWS Security Hub** aggregates findings and triggers automated workflows via **AWS Lambda** for remediation

Figure 6.8: *Automated threat detection and remediation workflow using Amazon Inspector, GuardDuty, Security Hub, and AWS Lambda*

Continuous Compliance without Slowing Deployment

Traditional compliance checks happen at fixed intervals, often delaying releases. DevSecOps enables compliance validation to be an ongoing process without adding delays.

Example in AWS

- Use **AWS Config Rules** and **Conformance Packs** to continuously validate resources against frameworks like CIS, HIPAA, or PCI DSS
- Automate remediation with **AWS Systems Manager Automation Documents (SSM Documents)**
- Integrate compliance dashboards into **Security Hub** for real-time oversight

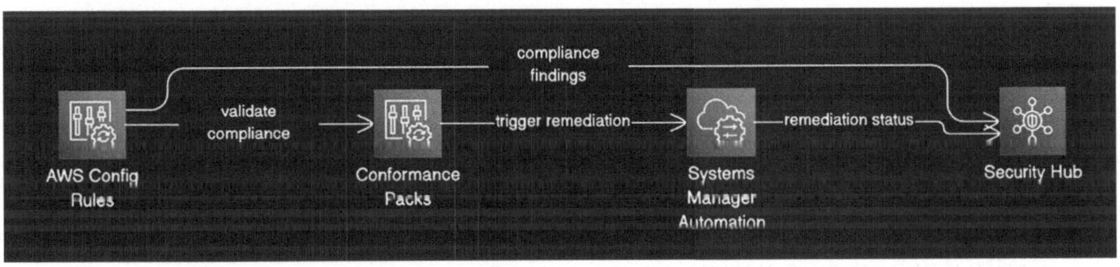

Figure 6.9: *Compliance validation and automated remediation workflow using AWS Config Rules, Conformance Packs, Systems Manager Automation, and Security Hub*

Improved Collaboration between Dev, Sec, and Ops Teams

DevSecOps fosters a shared responsibility model where security is no longer a "final checkpoint" owned solely by a security team, but a collective goal across all teams.

Example in AWS

- Developers integrate security tools into **CodePipeline** stages.
- Security engineers define guardrails via **Service Control Policies (SCPs)** and **IAM permission boundaries**.
- Operations teams maintain observability with **CloudWatch** and **X-Ray** for both performance and security issues.

Lower Security Incident Costs Through Proactive Prevention

Proactively addressing vulnerabilities in development or pre-deployment stages is far cheaper than post-incident recovery, regulatory fines, and reputation loss.

Examples in AWS

- Pre-deployment **CloudFormation Guard** rules prevent insecure infrastructure from ever being launched
- Automated key rotation with **AWS KMS** prevents credential compromise
- Threat modeling during planning reduces attack surface before a single resource is provisioned

Scalability of Security Processes with Growing Workloads

Automation ensures that as workloads and teams scale, security processes scale too—without requiring proportional increases in headcount.

Example in AWS

- Centralized **AWS Organizations** with SCPs enforce consistent policies across hundreds of accounts
- **AWS Control Tower** applies standardized guardrails at scale for new accounts
- **CloudFormation** and **AWS CDK** deliver pre-approved, security-hardened infrastructure templates

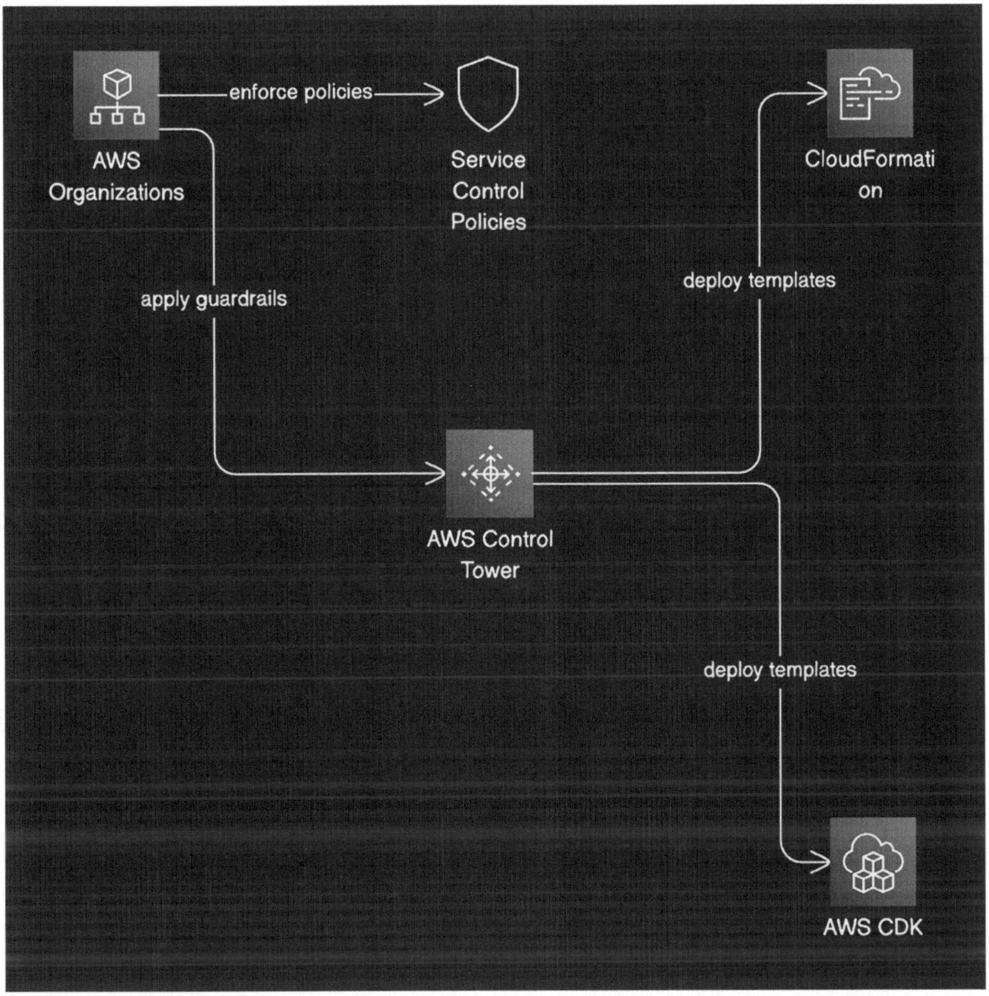

Figure 6.10: *Centralized governance and automated deployment using AWS Organizations, Service Control Policies, AWS Control Tower, CloudFormation, and AWS CDK*

Stronger Alignment with Regulatory Requirements

DevSecOps frameworks, when combined with AWS services, enable organizations to meet and maintain compliance requirements with minimal manual intervention.

Example in AWS

- **AWS Audit Manager** automates evidence collection for audits
- **Amazon Macie** identifies and protects sensitive data to meet privacy regulations

- Continuous encryption enforcement with **AWS KMS** and **S3 bucket policies** ensures compliance with data protection mandates

Future of DevSecOps

As cloud environments evolve, DevSecOps will continue to mature through greater automation, predictive intelligence, and tighter integration into developer workflows. The following topics explore where the discipline is headed next.

Increased Use of AI/ML for Automated Threat Detection

Artificial Intelligence (AI) and Machine Learning (ML) will play an even bigger role in detecting anomalies, identifying zero-day threats, and predicting attack patterns before they happen.

Example in AWS

- **Amazon GuardDuty** already uses ML to detect anomalous behavior based on VPC Flow Logs, DNS logs, and CloudTrail data
- **Amazon Detective** applies ML to investigate complex security incidents by building a graph of related activities
- Future integrations may enable predictive security–spotting attack vectors before they are exploited

Tighter Integration of Security Tools Within Developer IDEs

Security checks will move even closer to the developer's workflow, integrating directly into IDEs such as VS Code, JetBrains, and AWS Cloud9. Developers will be able to catch vulnerabilities before code even reaches version control.

Example in AWS

- AWS could extend **CodeWhisperer** to recommend security best practices in real time
- IDE plugins could run `cfn-nag` or **CloudFormation Guard** scans on infrastructure code before committing changes

Expansion of Security-as-Code Frameworks

Security will increasingly be defined, managed, and enforced through code, just like infrastructure. This makes security policies portable, version-controlled, and testable.

Example in AWS

- **AWS CloudFormation Guard**, **Open Policy Agent (OPA)**, and **Terraform Sentinel** for policy enforcement
- Automated integration with **CodePipeline** to fail builds that don't meet security baselines

Greater Emphasis on Supply Chain Security for Software Components

With attacks increasingly targeting software supply chains, organizations will focus on validating and securing every dependency, container image, and third-party library.

Example in AWS

- **Amazon ECR Image Scanning** to detect vulnerabilities before pushing images to production
- **AWS CodeArtifact** with signed packages to ensure code integrity
- **Integration of Software Bill of Materials (SBOM)** tools into CI/CD pipelines

Serverless and Container Security Automation as Defaults

Serverless architectures and containers will continue to dominate cloud deployments, and security automation will become a built-in expectation rather than an optional step.

Example in AWS

- **AWS Lambda** security scanning for code and dependencies before deployment
- **ECS/EKS with Amazon Inspector** to automatically check running workloads for CVEs
- Security controls automatically applied during build stages with **CodeBuild**

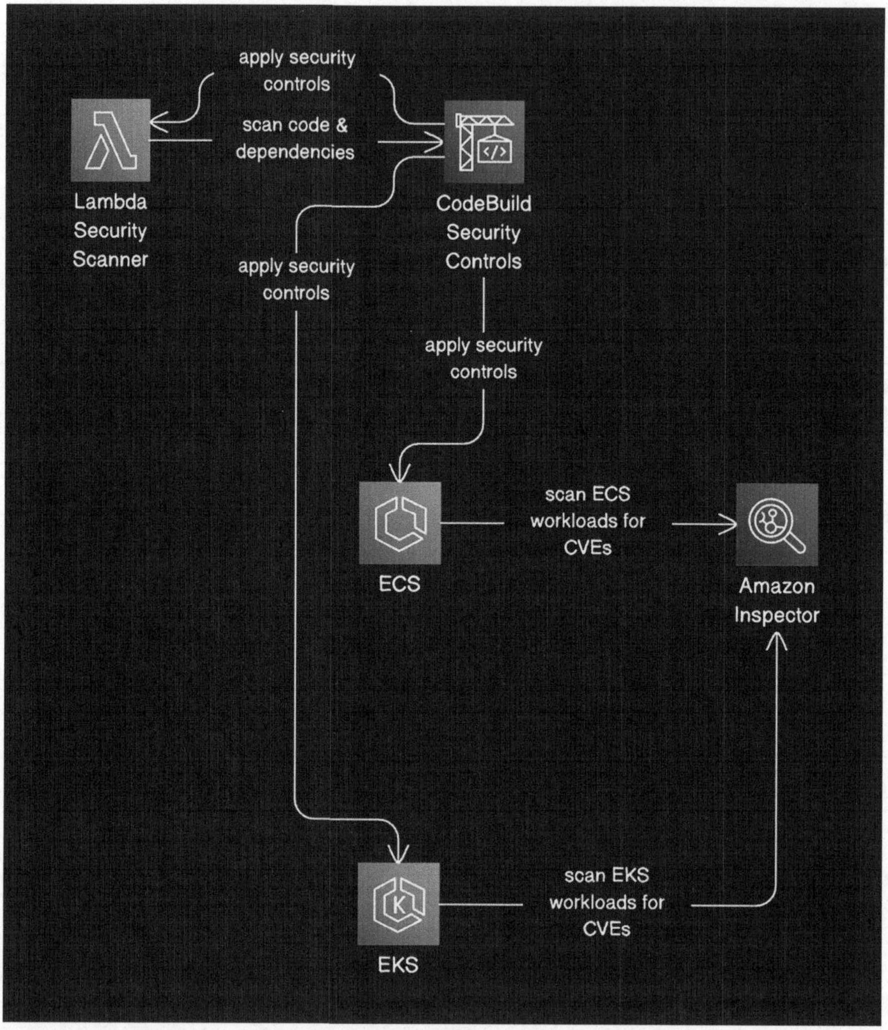

***Figure 6.11:** Security scanning workflow applying controls to Lambda, ECS, and EKS workloads, with Amazon Inspector detecting vulnerabilities in container environments*

Industry-Specific Compliance Automation Blueprints

AWS and other cloud providers offer ready-made compliance automation templates tailored for specific industries, which reduce the time that goes into ensuring continuous adherence and compliance with the existing rules.

Example in AWS

- **AWS Control Tower** with healthcare-ready blueprints for HIPAA compliance

- Financial services templates for **PCI DSS** implemented with **AWS Config Conformance Pack**.
- **Prebuilt AWS Audit Manager** frameworks for government standards like FedRAMP

Key Takeaways and Best Practices

As we conclude our exploration of DevSecOps and security automation on AWS, let us briefly review the associated key best practices:

- **Shift Left with Security**: Integrate security earlier in the development lifecycle to catch issues before they reach production
- **Automate Everything Possible**: Security testing, compliance checks, and remediation should all be automated to ensure consistency and reduce manual effort
- **Use Infrastructure as Code**: Define your infrastructure using code to ensure consistent, secure deployments and enable automated security validation
- **Implement Continuous Monitoring**: Set up real-time monitoring for security events and automate responses to threats
- **Establish Security Gates**: Define security requirements that must be met before code can progress through the pipeline
- **Practice Defense in Depth**: Layer security controls throughout your application and infrastructure
- **Regular Security Training**: Ensure everyone in the organization understands their role in maintaining security
- **Leverage AWS Native Security Services**: Take advantage of the integrated security services AWS provides, such as GuardDuty, Security Hub, and Inspector

Conclusion

DevSecOps represents a significant cultural and technical transformation in how organizations approach security. By integrating security throughout the development lifecycle and leveraging AWS's powerful automation capabilities, organizations can deliver secure applications faster without sacrificing quality.

The tools and practices we have explored in this chapter—from automated security testing to infrastructure as code validation—provide a strong foundation for implementing DevSecOps in AWS environments. As security threats continue to evolve, this automated and integrated approach to security becomes increasingly important for maintaining robust cloud security postures.

In the next chapter, we will build on these concepts by exploring how to implement specific security controls for data protection and encryption, ensuring that your applications not only pass security tests but also effectively protect sensitive information.

Points to Remember

- DevSecOps integrates security throughout the software development lifecycle rather than treating it as an afterthought.
- AWS provides numerous services for automating security controls, including AWS Config, CodePipeline, and CloudFormation.
- Infrastructure as Code enables security to be baked into infrastructure from the beginning and validated before deployment.
- Continuous compliance monitoring with AWS Config helps ensure resources remain secure over time.
- Security automation reduces the risk of human error and ensures consistent application of security controls.

Multiple Choice Questions

1. Which AWS service helps automate compliance monitoring and auditing of resource configurations?
    a. AWS Inspector
    b. AWS Config
    c. AWS GuardDuty
    d. AWS Security Hub
2. In a DevSecOps approach, when should security be integrated into the development process?
    a. At the end of the development cycle
    b. During the testing phase
    c. Throughout the entire development lifecycle
    d. Only after deployment

3. Which of the following is NOT a benefit of Infrastructure as Code in a DevSecOps context?
    a. Consistent security configurations
    b. Version control of infrastructure
    c. Manual approval processes
    d. Template validation before deployment
4. Which AWS service would you use to automatically check CloudFormation templates for security issues in a CI/CD pipeline?
    a. AWS Config
    b. AWS CloudFormation Guard
    c. AWS Shield
    d. AWS KMS
5. What is the primary purpose of AWS Secrets Manager in a DevSecOps pipeline?
    a. Encrypting data at rest
    b. Securely storing and managing sensitive credentials
    c. Monitoring for security events
    d. Scanning code for vulnerabilities

Answers

1. b
2. c
3. c
4. b
5. b

References

- AWS Security Documentation: https://docs.aws.amazon.com/security/
- AWS DevOps Documentation: https://aws.amazon.com/devops/
- AWS Config Documentation: https://aws.amazon.com/config/
- AWS CloudFormation Documentation: https://aws.amazon.com/cloudformation/
- AWS Secrets Manager Documentation: https://aws.amazon.com/secrets-manager/

CHAPTER 7
Exam Overview and Study Tips

Introduction

Welcome to this pivotal point in your journey to achieve the AWS Certified Security Specialty certification! This chapter serves as your comprehensive guide to understand the structure of the AWS Security Specialty exam and develop effective study strategies techniques to navigate the exam successfully. The certification validates your specialized knowledge in securing AWS environments, which is an increasingly valued cross-industry skill as organizations embark upon their cloud migration journeys.

As cyber threats continue to evolve in sophistication and frequency, companies actively seek professionals who can design, implement, and manage robust security controls in cloud environments. The AWS Security Specialty certification validates your ability to meet these demands, while showcasing your expertise in areas like identity and access management, data protection, infrastructure security, logging and monitoring, and incident response within AWS.

In this chapter, we will explore the AWS exam format, domain coverage, and effective preparation strategies to help you in the process. We will provide insights into the types of questions you might encounter, time management techniques, and practice questions that simulate the actual exam experience. By the end of this chapter, you will have a clear understanding of what to expect from the exam and how to approach your final preparation phase confidently.

Structure

In this chapter, we will cover the following topics:

- Exam Format and Structure
  - Overview of the Exam
  - Scoring Methodology

  - Exam Interface and Navigation
  - Registration Process and Requirements
- Question Types and Analysis
  - Multiple Choice Questions
  - Multiple Response Questions
  - Scenario-Based Questions
  - Question Analysis Strategies
  - Common Question Pitfalls
- Preparation Strategies
  - Creating a Study Plan
  - Focus on Key AWS Security Services
  - Hands-on Practice
  - Using the Official Exam Guide
  - Learning from AWS Documentation
  - Joining Study Groups and Forums
- Time Management Techniques
  - Before the Exam
  - During the Exam
  - Strategies for Different Question Types
  - Handling Difficult Questions
- Study Resources and Tools
  - Official AWS Resources
  - Third-Party Resources
  - Hands-On Labs and Workshops
  - Community Resources
  - Building Your Own Study Materials
- Practice Questions and Detailed Solutions
  - Domain 1: Incident Response
  - Domain 2: Logging and Monitoring
  - Domain 3: Infrastructure Security
  - Domain 4: Identity and Access Management
  - Domain 5: Data Protection

    - Domain 6: Management and Security Governance
    - Advanced Scenario Questions
- Final Preparation Checklist
    - Two Weeks Before the Exam
    - One Week Before the Exam
    - Day Before the Exam
    - Exam Day
    - Post-Exam Next Steps

Exam Format and Structure

Before diving into the details of the AWS Certified Security Specialty exam, it's important to understand how the test is structured and what to expect on exam day. This section outlines the overall format, duration, question types, scoring methodology, and delivery methods used for the certification. Having a clear picture of these elements will help you plan your preparation strategy, manage time effectively during the exam, and approach each question with confidence.

Overview of the Exam

The AWS Certified Security Specialty (SCS-C02) exam is designed to validate your specialized knowledge and skill in securing AWS environments. It is a rigorous assessment that requires thorough preparation and a deep understanding of AWS security services, principles, and best practices.

Here are the key aspects of the exam format:

- **Duration**: 170 minutes (2 hours and 50 minutes)
- **Number of Questions**: 65 questions
- **Question Types**: Multiple-Choice and Multiple-Response
- **Delivery Method**: Testing center or online proctored exam
- **Passing Score**: 750 out of 1,000
- **Cost**: $300 USD
- **Available Languages**: English, Japanese, Korean, and Simplified Chinese
- **Validity Period**: 3 years

The AWS Certified Security Specialty exam is specifically designed for individuals who perform a security role with at least two years of hands-on experience securing

AWS workloads. It validates a candidate's ability to effectively demonstrate their knowledge in the following areas:

- Securing AWS workloads and applications
- Implementing monitoring and logging solutions
- Protecting network infrastructure
- Managing identity and access
- Applying data protection mechanisms
- Responding to security incidents

It is worth noting that out of 65 questions, only 50 are scored, while the remaining15 are unscored and are used by AWS for further research purposes. You will not know which questions are unscored, so it is important to treat every question with equal importance.

Scoring Methodology

The AWS Security Specialty exam uses a scaled scoring system ranging from 100 to 1000, with the minimum passing score being 750. This method allows AWS to maintain a consistent standard regardless of the specific exam version one takes.

The exam does not have negative marking, which means that you will not lose points for incorrect answers. This is important to remember for your exam strategy–you must always answer a question despite being unsure, rather than leaving it blank.

AWS does not provide detailed information about their exact scoring algorithms, but here are some important points:

- **Scaled Scoring**: Your raw score is based on the number of questions you answer correctly and is then converted into a scaled score between 100 and 1000.
- **Passing Threshold**: The passing score of 750 reflects a specific level of competence, not the percentage of correct answers.
- **Question Weightage**: Some questions may be awarded a different weightage based on the level of difficulty. However, AWS does not publicly disclose the questions that carry more weight marks-wise.
- **Statistical Adjustment**: AWS may adjust scores based on a statistical analysis of all test-takers' performance.

After completing the exam, you will receive a "pass" or "fail" result immediately. A detailed score report will follow via email, typically within five business days, which breaks down your performance in different domain area.

Exam Tip: *Do not spend too much time on any single question. If you are unsure,* *mark it for review and move on. You can always revisit it if you have time remaining. This strategy maximizes your chances of answering all the questions within the time limit.*

Exam Interface and Navigation

While taking the AWS Certified Security Specialty exam, you will encounter a user interface designed to facilitate efficient navigation and question management. Being familiar with this interface can reduce anxiety and improve your performance in the exam.

The interface includes several key features as follows:

- **Question Navigator**: A panel that displays all question numbers, allowing you to jump to any question directly
- **Mark for Review**: A feature that lets you flag questions you want to revisit later
- **Time Remaining**: A countdown timer showing the time you have left to complete the exam
- **Calculator**: A basic calculator so that you might need during the exam
- **Question Progress**: Visual indicators that show which questions you have answered, which are unanswered, and which are marked for review

Here is a typical workflow to navigate the exam:

1. **Review Instructions**: Take a moment to read all exam instructions carefully
2. **Question Navigation**: Use the question navigator to move between questions
3. **Answering Questions**: Select your answer(s) for each question. For Multiple Choice questions, select one option; for Multiple Response, select two or more options
4. **Marking Questions**: If you are unsure about a question, use the "Mark for Review" feature to flag it for reviewing later
5. **Review Screen**: After answering all the questions, you will reach a review screen showing the questions that are answered, unanswered, or marked for review
6. **Final Review**: Use the remaining time to review the marked questions before submitting

Familiarizing yourself with the interface before the exam can help reduce anxiety and improve how you manage your time. AWS also provides a demo of the exam interface on their website that you can practice with.

Registration Process and Requirements

Registering for the AWS Certified Security Specialty exam involves several steps that ensure you are properly prepared and verified for the assessment.

Prerequisites

While there are no formal prerequisites for taking the Security Specialty exam, AWS recommends a candidate to:

- Possess at least 2 years of hands-on experience in securing AWS workloads
- Have more than 5 years of IT security experience in designing and implementing security solutions
- Be familiar with security controls for workloads on AWS

Registration Steps

To appear for the AWS Certified Security Specialty exam, you need to complete a few simple registration steps. Follow the process below to create your account, select your exam type, and schedule your test.

1. **Create an AWS Certification Account**: If you do not already have one, create an account on the AWS Certification Portal
2. **Select the Exam**: Visit the AWS Certified Security Specialty exam page and choose your preferred testing method:
   a. In-person at a testing center
   b. Online proctored exam
3. **Schedule the Exam**: Select your preferred date, time, and location if you are opting for in-person testing centers, or verify that your system meets the requirements for online proctored exams.
4. **Payment**: Pay the $300 USD exam fee. Corporate training credits or discount vouchers can be applied at this stage
5. **Confirmation**: You will receive a confirmation email with details about your exam appointment and preparation resources

Online Proctored Exam Requirements

If you choose to take the exam online, you will need to ensure:

- A quiet, private room where you will not be disturbed
- A computer with a webcam, microphone, and stable internet connection

- No additional monitors or devices connected
- A clean desk with no materials except those permitted by the proctor
- Valid government-issued photo identification

Testing Center Requirements

For in-person exams:

- Arrive at least 15 minutes early
- Bring valid government-issued photo identification
- Be prepared for security procedures, including possible biometric verification

Exam Accommodations

AWS provides reasonable accommodations for individuals with documented disabilities. Requests should be submitted during the registration process and at least 30 days before the exam date.

Rescheduling Policy

You can reschedule your exam up to 24 hours before your appointment without additional fees. The exam fees is forfeited in case of cancellations requested in less than 24 hours in-advance, or no-shows.

Exam Tip: *Consider scheduling your exam for a time when you are the most alert and focused. Morning slots work best for some candidates, while others perform better in afternoon sessions.*

Question Types and Analysis

The AWS Security Specialty exam includes various questions designed to test your knowledge, analytical skills, and ability to apply AWS security concepts to real-world scenarios. Understanding the structure and approach for every type of question can improve your performance significantly.

Multiple Choice Questions

Multiple-Choice questions are followed by four options, where only one is the correct answer. These questions test your knowledge of AWS security concepts, services, and best practices.

Characteristics

- One correct answer out of four options

- Tests recall of facts, understanding of concepts, or application of knowledge
- May include scenarios or direct knowledge-based questions
- Often includes distracters (incorrect options) that seem plausible

Example

Which AWS service would you use to automatically discover, classify, and protect sensitive data stored in Amazon S3?

a. Amazon Inspector

b. Amazon Macie

c. AWS Shield

d. Amazon GuardDuty

Answer: 'b'

Explanation: Amazon Macie is a fully-managed data security and data privacy service that employs Machine Learning and pattern matching to discover and protect sensitive data in AWS. Amazon Inspector is used for vulnerability management, AWS Shield provides DDoS protection, while Amazon GuardDuty is a threat detection service.

Approach Strategy

1. Read the question carefully, identifying key terms and requirements
2. Try to arrive at a probable answer before looking at the options
3. Evaluate every option against your knowledge in a systematic way
4. Eliminate obviously incorrect options
5. Compare remaining options to determine the most accurate answer

Multiple-Response Questions

Multiple-Response questions require you to select two or more correct answers from a list of options. These questions often test your deeper understanding of AWS security services and their capabilities.

Characteristics

- Two or more correct answers out of five or more options
- The question will indicate how many answers to select (e.g., "Select TWO")
- Tests broader knowledge and understanding of related concepts
- Often presents closely related options that require careful discrimination

Example

Which of the following are valid methods for encrypting data at rest in Amazon S3? (Select TWO)

a. Server-side encryption with Amazon S3-managed keys (SSE-S3)

b. Client-side encryption with customer-managed keys

c. Server-side encryption with AWS CloudFront

d. Server-side encryption with AWS KMS-managed keys (SSE-KMS)

e. Using AWS Shield for data encryption

Answers: 'a' and 'd'

Explanation: Amazon S3 supports server-side encryption with S3-managed keys (SSE-S3) and with AWS KMS-managed keys (SSE-KMS). Client-Side encryption is a valid approach but is managed by the client, not Amazon S3. AWS CloudFront is a content delivery network, not an encryption service. AWS Shield is a DDoS protection service, not an encryption service.

Approach Strategy

1. Note the number of correct answers required
2. Evaluate every option independently
3. Mark the options that are definitely correct or incorrect options
4. Compare the remaining options to determine the correct ones
5. Double-check that you have selected the exact number of answers required

Scenario-Based Questions

Scenario-Based questions present a real-world situation and ask you to apply your AWS security knowledge to solve a problem or identify the best solution. These questions test your ability to apply concepts rather than simply recalling facts.

Characteristics

- Longer descriptions providing context and requirements
- Tests application of knowledge to realistic situations
- Often involves multiple AWS services and security concepts
- May require analyzing trade-offs between different approaches

Example

A financial services company has deployed a three-tier web application in AWS. The application stores sensitive customer data in an Amazon RDS database. The company's security team has identified the following requirements:

- All data must be encrypted at rest and in transit
- Access to the database should be limited to the application tier only
- All API calls must be logged and monitored for suspicious activity
- The solution must comply with financial services regulations

Which combination of AWS services and configurations would BEST meet these requirements?

a. Use RDS with default encryption, place the database in a public subnet, enable CloudTrail, and use AWS Artifact for compliance documentation

b. Use RDS with KMS encryption, place the database in a private subnet, configure security groups to allow access only from the application tier, enable CloudTrail with log file validation, and use AWS Config for compliance monitoring

c. Use EC2 with encrypted EBS volumes for the database, place it in a private subnet, use network ACLs to restrict access, enable VPC Flow Logs, and use AWS Shield for compliance

d. Use RDS with SSL/TLS, place the database in a public subnet with restrictive security groups, enable CloudTrail, and use AWS WAF for compliance

Answer: 'b'

Explanation: Option B meets all requirements: RDS with KMS encryption addresses data encryption at rest, private subnet placement with security group rules limits access to the application tier, CloudTrail with log file validation provides comprehensive logging, and AWS Config helps monitor compliance with regulations.

Approach Strategy

1. Carefully analyze the scenario to identify all requirements
2. Break down the requirements into specific technical needs
3. Evaluate each option against all requirements
4. Eliminate options that fail to meet one or more requirements
5. Select the option that best addresses all requirements

Question Analysis Strategies

Developing a structured approach to analyzing exam questions can help you identify the correct answers more efficiently:

1. **Read the Question Carefully**: Pay attention to what is being asked and identify key terms or requirements. Look for qualifiers such as "MOST," "LEAST," "BEST," or "NOT" which can completely change the meaning of a question
2. **Identify the Context of the Scenario**: Determine if the question is about a specific AWS service, security concept, or architecture pattern. Understanding the context helps narrow down the relevant knowledge areas
3. **Analyse the Requirements**: For scenario-based questions, identify the explicit and implicit requirements. Explicit requirements are directly stated, while implicit requirements are implied by the context or industry standards
4. **Eliminate Obviously Incorrect Options**: Before selecting your answer, eliminate options that are clearly wrong to narrow down your choices. This improves your odds of selecting the correct answer
5. **Apply AWS Best Practices**: When evaluating options, consider AWS security best practices and the Well-Architected Framework's security pillar guidance
6. **Consider Trade-Offs**: For complex scenarios, assess the trade-offs between different approaches (cost, complexity, security, scalability) to identify the most appropriate solution
7. **Verify Your Answer**: Before moving on, verify that your selected answer(s) actually address the question being asked. It is easy to get distracted by technically correct information that does not answer the specific question

Common Question Pitfalls

Be aware of these common pitfalls that can lead to incorrect answers:

- **Misreading the Question**: Failing to notice key words such as "NOT" or "EXCEPT" that invert the meaning of what's being asked
- **Overlooking Qualifiers**: Missing modifiers like "MOST appropriate" or "LEAST secure" that indicate you need to compare options rather than just identify correct statements
- **Assuming Unmentioned Details**: Adding assumptions beyond what's stated in the question can lead to selecting incorrect answers based on imagined constraints

- **Selecting Familiar Options**: Choosing an option because it is a service or technique you are familiar with, rather than because it best addresses the question
- **Overcomplicating Simple Questions**: Sometimes questions are straightforward tests of service knowledge, not complex scenarios requiring nuanced analysis
- **Missing Service Limitations**: Selecting options without considering service limitations or constraints that would make them impractical for the scenario
- **Being Distracted by Partially Correct Options**: In multiple-choice questions, options may contain some correct information but still not be the best answer

Exam Tip: *For multiple-response questions, read each option independently and decide if it is correct based on the question. Do not try to find relationships between the options unless it is specifically indicated.*

Preparation Strategies

Preparing for the AWS Security Specialty exam requires a structured approach and consistent effort. Here are effective strategies to help you build a solid foundation and master the exam content.

Create a Study Plan

A well-structured study plan is essential for effective preparation. Consider the following steps:

1. **Assess Your Current Knowledge**: Start by taking a practice test to identify your strengths and weaknesses. This baseline assessment will help you focus your studies on areas that need improvement
2. **Allocate Study Time Based on Domain Weightage**: Distribute your study time according to the domain weightage. For example, since Infrastructure Security (26%) and Data Protection (22%) have the highest weightage, allocate proportionally more time to these domains
3. **Set Realistic Goals**: Define what you want to achieve in each study session and track your progress. Break down your preparation into manageable chunks, focusing on specific services or concepts in each session
4. **Create a Timeline**: Work backward from your exam date to create a timeline for covering all domains. Include buffer time for revision and practice exams

5. **Schedule Regular Study Sessions**: Consistent, shorter study sessions are often more effective than occasional marathon sessions. Aim for 1-2 hours of focused study several times per week
6. **Incorporate Different Learning Methods**: Combine reading, hands-on practice, video courses, and practice questions to reinforce your understanding from different angles
7. **Include Regular Review Sessions**: Schedule time to revisit previously covered topics to reinforce your understanding and combat the forgetting curve

Sample 8-Week Study Plan

The following sample 8-week study plan provides a structured approach to help you cover all exam domains efficiently. It balances theory, hands-on practice, and review sessions to ensure consistent progress and comprehensive preparation for the AWS Certified Security Specialty exam.

Week	Focus Area	Activities
Week 1	Introduction and IAM	Study IAM concepts, policies, roles, and federation. Complete hands-on labs with IAM
Week 2	Infrastructure Security Part 1	Study VPC, Security Groups, NACLs, and network security. Complete related hands-on labs
Week 3	Infrastructure Security Part 2	Study AWS WAF, Shield, Firewall Manager, and edge security. Complete related hands-on labs
Week 4	Data Protection	Study KMS, CloudHSM, encryption options, Secrets Manager, and Certificate Manager. Complete related hands-on labs
Week 5	Logging and Monitoring	Study CloudTrail, CloudWatch, VPC Flow Logs, and Security Hub. Complete related hands-on labs
Week 6	Incident Response	Study GuardDuty, Detective, and incident response procedures. Complete related hands-on labs
Week 7	Review and Practice	Review all domains. Take practice exams and identify weak areas for additional study
Week 8	Final Preparation	Focus on weak areas, take final practice exams, and review key concepts

Table 7.1: *Study Plan*

Focus on Key AWS Security Services

The exam heavily focuses on AWS security services and their capabilities. Make sure you have a deep understanding of the following:

Identity and Access Management Services

This section highlights the core AWS services used to manage identities, permissions, and access control across your cloud environment. Understanding these services and how they integrate is essential for enforcing least privilege, enabling secure authentication, and maintaining centralized access management.

- **IAM Roles**: Understand delegation, cross-account access, service roles, and role assumption
- **IAM Policies**: Master policy types (identity-based, resource-based), policy structure, and policy evaluation logic
- **Permission Boundaries**: Know how to use permission boundaries to limit maximum permissions
- **AWS Organizations**: Understand organization structure, Service Control Policies (SCPs), and organizational units
- **AWS SSO**: Configure Single Sign-On for multiple AWS accounts and applications
- **AWS Directory Service**: Implement Microsoft Active Directory integration options
- **Amazon Cognito**: Manage customer identity and access for applications

Logging and Monitoring Services

Effective logging and monitoring form the backbone of AWS security visibility. This section outlines the key AWS services that enable continuous monitoring, log analysis, and automated alerting, helping you detect anomalies, maintain compliance, and respond to incidents proactively.

- **AWS CloudTrail**: Configure organization-wide trails, log file validation, and multi-region logging
- **Amazon CloudWatch**: Set up metrics, alarms, dashboards, and automated responses
- **VPC Flow Logs**: Implement network traffic monitoring and analysis
- **AWS Config**: Establish configuration monitoring, compliance rules, and remediation
- **AWS Security Hub**: Enable consolidated security findings and compliance checks
- **Amazon Athena**: Query and analyze logs using SQL
- **Amazon Detective**: Analyze and visualize security events to identify root causes

Infrastructure Security Services

Infrastructure security in AWS focuses on protecting network boundaries, controlling traffic, and enforcing defense-in-depth principles. The following services help you design, monitor, and manage secure network environments across your AWS infrastructure:

- **Amazon VPC**: Design secure network architectures with multiple layers of defense
- **Security Groups and NACLs**: Implement effective traffic filtering at instance and subnet levels
- **AWS WAF**: Configure web application firewall rules to protect against common vulnerabilities
- **AWS Shield**: Understand Standard vs. Advanced DDoS protection features
- **AWS Firewall Manager**: Implement centralized security policy management
- **AWS Network Firewall**: Deploy stateful and managed network firewall service
- **AWS Transit Gateway**: Configure secure connectivity between multiple VPCs
- **Amazon Inspector**: Implement automated vulnerability assessment

Data Protection Services

Securing data - whether at rest, in transit, or in use - is a foundational aspect of cloud security. This section introduces AWS data protection services that safeguard sensitive information through encryption, key management, and secure credential handling.

- **AWS KMS**: Master key management, key policies, grants, and key usage in AWS services
- **AWS CloudHSM**: Understand hardware security module use cases and integration
- **AWS Secrets Manager**: Implement secure credential storage with automatic rotation
- **AWS Certificate Manager**: Manage SSL/TLS certificates for secure communications
- **Amazon S3**: Configure bucket policies, encryption, and access controls
- **Amazon Macie**: Set up sensitive data discovery and protection

Incident Response Services

A well-prepared incident response strategy enables organizations to detect, investigate, and remediate security threats swiftly. The following services help automate detection, orchestrate responses, and maintain control during security incidents:

- **Amazon GuardDuty**: Configure threat detection with custom findings and automated responses
- **AWS Security Hub**: Establish a unified view of security alerts and compliance status
- **Amazon EventBridge**: Create event rules to automate security responses
- **AWS Lambda**: Develop automated remediation functions
- **AWS Systems Manager**: Implement secure instance management and patch compliance

Service Cross-Cutting Knowledge

For each service, ensure you understand:

- Integration points with other AWS services
- Security best practices and common misconfigurations
- Scalability considerations for enterprise environments
- Cost implications of different security configurations
- Automation capabilities and limitations

Example Study Approach for a Single Service

Let's take AWS KMS as an example of a deep-dive study approach:

- **Purpose and Core Concepts**
    - Understand KMS's role in AWS encryption ecosystem
    - Master key concepts: CMKs, key policies, grants, aliases
    - Know the difference between AWS-managed and customer-managed keys
- **Service Configuration**
    - Configure different key types (symmetric vs. asymmetric)
    - Set up key policies and IAM policies for access control
    - Implement key rotation strategies
- **Integration Points**
    - Study how S3, RDS, EBS, Lambda, and other services use KMS
    - Understand cross-account key usage scenarios
    - Learn about envelope encryption implementation

- **Best Practices**
  - Review AWS documentation on KMS best practices
  - Understand key monitoring and auditing approaches
  - Learn key usage patterns for different compliance requirements
- **Hands-on Practice**
  - Create a CMK with custom key policy
  - Encrypt and decrypt data using different methods
  - Configure automatic key rotation
  - Set up cross-account key sharing
- **Common Exam Scenarios**
  - Key compromise response procedures
  - Multi-region encryption requirements
  - Compliance-focused key management

Hands-on Practice

Theoretical knowledge alone is not sufficient for the AWS Security Specialty exam. Implementing what you learn through hands-on practice is crucial for solidifying concepts and understanding real-world application.

Setting Up a Practice Environment

- **AWS Free Tier Account**: Create an AWS account to practice with minimal costs. Many security services offer free tier benefits.
- **Sandboxed Environment**: Create a dedicated AWS Organization with separate accounts for experimentation without affecting production environments.
- **Infrastructure as Code (IaC)**: Use AWS CloudFormation or Terraform to quickly provision and tear down environments for practice.
- **AWS CloudShell**: Utilize the browser-based shell for quick CLI practice without installing tools locally.

Key Hands-On Labs to Complete

Hands-on practice is essential to reinforce theoretical knowledge and prepare effectively for the AWS Certified Security Specialty exam. The following lab exercises are organized by domain to help you apply security concepts in real AWS environments and gain practical experience with key services.

- **IAM Security Labs**
  - Create a comprehensive IAM permission structure with least privilege
  - Implement permission boundaries for delegated administration
  - Configure cross-account access with IAM roles
  - Set up SAML federation with an identity provider
- **Network Security Labs**
  - Design a multi-tier VPC architecture with security groups and NACLs
  - Implement AWS Network Firewall for east-west traffic inspection
  - Configure VPC endpoints for secure service access
  - Set up AWS WAF with custom rules to protect web applications
- **Data Protection Labs**
  - Implement S3 bucket policies and encryption
  - Configure KMS for cross-account encryption
  - Set up automatic rotation of database credentials with Secrets Manager
  - Deploy certificate management with ACM for public and private endpoints
- **Logging and Monitoring Labs**
  - Create a centralized logging architecture for multiple accounts
  - Set up real-time alerting for security events
  - Configure automated compliance checks with AWS Config
  - Implement log analysis with Athena and QuickSight
- **Incident Response Labs**
  - Develop GuardDuty custom findings and automated responses
  - Create an incident response runbook for specific security scenarios
  - Simulate security incidents and practice response procedures
  - Implement automated remediation with Lambda and EventBridge

Detailed Lab Example: Secure Multi-Tier Application Architecture

This comprehensive lab combines multiple security aspects:

- **Setup Phase**
  - Create a multi-account structure with AWS Organizations
  - Implement SCPs for guardrails

- Configure CloudTrail for organization-wide logging
- **Network Configuration**
  - Design VPCs with public, private, and isolated tiers
  - Implement proper security groups and NACLs
  - Configure Transit Gateway for secure inter-VPC communication
  - Set up VPC endpoints for AWS services
- **Application Deployment**
  - Deploy web servers in the public tier
  - Place application servers in the private tier
  - Deploy databases in the isolated tier
  - Implement IAM roles for EC2 instances
- **Security Controls**
  - Configure WAF and Shield for front-end protection
  - Implement KMS encryption for data at rest
  - Set up CloudWatch alarms for suspicious activities
  - Deploy GuardDuty for threat detection
- **Testing and Validation**
  - Verify proper segmentation with connectivity tests
  - Conduct penetration testing within allowed boundaries
  - Simulate security incidents and verify detection
  - Review logs and monitoring effectiveness

AWS Workshops and Tutorials

AWS provides free workshops and tutorials specifically focused on security topics:

- **AWS Security Workshop**: Comprehensive security labs covering multiple domains
- **AWS Well-Architected Labs**: Hands-on labs aligned with the Security Pillar
- **Amazon GuardDuty Workshop**: Threat detection and response scenarios
- **AWS Identity Workshop**: Advanced IAM and identity management scenarios

Exam Tip: *Document your hands-on practice with notes about configurations, challenges encountered, and solutions implemented. This documentation becomes a valuable study reference and helps reinforce your learning.*

Using the Official Exam Guide

AWS provides an official exam guide for the Security Specialty certification. This guide outlines the exam objectives, recommended AWS services, and the types of questions you can expect. Use this guide as a roadmap for your studies to ensure you cover all required topics.

Key Components of the Exam Guide

This section explains what the official exam guide contains and how each part helps you understand the scope, depth, and logistics of the SCS-C02 exam.

- **Exam Overview**: Provides information about exam structure, scoring, and logistics
- **Domain Descriptions**: Details the knowledge areas within each domain and their relative weightings
- **Content Outline**: Lists specific topics and services covered in each domain
- **Sample Questions**: Offers examples of the types of questions you will encounter

How to Use the Exam Guide Effectively

Use the following tips to turn the exam guide into a practical study roadmap that keeps you focused, efficient, and aligned with the exam blueprint:

- **Create a Study Checklist**: Convert each bullet point in the content outline into a checklist item to track your progress
- **Map Resources to Domains**: For each domain and topic, identify specific learning resources such as documentation, videos, and labs
- **Prioritize Based on Weightings**: Allocate study time proportionally based on domain weightings
- **Use as a Final Review Tool**: Before the exam, review the guide to identify any topics you might have missed

Learning from AWS Documentation

AWS Documentation is the most authoritative source for information about AWS services and features. While it can be extensive, focusing on specific sections can dramatically improve your understanding.

Key Documentation Resources

Start with these high-value documentation hubs to get authoritative, exam-relevant information quickly.

- **Security, Identity, and Compliance Documentation**: Comprehensive documentation for all security-related services
- **AWS Security Best Practices**: Whitepapers covering security recommendations across multiple domains
- **Service-Specific Security Documentation**: Each AWS service has a dedicated security chapter in its documentation
- **AWS Well-Architected Framework: Security Pillar**: Design principles and best practices for security in the cloud

How to Use AWS Documentation Effectively

Apply the following strategies to read faster, retain more, and translate docs into actionable knowledge:

- **Start with Overviews**: Begin with service overviews to understand core concepts before diving into details
- **Focus on Key Concepts**: Prioritize understanding key concepts, such as how KMS encryption works or IAM policy evaluation logic
- **Study Architecture Diagrams**: Pay close attention to architecture diagrams that illustrate service interactions and security controls
- **Review FAQs**: Service FAQs often address common questions and clarify misconceptions.
- **Explore Tutorial Sections**: Tutorial sections provide step-by-step guidance for implementing security features

Joining Study Groups and Forums

Connecting with others preparing for the same exam can provide valuable insights and support:

Community Resources

Use these communities to ask questions, compare notes, and learn from real-world experiences across the AWS security space.

- **AWS Certification Forums**: Platforms such as the r/AWSCertifications

Subreddit and the AWS Certification Slack community are good places to ask questions about the exam and share experiences

- **Study Groups**: Join or form study groups to discuss challenging concepts and quiz each other on them. Virtual study groups can be found on platforms like Meetup or LinkedIn
- **AWS Events**: Attend AWS meet-ups, webinars, and conferences focused on security topics to learn from experts and network with peers
- **AWS Hero and Ambassador Content**: Follow content created by AWS Heroes and Ambassadors who often share exam tips and deep dives into security topics

Benefits of Community Learning

The points below highlight why studying with others can clarify concepts, surface blind spots, and keep you motivated.

- **Alternative Explanations**: Different explanations of complex topics can help clarify your understanding
- **Experience Sharing**: Learn from others' exam experiences and preparation strategies
- **Knowledge Gaps**: Discover topics you might have overlooked in your individual studies
- **Motivation and Accountability**: Regular interaction with peers can help maintain motivation and study consistency
- **Resource Sharing**: Exchange useful resources, practice questions, and study notes

How to Contribute to Communities

Follow these practices to ask better questions, share value, and elevate discussions for everyone.

- **Ask Focused Questions**: When seeking help, ask specific, well-defined questions rather than broad queries
- **Share Your Knowledge**: Explaining concepts to others reinforces your own understanding.
- **Provide Feedback on Resources**: Share your experience with different study materials to help others
- **Organize Study Sessions**: Take initiative in organizing topic-specific study sessions

Time Management Techniques

With 65 questions to answer in 170 minutes, effective time management is crucial for exam success. Here are strategies to help you navigate the exam efficiently:

Before the Exam

Prepare deliberately with these steps so you arrive confident, calibrated, and ready to execute your plan.

- **Practice with Timed Tests**: Regularly take practice exams under timed conditions to build your pacing skills. Start with domain-specific quizzes before moving to full-length exams
- **Analyse Your Timing Patterns**: Track how long you spend on different question types to identify areas where you might need to improve your speed
- **Develop a Question Approach Strategy**: Create a systematic approach for different question types:
    - For straightforward knowledge questions: Answer quickly if you know it, mark for review if unsure
    - For scenario-based questions: Take time to analyse requirements before evaluating options
    - For calculation questions: Use a structured approach to avoid errors
- **Get Familiar with the Exam Interface**: Use the AWS practice exam interface to understand the navigation and features, such as the question review screen and calculator
- **Establish Personal Time Markers**: Decide on time checkpoints to assess your progress during the exam (for example, question 20 by 50 minutes, question 40 by 100 minutes).

During the Exam

Use the following techniques to control your pace, make sound decisions, and maximize your score.

- **Time Allocation Strategies:**
    - **Overall Pace**: With 170 minutes for 65 questions, you have approximately 2.6 minutes per question on average
    - **Adaptive Pacing**: Spend less time (1-2 minutes) on straightforward questions and more time (3-4 minutes) on complex scenarios
    - **Progress Monitoring**: Check your pace at 30-minute intervals

- **Question Prioritization Techniques:**
  - **First Pass**: Answer all questions you are confident about immediately
  - **Marking Strategy**: Use the "Mark for Review" feature for:
    - Questions you are unsure about
    - Questions that seem time-consuming
    - Questions you want to double-check
  - **Second Pass**: Return to marked questions with your remaining time
- **Handling Difficult Questions:**
  - **30-Second Assessment**: Spend 30 seconds determining if you can answer the question quickly
  - **Elimination Method**: Even if you are unsure, eliminate obviously incorrect options to improve guessing odds
  - **Move On Rule**: If you spend more than 3 minutes without progress, mark it and move on
  - **Educated Guessing**: Never leave a question unanswered, as there is no penalty for wrong answers
- **Time-Saving Approaches**:
  - **Read the Question First**: Understand what's being asked before analysing the scenario details
  - **Identify Key Words**: Look for words like "MOST," "LEAST," "BEST," or "NOT" that indicate the specific requirement
  - **Focus on Requirements**: For scenario questions, identify the explicit requirements before evaluating options
  - **Avoid Second-Guessing**: Trust your initial answer unless you have a specific reason to change it
- **End-of-Exam Strategy**:
  - **Reserve Review Time**: Save the last 15-20 minutes to review flagged questions
  - **Question Verification**: Check that you have answered all questions
  - **Answer Consistency**: Ensure your answers are consistent with AWS best practices

Strategies for Different Question Types

Tailor your approach using the playbooks below to handle each question style efficiently and accurately.

Multiple-Choice Questions

- Read all options before selecting an answer
- Eliminate obviously incorrect options first
- Look for qualifiers in the question that narrow down the correct answer
- Average time: 1-2 minutes

Multiple-Response Questions

- Note how many answers are required
- Evaluate each option independently
- Verify you have selected the exact number of answers required
- Average time: 2-3 minutes

Scenario-Based Questions

- Identify all requirements in the scenario
- Match requirements to AWS services and features
- Evaluate each option against all requirements
- Average time: 3-4 minutes

Calculation or Configuration Questions

- Use a structured approach for any calculations
- Break complex configurations into smaller steps
- Verify your solution meets all requirements
- Average time: 2-3 minutes

Handling Difficult Questions

When you're stuck, use these decision rules to protect your timing while still improving your odds.

- **When You do Not Know the Answer**
    - Eliminate the obviously incorrect options
    - Look for clues in the question itself
    - Consider AWS best practices and the Well-Architected Framework
    - Make an educated guess based on your knowledge of AWS security principles
- **When Multiple Options Seem Correct**
    - Reread the question focusing on qualifiers such as "MOST" or "BEST"

  - Look for subtle differences between options
  - Consider factors such as cost, complexity, security, and management overhead
  - Choose the option that best aligns with AWS recommended best practices
- **When You Are Running Out of Time**
  - Focus on answering all questions rather than perfecting answers to difficult ones
  - Use the remaining time to review unanswered questions
  - Make educated guesses rather than leaving questions blank

Time Management Challenge: In practice exams, try to complete each domain's questions within a time proportional to its exam weightage. For example, Infrastructure Security (26%) should take approximately 44 minutes of your total exam time.

Study Resources and Tools

A variety of resources can support your preparation for the AWS Security Specialty exam. Here is a comprehensive list to help you build a robust study arsenal:

Official AWS Resources

Build a balanced prep stack with the official materials, third-party courses, and hands-on labs listed as follows:

- **AWS Documentation**
  - Security, Identity, and Compliance documentation
  - Service-specific security sections
  - AWS Security Best Practices whitepaper
  - AWS Well-Architected Framework: Security Pillar
  - AWS Security Reference Architecture (AWS SRA)
- **AWS Training and Certification**
  - AWS Certified Security – Specialty Official Practice Exams
  - AWS Security Learning Path courses
  - AWS Digital Training courses focused on security
  - AWS Classroom Training: Security Engineering on AWS
- **AWS Security Blog**
  - Articles on AWS security services, features, and best practices

- Real-world security implementation examples
- Updates on new security features and services

- **AWS Well-Architected Labs**
  - Hands-on labs aligned with the Security Pillar
  - Self-paced labs covering various security topics
  - Real-world scenarios with step-by-step instructions
- **AWS Samples on GitHub**
  - Sample code for security implementations
  - Security automation examples
  - Architecture patterns for secure deployments

Third-Party Resources

Augment your prep with these reputable books, courses, and practice exams.

- **Study Guides and Books:**
  - "AWS Certified Security Specialty Study Guide" by Zeal Vora
  - "AWS Certified Security Specialty All-in-One Exam Guide" by Tracy Wallace
  - "AWS Security Cookbook" for practical implementation examples
- **Online Courses:**
  - A Cloud Guru AWS Security Specialty Course
  - Whizlabs AWS Certified Security Specialty Course
  - Udemy Courses by Stephane Maarek or Adrian Cantrill
  - Pluralsight AWS Security Paths
- **Practice Exams:**
  - Whizlabs Practice Tests
  - Tutorials Dojo Practice Exams
  - A Cloud Guru Practice Exams
  - Digital Cloud Training Practice Tests
- **Flashcards and Quick References:**
  - Anki Flashcards for Spaced Repetition Learning
  - Tutorials Dojo Cheat Sheets
  - Self-Created Service Comparison Tables
  - Visual Study Aids for Complex Concepts

Hands-on Labs and Workshops

Turn concepts into muscle memory using guided and DIY lab work.

- **AWS Workshops**: security.awsworkshop.io provides hands-on security labs covering various domains:
    - Identity Federation Workshop
    - Security Automations Workshop
    - Incident Response Simulation
    - Threat Detection and Response Workshop
- **QwikLabs**: Guided labs on AWS security services and configurations:
    - Introduction to AWS Security
    - Securing VPC Resources
    - Implementing Encryption with AWS KMS
    - Managing Access with IAM
- **AWS Security Incident Response Simulations**:
    - Practical exercises for responding to security incidents
    - Scenario-based learning for incident handling
    - Practice implementing security controls in response to threats
- **DIY Labs**:
    - Create security-monitoring solutions
    - Implement encrypted data storage with access controls
    - Build a multi-tier application with security controls
    - Set up an identity federation with external providers

Community Resources

Tap these channels to ask, share, and learn continuously throughout your prep.

- **AWS Community Forums**
    - AWS Security Forum
    - AWS Identity Management Forum
    - AWS Certification Forum
- **Reddit Communities**
    - r/aws for general AWS discussions
    - r/awscertifications for certification-specific advice

- r/cloudsecurity for broader cloud security topics
- **AWS Security Slack Channels**
  - AWS Community Slack (#security channel)
  - AWS Security Specialty Study Group Slack
  - DevSecOps community channels
- **GitHub Repositories**
  - flAWS challenges for security practice
  - AWS security automation scripts
  - CloudFormation and Terraform security templates

Building Your Own Study Materials

Creating your own study materials can significantly enhance retention and understanding:

- **Personal Knowledge Base**
  - Create a digital notebook with key concepts, diagrams, and service comparisons
  - Organize by exam domains for easy reference
  - Include personal notes from hands-on experiences
  - Update regularly as you learn new concepts
- **Service Comparison Charts**
  - Create tables comparing similar services (for example, security group vs. NACL)
  - Map services to security use cases
  - Note integration points between services
  - Highlight key limitations and best practices
- **Security Architecture Diagrams**
  - Create reference diagrams for common security architectures
  - Visualize service interactions and security controls
  - Map security services to the AWS Well-Architected Framework
- **Personal Cheat Sheets**
  - Develop quick reference guides for complex topics
  - Create command references for CLI operations
  - List key policy examples for common scenarios

   - Document troubleshooting procedures

Resource Management Tip: *Create a central repository or folder structure to organize all your resources by domain and topic. Include links to official documentation, your notes, and practice exercises for each area.*

Practice Questions and Detailed Solutions

To help you assess your understanding and prepare for the exam, here are some sample questions covering different domains, along with detailed explanations.

Domain 1: Threat Detection and Incident Response

Question 1: Your security team has detected unauthorized access to an EC2 instance in your AWS environment. Which combination of AWS services would be MOST effective for investigating this incident? (Select TWO)

a. AWS CloudTrail and Amazon CloudWatch Logs

b. Amazon Connect and AWS Lambda

c. AWS Secrets Manager and AWS KMS

d. Amazon Inspector and Amazon QuickSight

e. AWS Systems Manager Session Manager and VPC Flow Logs

Answers: 'a' and 'e'

Explanation

- **AWS CloudTrail** records API calls, which can help identify who accessed the EC2 instance and what actions they performed. CloudTrail logs would show events like console logins, API calls to modify security groups, or changes to IAM permissions that might have enabled the unauthorized access.
- **VPC Flow Logs** capture network traffic to and from the instance, while identifying suspicious connections. They provide visibility into IP addresses, ports, and traffic volumes, which can reveal command and control servers or data exfiltration attempts.
- **AWS Systems Manager Session Manager** allows secure shell access to investigate the instance without needing to open additional ports. This provides a way to examine the internal state of the instance without compromising its security further.

Amazon Connect is a contact center service unrelated to security investigation. AWS Secrets Manager manages secrets but does not investigate incidents. AWS KMS manages encryption keys but it is not a primary investigation tool. Amazon Inspector is for vulnerability assessment, not incident investigation. Amazon QuickSight is a business intelligence service, not specifically designed for security investigations.

Question 2: After discovering a potential security breach, your security team needs to implement a containment strategy. Which actions should be taken to contain the incident effectively? (Select TWO)

a. Permanently terminate all potentially compromised resources and create new ones

b. Change all IAM user passwords and delete access keys

c. Isolate affected instances by modifying security groups to restrict traffic

d. Create an AMI of compromised instances for forensic analysis

e. Immediately apply all pending patches to potentially affected systems

Answers: 'c' and 'd'

Explanation

- **Isolating affected instances** (option C) is a crucial containment strategy to prevent lateral movement of attackers. By modifying security groups to restrict traffic, you can isolate compromised resources while maintaining them for investigation.
- **Creating an AMI** (option D) preserves the state of compromised instances for forensic analysis, which is essential for understanding the attack and improving future security.

Option A (terminating resources) may destroy valuable forensic evidence. Option B (changing all passwords) is too broad and might alert attackers. Option E (applying patches) could potentially destroy forensic evidence and does not directly contain the incident.

Domain 2: Logging and Monitoring

Question 3: A security architect needs to implement a centralized logging solution for a multi-account AWS environment. The solution must capture all API activities, ensure logs cannot be tampered with, and allow for efficient querying. Which solution meets these requirements?

a. Configure CloudTrail in each account with logs stored in account-specific S3 buckets

b. Set up a central logging account, configure organization-wide CloudTrail, enable log file validation, and use Athena for querying

c. Enable CloudWatch Logs in each account and set up cross-account subscriptions

d. Deploy third-party logging agents on all instances and store logs in Amazon Redshift

Answer: 'b'

Explanation

The requirements call for centralized logging, tamper-proof logs, and efficient querying. Option B meets all requirements by:

- Creating a centralized logging structure using AWS Organizations and CloudTrail
- Enabling log file validation to ensure logs cannot be tampered with (this creates digest files that can be used to verify log integrity)
- Using Amazon Athena for efficient SQL-based querying of CloudTrail logs stored in S3

Option A does not provide centralized logging. Option C does not ensure logs cannot be tampered with. Option D involves unnecessary complexity with third-party agents and does not address API activity logging specifically.

Question 4: Your security team needs to monitor for and respond to unauthorized changes to security groups in your AWS environment. Which combination of AWS services should be used to implement this solution? (Select TWO)

a. AWS Config rules to detect security group changes

b. CloudWatch Events (EventBridge) to trigger automated responses

c. AWS Trusted Advisor to recommend security improvements

d. Amazon Inspector to scan for security group vulnerabilities E. AWS Shield to protect against malicious security group changes

Answers: 'a' and 'b'

Explanation

- **AWS Config rules** (option A) can monitor security group configurations and detect changes that violate policy. Config provides continuous monitoring and can identify when security groups are modified to allow overly permissive inbound or outbound traffic.

- **CloudWatch Events/EventBridge** (option B) can trigger automated responses when security group changes are detected, such as notifying security personnel or reverting unauthorized changes.

AWS Trusted Advisor (option C) provides recommendations but does not monitor real-time changes. Amazon Inspector (option D) assesses applications for vulnerabilities but does not monitor security group changes. AWS Shield (option E) is for DDoS protection, not security group monitoring.

Domain 3: Infrastructure Security

Question 5: A company is designing a multi-tier web application in AWS. The application consists of a web tier, application tier, and database tier. Which combination of security controls would provide the MOST secure network architecture? (Select TWO)

a. Place all tiers in the same subnet with security groups controlling access between tiers

b. Use separate subnets for each tier with network ACLs controlling traffic between subnets

c. Configure security groups to allow only necessary traffic between tiers

d. Place all tiers in a public subnet and use AWS WAF to filter malicious traffic

e. Configure the VPC to use a NAT gateway for outbound internet access from private subnets

Answers: 'b' and 'c'

Explanation

The most secure network architecture for a multi-tier application includes:

- **Network segmentation** (Option B): Separate subnets for each tier provide logical isolation, with network ACLs adding a layer of security at the subnet level. This follows the principle of Defense-in-Depth
- **Least privilege access** (Option C): Security groups should allow only necessary traffic between tiers, following the principle of least privilege. For example, only the web tier should receive internet traffic, and only the application tier should access the database tier
- **Private subnets** (implied in Option B and supported by Option E): Database and application tiers should be in private subnets, with only the web tier potentially in a public subnet

Option A lacks proper network segmentation. Option D places all tiers in a public subnet, which is insecure for application and database tiers. Option E is a good practice for enabling outbound internet access from private subnets, but it does not address overall architecture security.

Question 6: A company needs to secure their internal API endpoints that are accessed by applications running in multiple VPCs. The solution should be scalable, minimize latency, and maintain private connectivity. Which solution is MOST appropriate?

a. Deploy the API endpoints with public IPs and use security groups to restrict access

b. Use VPC peering between all VPCs that need to access the API endpoints

c. Implement a Transit Gateway to connect all VPCs and control routing

d. Set up AWS PrivateLink (Interface VPC Endpoints) for the API services

Answer: 'd'

Explanation: AWS PrivateLink (Interface VPC Endpoints) is the most appropriate solution because it:

- Provides private connectivity to services across different VPCs without requiring public internet access
- Offers low latency by keeping traffic within the AWS network
- Scales automatically to handle increased traffic
- Maintains security by eliminating exposure to the public internet
- Simplifies network architecture compared to VPC peering or Transit Gateway for service access

Option A exposes the API to the internet, creating unnecessary security risk. Option B requires creating and managing multiple peering connections, which does not scale well as the number of VPCs increases. Option C (Transit Gateway) is a viable solution for general VPC connectivity but adds more complexity than needed just for API access.

Domain 4: Identity and Access Management

Question 7: A company needs to grant temporary access to AWS resources for a contractor. Which approach provides the MOST secure and manageable solution?

a. Create an IAM user with an access key and password, then delete the user when the contract ends

b. Create an IAM role with necessary permissions and a trust policy allowing the contractor to assume the role

c. Add the contractor's identity to an IAM group that has the required permissions

d. Share AWS account credentials with time restrictions

Answer: 'b'

Explanation

IAM roles provide temporary, limited-privilege credentials that automatically expire, making them ideal for third-party access scenarios. Option B is the most secure approach because:

- It avoids creating permanent credentials
- It uses automatic expiration
- It enables easy permission updates if requirements change
- It provides an audit trail of role assumptions

Option A creates long-term credentials that require manual cleanup. Option C requires creating a permanent IAM user. Option D violates AWS best practices by sharing account credentials.

Question 8: Your organization manages multiple AWS accounts and wants to centralize IAM user management while enforcing consistent permissions across all accounts. Which combination of AWS services and features should you implement? (Select TWO)

a. AWS Control Tower with Service Control Policies b. AWS Organizations with Service Control Policies c. AWS IAM Identity Center (formerly AWS Single Sign-On) d. Cross-account IAM roles with resource-based policies e. Amazon Cognito with user pools

Answers: 'b' and 'c'

Explanation

- **AWS Organizations with Service Control Policies (SCPs)** (Option B) provides account management with centralized policy control. SCPs act as guardrails by setting permission boundaries that can't be exceeded, even by account administrators
- **AWS IAM Identity Center** (Option C) provides centralized user management and single sign-on capabilities for multiple AWS accounts. Users can be managed centrally and granted specific permissions to use multiple accounts

AWS Control Tower (option A) includes Organizations and SCPs but adds additional governance capabilities beyond what's needed for this scenario. Cross-account roles (option D) can be useful but do not provide centralized user management.

Amazon Cognito (option E) is primarily for application user management, not AWS administrative access.

Domain 5: Data Protection

Question 9: A financial services company needs to encrypt sensitive customer data stored in Amazon RDS PostgreSQL. The company's security policy requires the ability to audit and control access to encryption keys. Which solution meets these requirements?

a. Enable default RDS encryption using AWS-managed keys

b. Use RDS with AWS KMS customer managed keys (CMKs) and enable AWS CloudTrail

c. Use RDS with client-side encryption and store keys in AWS Secrets Manager

d. Deploy a self-managed database on EC2 with encrypted EBS volumes

Answer: 'b'

Explanation

The requirements focus on encryption with auditable key access control. Option B meets all requirements by:

- Using RDS encryption with customer managed keys, which gives the company control over the key policy
- Leveraging AWS KMS for key management, which integrates with IAM for access control
- Enabling CloudTrail to audit all key usage and management actions

Option A uses AWS-managed keys, which do not provide the required control. Option C introduces unnecessary complexity with client-side encryption. Option D requires managing the database software, which is less efficient than using RDS.

Question 10: Your company stores its sensitive documents in an Amazon S3 bucket. You need to implement a solution that prevents accidental or intentional deletion of these documents for a retention period of 7 years. Which combination of S3 features should you implement? (Select TWO)

a. S3 Versioning with lifecycle policies

b. S3 Object Lock in compliance mode

c. S3 server-side encryption with KMS

d. S3 cross-region replication E. S3 Intelligent-Tiering storage class

Answers: 'a' and 'b'

Explanation

- **S3 Versioning with lifecycle policies** (Option A) protects against accidental deletion by preserving previous versions of objects. Even if an object is deleted, the previous versions remain available, and lifecycle policies can manage version retention
- **S3 Object Lock in compliance mode** (Option B) prevents objects from being deleted or overwritten during a specified retention period, even by users with administrative permissions. This provides a strong control for regulatory

Option C (encryption) protects data confidentiality but does not prevent deletion. Option D (cross-region replication) provides redundancy but does not prevent deletion in both regions. Option E (Intelligent-Tiering) is a storage class for cost optimization, not for preventing deletion.

Domain 6: Management and Security Governance

Question 11:

Your organization wants to ensure that no user or role in any AWS account can create resources in AWS regions outside of us-east-1 and us-west-2. The organization uses multiple AWS accounts managed under AWS Organizations. What is the most effective way to enforce this policy?

a. Create an IAM policy that denies region-based actions and attach it to all users and roles

b. Use AWS Config rules to detect resource creation in unauthorized regions

c. Define a Service Control Policy (SCP) that denies access to all regions except us-east-1 and us-west-2

d. Use IAM permission boundaries for all roles to limit regional access

Answer: 'c'

Explanation

SCPs are the most effective way to centrally enforce policies across multiple AWS accounts in an organization.

Option C correctly uses an SCP to deny actions in all regions except the allowed ones, providing a governance-level control.

Option A is not scalable and relies on consistent IAM usage.

Option B can detect violations but does not prevent them.

Option D is role-specific and cannot enforce account-wide restrictions.

Question 12: Your compliance team wants to ensure that all EC2 instances launched in the organization are using approved instance types only. If any instance is launched with an unauthorized type, it should be flagged and remediated automatically. Which AWS service should you use to implement this control?

a. AWS Systems Manager

b. AWS CloudTrail

c. AWS Config with custom rules and remediation

d. IAM policy with deny statements for EC2 actions

Answer: 'c'

Explanation

AWS Config allows you to define custom rules (or use managed ones) to check for compliance such as approved instance types.

Automatic remediation can be triggered via AWS Config and AWS Systems Manager Automation to stop or tag non-compliant resources.

Option A (SSM) does not natively enforce compliance.

Option B (CloudTrail) provides audit logs but does not enforce or remediate.

Option D (IAM) can restrict usage, but it is complex to manage and does not remediate violations automatically.

Advanced Scenario Questions

Question 12: A multinational company is implementing a multi-account AWS environment for its global operations. The security team needs to establish centralized security controls while allowing regional teams to manage their resources. Which architecture BEST meets these requirements?

a. Create a single AWS account with separate VPCs for each region and IAM roles for regional teams

b. Create an AWS Organization with a security account, implement Service Control Policies, and use AWS Config aggregators

c. Create separate AWS accounts for each region and use cross-account IAM roles for the security team

d. Deploy AWS Control Tower in each region with guardrails customized for regional requirements

Answer: 'b'

Explanation

Option B provides the most comprehensive solution that balances centralized security with regional autonomy:

- AWS Organizations enables hierarchical account management with Organizational Units (OUs) that can be structured around regions or business functions
- Service Control Policies (SCPs) provide guardrails that prevent member accounts from violating security policies, regardless of IAM permissions
- A dedicated security account centralizes security services such as GuardDuty, Security Hub, and IAM Access Analyzer
- AWS Config aggregators provide visibility into resource configurations across all accounts from a central location

Option A lacks proper segregation of duties and does not scale well. Option C provides account isolation but lacks centralized policy enforcement. Option D is incorrect because AWS Control Tower is deployed once for the organization, not in each region.

Question 13: Your organization has implemented a CI/CD pipeline for application deployment to AWS. The security team needs to integrate automated security testing into the pipeline without significantly impacting deployment speed. Which combination of approaches would be MOST effective? (Select TWO)

a. Manually review all code changes before allowing deployment to production

b. Integrate Static Application Security Testing (SAST) tools in the build phase

c. Implement AWS CodeGuru for automated code reviews in the pipeline

d. Require security team approval for every deployment

e. Deploy to a staging environment with dynamic security testing before production release

Answers: 'b' and 'e'

Explanation

- Integrating SAST tools in the build phase (option B) facilitates early detection of security issues without significantly impacting pipeline speed. These tools can identify vulnerabilities, insecure coding patterns, and potential security flaws during the development process
    - Deploying to a staging environment with dynamic testing (option E) allows one to conduct more comprehensive security testing, including

runtime analysis and penetration testing, in an environment that mimics production without affecting actual systems

Options A and D introduce manual processes that would significantly slow down the pipeline. Option C (CodeGuru) is useful but would typically be used alongside other testing approaches rather than as a complete solution.

Final Preparation Checklist

As exam day approaches, use this checklist to ensure you are fully prepared:

Two Weeks before the Exam

Run a diagnostic, target weak areas, and tune your pacing strategy.

- Complete a full-length practice exam
  - Identify weak areas that need additional focus
  - Analyze your timing and adjust your exam strategy
  - Review incorrect answers to understand knowledge gaps
- Review AWS documentation for services you are less comfortable with
  - Focus on service features, limitations, and integration points
  - Study configuration options and security best practices
  - Understand service-specific security controls
- Practice hands-on labs for key security services
  - Implement logging and monitoring solutions
  - Configure encrypted data storage with proper key management
  - Set up identity federation and permission boundaries
  - Create automated security responses with EventBridge and Lambda
- Join a study group or forum to discuss challenging concepts
  - Post questions about topics you find difficult
  - Participate in discussions about exam experiences
  - Share resources and study strategies
- Create mind maps for complex security architectures
  - Map services to security domains
  - Visualize relationships between services
  - Document common integration patterns

One Week before the Exam

Re-assess progress, tighten techniques, and prepare concise summaries.

- Take another practice exam to examine your improvement
    - Focus on timing and question analysis strategies
    - Identify any remaining weak areas
    - Practice skipping and returning to difficult questions
- Review exam-specific tips and common pitfalls
    - Study the question analysis strategies from this chapter
    - Review time management techniques
    - Understand common misconceptions and distractors
- Create a one-page summary of key services, their features, and use cases
    - Focus on distinguishing features between similar services
    - List common integration scenarios
    - Note key limitations and constraints
- Ensure you understand all five domains and their key concepts
    - Review the domain weightings and focus areas
    - Verify your understanding of core concepts in each domain
    - Create flashcards for quick review of challenging topics
- Practice explaining complex concepts in simple terms
    - Security architectures
    - Encryption methods and key management
    - Identity federation
    - Incident response procedures
- Review AWS Well-Architected Framework: Security Pillar
    - Understand how exam questions align with framework principles
    - Review design principles and best practices
    - Map services to security objectives

Day before the Exam

Keep it light: review essentials, set up logistics, and prioritize rest.

- Light review of your summary notes
    - Avoid deep study or new topics

- Focus on reinforcing key concepts
- Review service capabilities and integration points

- Verify exam details
  - Confirm testing center location and directions (for in-person exams)
  - Check technical requirements (for online exams)
  - Prepare any required software or systems (for online exams)
- Prepare required identification documents
  - Government-issued photo ID
  - Secondary ID if required
  - Any additional documentation specified in your exam confirmation
- Set up your testing environment (for online exams)
  - Clean your desk area
  - Ensure good lighting and a comfortable seating arrangement
  - Test your internet connection
  - Close unnecessary applications and browser tabs
- Get a good night's sleep
  - More valuable than last-minute cramming
  - Ensures mental alertness during the exam
  - Reduces anxiety and improves decision-making

Exam Day

Execute your plan: manage time, stay calm, and use review features wisely.

- Arrive early for an in-person exam or set up your space for an online exam
  - Plan to arrive at least 30 minutes early for in-person exams
  - Log in 15-30 minutes early for online exams
  - Complete system checks and identity verification promptly
- Use relaxation techniques if you feel anxious
  - Deep breathing exercises
  - Positive visualization
  - Progressive muscle relaxation
  - Mental rehearsal of your exam strategy

- Read each question carefully and manage your time
    - Identify key requirements and constraints
    - Watch for qualifier words (MOST, LEAST, BEST)
    - Monitor your progress against time checkpoints
    - Use the marking feature for questions you want to revisit
- Use the provided resources
    - Calculator for any necessary calculations
    - Notepad for working through complex scenarios
    - Review screen to identify unanswered questions

Final Exam Tip: *Trust your preparation. By the time you take the exam, you should have a solid understanding of AWS security concepts and services. Stay calm, read the questions carefully, and apply the knowledge you have gained throughout your preparation.*

Post-Exam Next Steps

Regardless of the exam outcome, consider these next steps:

If You Pass:

- Share your certification on professional networks
- Plan for maintaining and enhancing your skills
- Consider complementary certifications (AWS Advanced Networking, DevOps)
- Apply your knowledge to real-world projects

If You Need to Retake:

- Analyse the domains where you scored lowest
- Focus your study on weak areas
- Try different study resources
- Increase hands-on practice
- Schedule your retake after sufficient preparation

For All Candidates:

- Continue building practical skills through projects
- Stay updated on new AWS security services and features
- Contribute to the AWS security community
- Apply security principles in your professional work

Conclusion

This chapter has provided a comprehensive overview of the AWS Certified Security Specialty exam, including its structure, content domains, preparation strategies, and practice questions. Remember that success in this exam requires both theoretical knowledge and practical experience with AWS security services.

The AWS Security Specialty certification represents a significant achievement in the field of cloud security. It validates your ability to implement and manage security controls across a wide range of AWS services and architecture patterns. Beyond the certification itself, the knowledge and skills you have developed during your preparation will serve you well when designing, implementing, and maintaining secure AWS environments.

As you continue your preparation, focus on understanding the "why" behind each security practice rather than just memorizing facts. This deeper knowledge will not only help you pass the exam but also make you a more effective security professional in real life. Security is an ongoing journey, not a destination–the learning habits you have established during your certification preparation will be a great addition to your existing skills as the cloud security landscape continues to evolve.

In the next chapter, "Final Practice Test and Real-World Applications," we will explore the practical applications of AWS security through real-world case studies and advanced scenarios that will provide you with additional context to apply your knowledge in professional environments. We will also provide a comprehensive practice test that simulates the actual exam experience, helping you assess your readiness and build confidence for the exam.

Points to Remember

- The exam consists of 65 questions (50 scored, 15 unscored) to be completed in 170 minutes
- Five domains are covered, with Infrastructure Security (26%) and Data Protection (22%) having the highest weightage
- Both multiple-choice and multiple-response questions will be included
- There is no penalty for wrong answers, so always provide an answer
- Having hands-on experience is crucial for exam success
- Focus on understanding AWS security services, their capabilities, limitations, and integrations
- Review official AWS documentation for the most accurate and up-to-date information
- Take multiple practice exams to assess your readiness

- Use time management strategies during the exam
- Create a structured study plan that covers all domains with emphasis on heavily weighted areas
- Practice explaining complex security concepts in simple terms
- Implement hands-on labs to reinforce theoretical knowledge
- Join study groups and forums to learn from peers
- Focus on understanding the reason or, the "why" behind security practices
- Develop an approach for analyzing and solving scenario-based questions

References

- **AWS Certified Security – Specialty Exam Guide (SCS-C02)** https://d1.awsstatic.com/training-and-certification/docs-security-spec/AWS-Certified-Security-Specialty_Exam-Guide.pdf
- **AWS Security Best Practices (Whitepaper)** https://docs.aws.amazon.com/whitepapers/latest/aws-security-best-practices/aws-security-best-practices.pdf
- **AWS Well-Architected Framework: Security Pillar** https://docs.aws.amazon.com/wellarchitected/latest/security-pillar/wellarchitected-security-pillar.pdf
- **AWS Security Documentation (Service docs hub)** https://docs.aws.amazon.com/security/
- **AWS Security Blog** https://aws.amazon.com/blogs/security/
- **AWS Security Reference Architecture (AWS SRA)** https://docs.aws.amazon.com/pdfs/prescriptive-guidance/latest/security-reference-architecture/security-reference-architecture.pdf
- **AWS Training & Certification – Security Specialty** https://aws.amazon.com/certification/certified-security-specialty/
- **AWS Workshops & Labs (Security category)** https://workshops.aws/categories/Security

CHAPTER 8
Final Practice Test and Real-World Applications

Introduction

You have made it to the final stretch of your AWS Security Specialty certification journey. In this chapter, we will put your knowledge to the test with a comprehensive practice exam designed to simulate the actual AWS Certified Security Specialty test. Each question is carefully crafted to cover the key domains and concepts you will encounter on exam day.

But this chapter is not just about testing your knowledge–it is about preparing you for real-world application of these security concepts. After completing the practice test, we will explore how the skills that you have acquired throughout this certification journey translate into practical, on-the-job scenarios. We shall also provide guidance on career opportunities in the AWS security space, and the next steps for your professional development.

Let us start with a full-length practice test that mirrors the format, difficulty level, and domain coverage of the actual AWS Security Specialty exam.

Structure

In this chapter, we will cover the following topics:

- Full-Length AWS Security Specialty Practice Test (65 questions)
- Test-taking Instructions and Strategies
- Detailed Answer Key with Explanations
- Real-World AWS Security Applications in:
    - Healthcare (HIPAA Compliance)

    - Financial Services (PCI DSS Compliance)
    - E-commerce (Scaling Securely During Peak Seasons)
    - Government (Secure Multi-Account Architecture)
- Career Advancement Opportunities with AWS Security Expertise
- Building your AWS Security Portfolio
- Next Steps after Certification for Continued Growth

Full-Length Practice Test

Instructions

This practice test consists of 65 multiple-choice and multiple-response questions, just like the actual AWS Security Specialty exam. You will have 170 minutes to complete the test, which aligns with the timing of the real exam. For multiple-response questions, be sure to select all applicable answers.

Remember these key test-taking strategies:

- Read each question carefully.
- Eliminate obviously incorrect answers.
- Manage your time effectively.
- Flag difficult questions to revisit later.
- Do not leave any questions unanswered.

Good luck!

Question 1: Your security team has received an alert from Amazon GuardDuty indicating potential cryptocurrency mining activity on an EC2 instance. What should be your FIRST response action?

a. Terminate the EC2 instance immediately

b. Take a snapshot of the instance for forensic analysis

c. Isolate the instance by modifying security groups

d. Patch the instance with the latest updates

Question 2: Your organization wants to improve its security incident detection and response capabilities in AWS. Which combination of services provides the MOST comprehensive solution for this requirement? (Select TWO)

a. Amazon Inspector and AWS Config

b. AWS Security Hub and Amazon GuardDuty

c. AWS CloudHSM and AWS KMS

d. Amazon CloudWatch and AWS CloudTrail

e. AWS Trusted Advisor and AWS Shield

Question 3: An AWS Lambda function in your account has been compromised, and is being used to launch attacks against other AWS accounts. Which of the following steps should you include in your incident response plan? (Select TWO)

a. Delete all Lambda functions in your AWS account

b. Review CloudTrail logs to identify the source of compromise

c. Update the Lambda function's code to remove the malicious components

d. Rotate all IAM user access keys in your account

e. Apply a restrictive IAM policy to the Lambda execution role

Question 4: Your organization has implemented an incident response framework for AWS workloads. Which of the following would be the MOST effective way to test the efficacy of this framework?

a. Conduct a penetration test on all AWS resources

b. Review security documentation with stakeholders

c. Perform a simulated security incident (table top exercise)

d. Deploy intrusion detection systems

Question 5: Your organization has experienced a data breach involving an S3 bucket. After containing the incident, which of the following actions should you take FIRST during the eradication phase?

a. Notify affected customers about the breach

b. Identify and eliminate the root cause of the breach

c. Restore data from backups

d. Document lessons learned

Question 6: During a security incident involving unauthorized access to an EC2 instance, which AWS service would provide the MOST detailed information about API calls made during the incident timeframe?

a. Amazon GuardDuty

b. AWS CloudTrail

c. AWS Config

d. Amazon Inspector

Question 7: Your organization needs to implement automated remediation for specific security findings. Which AWS service would be MOST appropriate for building these automated workflows?

a. AWS Lambda

b. AWS Systems Manager

c. AWS Step Functions

d. Amazon EventBridge

Question 8: Which of the following would be the MOST appropriate incident response action, if you discover a misconfigured S3 bucket that has been publicly accessible for an unknown period?

a. Immediately delete the S3 bucket and all objects

b. Remove public access, inventory exposed objects, and review access logs

c. Create a backup of the bucket before making any changes

d. Encrypt all objects in the bucket with AWS KMS

Question 9: Your organization needs to collect VPC flow logs from all AWS accounts in your organization for security monitoring. What is the MOST efficient way to implement this requirement?

a. Create an AWS Lambda function that enables flow logs for each VPC

b. Use AWS CloudFormation StackSets to deploy flow log configurations

c. Configure Service Control Policies (SCPs) to enforce flow log creation

d. Use AWS Config rules to detect and remediate missing flow logs

Question 10: Which of the following is the MOST comprehensive way to capture all AWS API calls made within your AWS account?

a. Enable AWS CloudTrail with a multi-region trail and log file validation

b. Configure Amazon CloudWatch Logs for all AWS services

c. Enable AWS Config recording for all resource types

d. Set up VPC Flow Logs for all VPCs

Question 11: Your company wants to detect when users are granted administrative privileges in IAM. Which combination of AWS services should you use for this purpose? (Select TWO)

a. AWS CloudTrail and Amazon CloudWatch Logs

b. AWS Config and AWS Firewall Manager

c. Amazon GuardDuty and AWS Shield

d. AWS Security Hub and AWS WAF

e. Amazon EventBridge and Amazon SNS

Question 12: Which CloudTrail event type captures non-API events in your AWS account, such as console sign-ins?

a. Management events

b. Data events

c. Insight events

d. Global service events

Question 13: Your organization needs to analyze CloudTrail logs for unusual API activity. Which AWS service would be the MOST effective for this use case?

a. Amazon Athena

b. Amazon QuickSight

c. Amazon RDS

d. Amazon DynamoDB

Question 14: Which of the following provides the MOST comprehensive visibility into the security posture of Lambda functions?

a. Amazon Inspector

b. AWS X-Ray

c. AWS CloudTrail

d. Amazon CloudWatch Lambda Insights

Question 15: Your organization needs to centralize security findings from multiple AWS services for analysis. Which service should you use?

a. AWS Control Tower

b. AWS Security Hub

c. AWS Organizations

d. AWS Artifact.

Question 16: Which combination of settings will provide the MOST secure configuration for CloudTrail? (Select TWO)

a. Enable log file integrity validation

b. Store logs in an S3 bucket with default encryption

c. Configure SNS notifications for log file delivery

d. Enable multi-region trail

e. Store logs in CloudWatch Logs

Question 17: Which AWS service provides the MOST effective protection against large-scale DDoS attacks targeting your web applications?

a. AWS WAF

b. Amazon Route 53

c. AWS Shield Advanced

d. Network ACLs

Question 18: Your application needs to communicate with an on-premises database securely over the public internet. Which solution provides the STRONGEST security for this connection?

a. Configure security groups to allow traffic only from specific IP addresses

b. Use Site-to-Site VPN with IPsec

c. Configure Network ACLs to filter traffic

d. Use Amazon API Gateway with resource policies

Question 19: Which of the following is the MOST secure way to allow multiple VPCs to communicate with each other?

a. Configure a NAT Gateway in each VPC

b. Use VPC peering connections

c. Set up a Transit Gateway with proper route tables

d. Configure Internet Gateways with routing tables

Question 20: Your organization needs to inspect all traffic entering and leaving your VPC. Which AWS service should you implement?

a. VPC Flow Logs

b. AWS Network Firewall

c. AWS Config

d. Security Groups

Question 21: Which AWS service provides protection against application layer attacks (Layer 7) on your web applications?

a. AWS Shield

b. Amazon GuardDuty

c. AWS WAF

d. Network ACLs

Question 22: Your organization needs to securely connect to multiple AWS services without traversing the public internet. Which solution should you implement?

a. AWS Direct Connect

b. VPC Endpoints

c. VPN Gateway

d. Internet Gateway with route tables

Question 23: Which combination of AWS security controls provides the MOST comprehensive protection for an EC2 instance? (Select TWO)

a. Security Groups

b. IAM Roles

c. Network ACLs

d. Host-based firewall

e. Resource-based policies

Question 24: You need to ensure that traffic between your application and database tiers is encrypted. Which of the following is the MOST secure approach?

a. Configure TLS on the application servers and database servers

b. Use VPC peering with security groups

c. Implement a Network Load Balancer

d. Deploy the application and database in the same subnet

Question 25: Which approach provides the MOST secure method for accessing an RDS database from AWS Lambda functions?

a. Configure the Lambda function in a VPC with appropriate security groups

b. Use IAM authentication for database access

c. Store database credentials in environment variables

d. Configure a NAT Gateway for outbound traffic

Question 26: Which AWS service allows you to federate Microsoft Active Directory users to AWS?

a. AWS IAM

b. AWS Cognito

c. AWS Directory Service

d. AWS Organizations

Question 27: Your organization needs to implement the principle of least privilege for IAM users. Which combination of features would BEST help achieve this? (Select TWO)

a. IAM Access Analyzer

b. AWS Organizations with SCPs

c. AWS Shield Advanced

d. AWS Config Rules

e. IAM Roles with managed policies

Question 28: Which of the following is the MOST secure approach for allowing EC2 instances to access S3 buckets?

a. Create IAM users and store access keys in the EC2 instance

b. Use IAM roles with instance profiles

c. Store AWS access keys in encrypted EBS volumes

d. Configure S3 VPC endpoints with bucket policies

Question 29: Your organization has multiple AWS accounts and needs to centrally manage IAM policies. Which service should you use?

a. AWS IAM Identity Center (successor to AWS Single Sign-On)

b. AWS Directory Service

c. AWS Organizations

d. AWS Control Tower.

Question 30: Which combination of features provides the MOST comprehensive protection against unintended permission escalation in IAM? (Select TWO)

a. IAM permission boundaries

b. Service Control Policies (SCPs)

c. IAM Access Advisor

d. Resource-based policies

e. AWS Shield Advanced

Question 31: Which statement is TRUE regarding AWS IAM roles compared to IAM users?

a. Roles provide temporary credentials, while users have long-term credentials

b. Roles can be assigned to AWS resources, but users cannot

c. Roles support multi-factor authentication, but users do not

d. Roles automatically rotate credentials, but users require manual rotation

Question 32: Your organization wants to implement a centralized identity management solution that supports SAML 2.0 for AWS access. Which service should you use?

a. Amazon Cognito

b. AWS IAM Identity Center (successor to AWS Single Sign-On)

c. AWS Directory Service

d. AWS Identity and Access Management

Question 33: Which AWS service helps you analyze identity and access management policies to validate that they provide the intended permissions?

a. AWS Config

b. AWS CloudTrail

c. AWS IAM Access Analyzer

d. AWS Security Hub

Question 34: Which AWS service provides the MOST secure way to manage and store encryption keys for other AWS services?

a. AWS Secrets Manager

b. AWS Key Management Service (KMS)

c. AWS Systems Manager Parameter Store

d. AWS Certificate Manager

Question 35: Your organization needs to encrypt data in an S3 bucket with customer-managed keys. Which solution should you implement?

a. S3 server-side encryption with Amazon S3-managed keys (SSE-S3)

b. S3 server-side encryption with AWS KMS keys (SSE-KMS)

c. S3 server-side encryption with customer-provided keys (SSE-C)

d. Client-side encryption with AWS KMS

Question 36: Which combination of AWS services would you use to automatically find, classify, and protect sensitive data? (Select TWO)

a. Amazon Macie

b. AWS Shield

c. AWS KMS

d. Amazon Detective

e. Amazon GuardDuty

Question 37: Your organization needs to securely store and automatically rotate database credentials. Which AWS service should you use?

a. AWS Systems Manager Parameter Store

b. AWS KMS

c. AWS Secrets Manager

d. AWS Certificate Manager

Question 38: Which S3 bucket policy element would you use to enforce the use of HTTPS for all requests to the bucket?

a. `aws: SecureTransport`

b. `aws: SourceIp`

c. `aws: PrincipalArn`

d. `awsRequestMethod`

Question 39: Your organization needs to implement a data loss prevention solution for objects stored in S3 buckets. Which service is the MOST suitable for this requirement?

a. Amazon GuardDuty

b. Amazon Macie

c. AWS CloudTrail

d. AWS Config

Question 40: Which AWS service provides encryption key management with FIPS 140-2 validated Hardware Security Modules (HSMs)?

a. AWS KMS

b. AWS CloudHSM

c. Amazon S3

d. AWS Certificate Manager

Question 41: Which feature would you use to track the usage history of an AWS KMS key?

a. CloudTrail logs

b. KMS key aliases

c. KMS key tags

d. KMS grants

Question 42: Your organization needs to implement field-level encryption for sensitive data transmitted through CloudFront. Which AWS service should you use in conjunction with CloudFront?

a. AWS Certificate Manager

b. AWS WAF

c. AWS KMS

d. AWS Secrets Manager

Question 43: Which AWS service helps you identify potential vulnerabilities in your Lambda functions' code?

a. Amazon Inspector

b. AWS Lambda@Edge

c. Amazon CodeGuru

d. AWS Config

Question 44: Which AWS service allows you to run security assessments against your EC2 instances?

a. Amazon Inspector

b. AWS Config

c. AWS Systems Manager

d. AWS Security Hub

Question 45: Your organization needs to implement security controls that apply to all AWS accounts in your organization. Which AWS service should you use?

a. AWS IAM

b. AWS Organizations with Service Control Policies

c. AWS Config

d. AWS Firewall Manager

Question 46: Which AWS service helps you detect and protect from DDoS attacks at both the network and application layers?

a. AWS Shield Advanced

b. AWS WAF.

c. Amazon GuardDuty

d. AWS Security Hub

Question 47: Your organization needs to implement a comprehensive security assessment solution for AWS resources. Which service should you use?

a. AWS Audit Manager

b. AWS Systems Manager

c. AWS Security Hub

d. AWS Config

Question 48: Which service would you use to validate that your AWS resources comply with your organization's security policies?

a. AWS Config

b. AWS Trusted Advisor

c. AWS CloudTrail

d. Amazon Inspector

Question 49: Your organization needs to ensure that all data in transit between AWS services is encrypted. Which approach is MOST effective?

a. Configure VPC endpoints for all AWS services

b. Use TLS/SSL for all API connections

c. Implement client-side encryption for all data

d. Configure HTTPS endpoints for all services

Question 50: Which AWS feature allows you to implement proactive security controls by preventing the deployment of resources that don't comply with your security policies?

a. AWS Config Rules

b. AWS CloudFormation Guard

c. AWS Service Control Policies

d. AWS IAM Policies

Question 51: Your organization needs to create a security assessment report to demonstrate compliance with regulatory requirements. Which AWS service should you use?

a. AWS Artifact

b. AWS Audit Manager

c. AWS Security Hub

d. AWS Trusted Advisor

Question 52: Which of the following provides the MOST secure method for storing and managing TLS certificates for use with AWS services?

a. Amazon S3 with server-side encryption
b. AWS Systems Manager Parameter Store
c. AWS Certificate Manager
d. AWS Secrets Manager

Question 53: Your organization needs to implement a solution that automatically remediates non-compliant AWS resources. Which combination of services would be MOST effective? (Select TWO)

a. AWS Config
b. AWS Lambda
c. AWS Systems Manager
d. AWS CloudTrail
e. AWS Trusted Advisor

Question 54: Which AWS service can detect anomalous API calls that might indicate unauthorized access to your AWS resources?

a. AWS CloudTrail
b. Amazon GuardDuty
c. AWS Config
d. Amazon Detective

Question 55: Your organization has strict requirements for controlling outbound traffic from your VPC to specific AWS services. Which AWS feature would be MOST effective for this requirement?

a. Network ACLs
b. Security Groups
c. VPC Endpoints with endpoint policies
d. Internet Gateway with route tables

Question 56: Which encryption option for EBS volumes provides the STRONGEST security control?

a. AWS-managed keys
b. Customer-managed keys in AWS KMS

c. Customer-managed keys in AWS CloudHSM

d. Customer-provided encryption keys

Question 57: Your organization needs to implement a comprehensive vulnerability management solution for containerized applications running on Amazon ECS. Which AWS service should you use?

a. Amazon Inspector

b. AWS Systems Manager

c. Amazon ECR Scan

d. AWS Config

Question 58: Which AWS service would you use to analyze CloudTrail logs to identify potential security issues and policy violations?

a. Amazon CloudWatch Logs Insights

b. Amazon Athena

c. Amazon QuickSight

d. Amazon Redshift

Question 59: Your organization needs to implement a solution that automatically remediates security misconfigurations. Which service combination would be MOST effective?

a. AWS Config Rules and AWS Systems Manager Automation

b. AWS Security Hub and AWS Lambda

c. Amazon GuardDuty and AWS Lambda

d. AWS Trusted Advisor and AWS CloudFormation

Question 60: Which AWS service enables you to enforce infrastructure compliance at scale across multiple AWS accounts?

a. AWS Control Tower

b. AWS Config

c. AWS Organizations

d. AWS Systems Manager

Question 61: Your organization needs to secure API access to your AWS resources. Which combination of services and features provides the MOST comprehensive solution? (Select TWO)

a. Amazon API Gateway with usage plans

b. AWS Lambda with resource-based policies

c. Amazon API Gateway with AWS WAF

d. AWS IAM with VPC endpoints

e. AWS Shield with Route 53

Question 62: Which AWS service helps you to Investigate Identity and Access Management (IAM) anomalies?

a. Amazon Detective

b. Amazon GuardDuty

c. AWS CloudTrail

d. AWS IAM Access Analyzer

Question 63: Your organization needs to implement a centralized solution for managing security findings across multiple AWS accounts and services. Which service should you use?

a. AWS Control Tower

b. AWS Security Hub

c. AWS Organizations

d. AWS IAM

Question 64: Which AWS service would you use to establish secure network connectivity between on-premises systems and AWS?

a. AWS Site-to-Site VPN

b. AWS Direct Connect

c. VPC Peering

d. AWS Transit Gateway

Question 65: Your organization needs to implement a solution that provides visibility into the overall security posture of your AWS resources. Which service should you use?

a. AWS Trusted Advisor

b. AWS Security Hub

c. AWS Config

d. AWS CloudTrail

Answer Keys and Explanations

Question 1: c

Explanation: When responding to a potential security incident, the first step should be to isolate the affected resource to prevent further compromise or damage. By modifying security groups, you can quickly isolate the EC2 instance from other resources, while preserving its state for forensic analysis. Terminating the instance (option a) may destroy valuable evidence. Taking a snapshot (option b) is important but should be done after isolation. Patching (option d) should only be done after investigation and remediation planning.

Question 2: b, d

Explanation: AWS Security Hub provides a comprehensive view of security alerts and compliance status, aggregating findings from multiple AWS services, including GuardDuty. Amazon GuardDuty is a threat detection service that continuously monitors for malicious activity and unauthorized behavior. Together with CloudWatch for monitoring and CloudTrail for API activity logging, these services create a robust security incident detection and response capability. Amazon Inspector and AWS Config are more focused on vulnerability assessment and compliance monitoring, while CloudHSM and KMS are focused on encryption services.

Question 3: b, e

Explanation: When responding to a compromised Lambda function, reviewing CloudTrail logs helps to identify the source and method of compromise, which is crucial for understanding the attack and preventing similar incidents. Applying a restrictive IAM policy to the Lambda execution role will immediately limit what the function can do, helping to contain the incident. Deleting all Lambda functions (option a) is an overreaction. Updating the code (option c) might be appropriate after investigation but is not a first response. Rotating all IAM user keys (option d) might be unnecessary, unless there is an evidence of broader compromise.

Question 4: c

Explanation: A table top exercise, or simulated security incident, is the most effective way to test an incident response framework because it allows the team to practice their response in a controlled environment without affecting production systems. This identifies gaps in procedures, roles, and communications. Penetration testing (option a) tests security controls, not the response framework. Documentation review (option b) is passive and does not test operational readiness. Deploying intrusion detection (option d) is a preventative measure, not a test of response capabilities.

Question 5: b

Explanation: After containing an incident, the eradication phase focuses on eliminating the root cause to prevent recurrence. Identifying and eliminating the root cause of the breach (such as insecure configurations, compromised credentials, or exploitation of vulnerabilities) is the first step in eradication. Notifying customers (option a) is a part of the communication plan but not eradication. Restoring data (option c) is part of the recovery phase. Documenting lessons learned (option d) is part of the post-incident activity.

Question 6: b

Explanation: AWS CloudTrail provides detailed logs of all API calls made within your AWS account, including information about the caller, the time of the call, the source IP address, the request parameters, and the response elements. This level of detail is essential for incident investigation and forensic analysis. While GuardDuty (option a) provides threat detection, it does not offer the comprehensive API logging of CloudTrail. AWS Config (option c) tracks resource configuration changes, and Amazon Inspector (option d) assesses vulnerabilities, but neither provides detailed API call information.

Question 7: c

Explanation: AWS Step Functions is ideal for building automated remediation workflows because it allows you to coordinate multiple AWS services into serverless workflows with visual workflows, error handling, and retry logic. While Lambda (option a) can execute code in response to events, Step Functions provides orchestration of complex workflows involving multiple Lambda functions and other AWS services. Systems Manager (option b) is more focused on operational management. EventBridge (option d) is an event bus service that routes events but does not provide the workflow orchestration capabilities of Step Functions.

Question 8: b

Explanation: When discovering a misconfigured S3 bucket with public access, the immediate priority is to remove public access to prevent further exposure. Next, you should inventory the exposed objects to understand what data may have been compromised, and review access logs to determine if unauthorized access occurred. These steps preserve evidence, while securing the environment. Immediately deleting the bucket (option a) would destroy evidence and potentially cause business disruption. Creating a backup (option c) is important, but secondary to stopping the exposure. Encrypting objects (option d) does not address the public access issue.

Question 9: b

Explanation: AWS CloudFormation StackSets provides the most efficient way to deploy standardized configurations, including VPC flow logs, across multiple AWS accounts. StackSets allows you to create, update, or delete stacks across multiple accounts and regions with a single operation. A Lambda function (option a) would require custom development and maintenance. Service Control Policies (option c) can enforce organizational policies but are not designed to create resources. AWS Config rules (option d) can detect missing flow logs but would require additional remediation steps.

Question 10: a

Explanation: Enabling AWS CloudTrail with a multi-region trail and log file validation provides the most comprehensive method to capture all AWS API calls. A multi-region trail captures API activity from all regions, ensuring complete coverage. Log file validation enables you to determine whether a log file was modified, deleted, or unchanged after CloudTrail delivered it. CloudWatch Logs (option b) captures application logs, not API calls. AWS Config (option c) records configuration changes, not all API calls. VPC Flow Logs (option d) capture network traffic, not API calls.

Question 11: a, e

Explanation: The most effective combination for detecting when users are granted administrative privileges is AWS CloudTrail with Amazon CloudWatch Logs, and Amazon EventBridge with Amazon SNS. CloudTrail logs all IAM actions, including policy attachments. CloudWatch Logs can analyze these logs for specific events. EventBridge can create rules to detect these events, and trigger notifications via SNS. AWS Config and Firewall Manager (option b) focus on resource configurations and network security. GuardDuty and Shield (option c) focus on threat detection and DDoS protection. Security Hub and WAF (option d) aggregate security findings, and protect web applications.

Question 12: a

Explanation: CloudTrail management events capture control plane operations on AWS resources, including non-API events such as console sign-ins. Data events (option b) capture data plane operations on resources (like S3 object-level operations). Insight events (option c) capture unusual API call rates or error rates. Global service events are not a separate category, but refer to events from global services like IAM, which are recorded in management events.

Question 13: a

Explanation: Amazon Athena is the most effective service for analyzing CloudTrail logs because it allows you to run SQL queries directly against log files stored in S3, without having to load the data into a separate database. This provides flexibility for ad-hoc analysis and investigation of unusual API activity. Amazon QuickSight (option b) is a visualization tool that could be used in conjunction with Athena but is not suited for direct log analysis. Amazon RDS (option c) and DynamoDB (option d) would require additional ETL processes to load and query the log data.

Question 14: d

Explanation: Amazon CloudWatch Lambda Insights provides the most comprehensive visibility into the security posture of Lambda functions because it offers detailed monitoring of performance metrics, errors, and operational issues that could indicate security problems. It provides visibility into memory utilization, CPU usage, latency, and errors that might indicate compromise. Amazon Inspector (option a) does not support Lambda functions directly. AWS X-Ray (option b) focuses on tracing requests through the application. CloudTrail (option c) logs API calls, but does not provide function-level visibility.

Question 15: b

Explanation: AWS Security Hub is specifically designed to centralize security findings from multiple AWS services, including GuardDuty, Inspector, Macie, IAM Access Analyzer, and Firewall Manager. It provides a comprehensive view of your security posture across accounts, and integrates with third-party security products. AWS Control Tower (option a) helps set up and govern multi-account environments. AWS Organizations (option c) manages multiple AWS accounts. AWS Artifact (option d) provides compliance reports and agreements.

Question 16: a, d

Explanation: The most secure CloudTrail configuration includes enabling log file integrity validation (option a) and configuring a multi-region trail (option d). Log file integrity validation ensures logs have not been tampered with, while a multi-region trail ensures that all API activity across all regions is captured. While S3 bucket encryption (option b) is important, server-side encryption with S3-managed keys (SSE-S3) is not the strongest encryption option; using KMS keys would be more secure. SNS notifications (option c) improve operational awareness, but do not enhance security directly. Storing logs in CloudWatch Logs (option e) is useful but does not improve security beyond what proper S3 configuration provides.

Question 17: c

Explanation: AWS Shield Advanced provides the most effective protection against large-scale DDoS attacks because it offers specialized DDoS mitigation, 24/7 access to the AWS DDoS Response Team, and cost protection from usage spikes due to DDoS attacks. While AWS WAF (option a) can help protect against application layer attacks, it is not designed specifically for large-scale DDoS attacks. Amazon Route 53 (option b) provides DNS services with some DDoS resilience, but not comprehensive protection. Network ACLs (option d) can filter traffic, but they are not designed to handle the scale of DDoS attacks.

Question 18: b

Explanation: Site-to-Site VPN with IPsec provides the strongest security for connecting to an on-premises database over the public internet because it creates an encrypted tunnel for all traffic. Security groups (option a) restrict traffic but do not encrypt it. Network ACLs (option c) filter traffic, but do not encrypt it. API Gateway with resource policies (option d) would be appropriate for API access, but not for direct database connectivity.

Question 19: c

Explanation: A Transit Gateway with proper route tables provides the most secure way to connect multiple VPCs because it enables centralized connectivity and security policy enforcement. It allows for fine-grained control over routing, and can be integrated with security services such as Network Firewall. NAT Gateways (option a) facilitate outbound internet connectivity, not VPC-to-VPC communication. VPC peering (option b) works well for a few VPCs but becomes complex with many VPCs. Internet Gateways (option d) connect VPCs to the internet, not to each other securely.

Question 20: b

Explanation: AWS Network Firewall is specifically designed to inspect traffic entering and leaving a VPC. It provides stateful inspection capabilities and can be configured with custom rules to filter traffic. VPC Flow Logs (option a) record network traffic but don't inspect or filter it. AWS Config (option c) tracks resource configurations, not network traffic. Security Groups (option d) control access to resources but don't provide deep packet inspection.

Question 21: c

Explanation: AWS WAF (Web Application Firewall) is specifically designed to protect against application layer (Layer 7) attacks on web applications. It can filter traffic based on patterns, IP addresses, and other criteria to block common attack vectors such as SQL injection and cross-site scripting. AWS Shield (option A) focuses on DDoS protection. Amazon GuardDuty (option b) provides threat detection but does not directly filter application traffic. Network ACLs (option d) operate at the network layer (Layer 4), not at the application layer.

Question 22: b

Explanation: VPC Endpoints allow you to privately connect your VPC to supported AWS services without requiring an internet gateway, NAT device, VPN connection, or AWS Direct Connect connection. This means traffic between your VPC and the AWS service does not leave the Amazon network, providing enhanced security. AWS Direct Connect (option a) provides dedicated connectivity to AWS but does not eliminate the need for internet-facing endpoints for AWS services. VPN Gateway (option c) and Internet Gateway (option d) both involve routing traffic over the internet.

Question 23: a, c

Explanation: The most comprehensive protection for an EC2 instance comes from a combination of Security Groups (option a) and Network ACLs (option c). Security Groups act as a firewall at the instance level, controlling inbound and outbound traffic with stateful inspection. Network ACLs provide an additional layer of defense at the subnet level with stateless filtering. Together, they create a defense-in-depth approach. IAM Roles (option b) control access to AWS APIs, not network traffic. Host-based firewalls (option d) can be useful but are not AWS-native controls. Resource-based policies (option e) are not applicable to EC2 instances directly.

Question 24: a

Explanation: Configuring TLS (Transport Layer Security) on both application servers and database servers ensures that all data in transit between these tiers is encrypted, providing the strongest security. VPC peering with security groups (option b) controls access but does not encrypt traffic. A Network Load Balancer (option c) distributes traffic but does not inherently provide encryption. Placing application and database in the same subnet (option d) does not provide encryption or necessary segmentation.

Question 25: a

Explanation: Configuring the Lambda function in a VPC with appropriate security groups is the most secure method for accessing an RDS database from Lambda. This approach ensures that the RDS database doesn't need to be exposed to the public internet, and the security groups can tightly control which Lambda functions can access the database. IAM authentication (option b) provides identity-based access but does not secure the network path. Storing credentials in environment variables (option c) addresses authentication, but not network security. A NAT Gateway (option d) enables outbound internet access but does not secure inbound database access.

Question 26: c

Explanation: AWS Directory Service allows you to connect your Microsoft Active Directory to AWS services, enabling federated access for AD users. AWS IAM (option

a) manages AWS identities but doesn't provide direct federation with Active Directory. AWS Cognito (option b) is primarily for web and mobile app authentication. AWS Organizations (option d) manages multiple AWS accounts, not external identity federation.

I will continue with the answer explanations and then proceed to the real-world applications section.

Question 27: a, b

Explanation: IAM Access Analyzer helps identify resources that are shared with external entities and can uncover overly permissive policies. AWS Organizations with Service Control Policies (SCPs) allows you to set permission guardrails across multiple accounts, enforcing least privilege at scale. These two features together provide powerful controls for implementing least privilege. AWS Shield Advanced (option c) is for DDoS protection. AWS Config Rules (option d) can monitor compliance but does not directly enforce least privilege. IAM Roles with managed policies (option e) can follow least privilege but lack the analytical capabilities of Access Analyzer.

Question 28: b

Explanation: Using IAM roles with instance profiles is the most secure approach for allowing EC2 instances to access S3 buckets because it eliminates the need to store long-term credentials on the instance and automatically rotates temporary credentials. Creating IAM users with access keys (option a) introduces the risk of key exposure. Storing access keys in encrypted EBS volumes (option c) still uses long-term credentials. S3 VPC endpoints with bucket policies (option d) control network access but do not address authentication.

Question 29: c

Explanation: AWS Organizations is designed to centrally manage policies, including IAM policies, across multiple AWS accounts. It provides features like Service Control Policies that can restrict permissions across all accounts in your organization. AWS IAM Identity Center (option a) provides single sign-on but not centralized policy management. AWS Directory Service (option b) is for Active Directory integration. AWS Control Tower (option d) sets up and governs environments but leverages Organizations for policy management.

Question 30: a, b

Explanation: IAM permission boundaries and Service Control Policies (SCPs) provide the most comprehensive protection against unintended permission escalation. Permission boundaries set the maximum permissions an entity can have, regardless of attached policies. SCPs set organization-wide permission guardrails that cannot be exceeded by account administrators. IAM Access Advisor (option c) shows service usage but doesn't prevent escalation. Resource-based policies (option d) control access to specific resources, but do not prevent broader escalation. AWS Shield Advanced (option e) is for DDoS protection, not permission management.

Question 31: a

Explanation: The key difference between IAM roles and users is that roles provide temporary security credentials, while users have long-term credentials (access keys). This makes roles more secure for many use cases as credentials are automatically rotated. Both roles and users can be assigned to AWS resources (statement b is false). Both roles and users support MFA (statement c is false). Roles have automatic credential rotation, but user credentials do not automatically rotate (statement d is partially true, but not the primary distinction).

Question 32: b

Explanation: AWS IAM Identity Center (successor to AWS Single Sign-On) is specifically designed as a centralized identity management solution that supports SAML 2.0 for AWS access. It allows you to manage user access to multiple AWS accounts from a central location. Amazon Cognito (option a) is primarily for customer identity management in applications. AWS Directory Service (option c) integrates with Microsoft Active Directory but does not provide the same centralized management for AWS access. AWS IAM (option d) manages identities within a single account, not centrally across accounts.

Question 33: c

Explanation: AWS IAM Access Analyzer analyzes resource-based policies to help identify resources shared with external entities and validate that policies provide only the intended permissions. It helps identify unintended access to resources and supports least privilege. AWS Config (option a) tracks resource configurations but does not analyze policies. AWS CloudTrail (option b) logs API activity but doesn't analyze policies. AWS Security Hub (option d) aggregates security findings, but does not perform policy analysis itself.

Question 34: b

Explanation: AWS Key Management Service (KMS) provides the most secure way to manage and store encryption keys for AWS services. It offers centralized control over the entire lifecycle of cryptographic keys used in AWS services and applications. AWS Secrets Manager (option a) is for storing secrets, not for managing encryption keys for services. Systems Manager Parameter Store (option c) can store parameters but does not provide the specialized key management features of KMS. AWS Certificate Manager (option d) manages SSL/TLS certificates, not encryption keys for AWS services.

Question 35: b

Explanation: S3 server-side encryption with AWS KMS keys (SSE-KMS) allows you to encrypt S3 objects with customer-managed keys in KMS, providing enhanced control over the encryption keys. SSE-S3 (option a) uses keys managed by Amazon S3, not by the customer. SSE-C (option c) uses customer-provided keys that must be managed outside AWS. Client-side encryption with AWS KMS (option d) requires implementing encryption in your application, before sending the data to S3.

Question 36: a, c

Explanation: Amazon Macie automatically discovers, classifies, and protects sensitive data by using machine learning to recognize sensitive data, such as Personally Identifiable Information (PII) or intellectual property. AWS KMS provides the encryption capabilities to protect the identified sensitive data. AWS Shield (option b) protects against DDoS attacks. Amazon Detective (option d) analyzes security events. Amazon GuardDuty (option e) detects threats, not the sensitive data.

Question 37: c

Explanation: AWS Secrets Manager is specifically designed to store, manage, and automatically rotate database credentials and other secrets. It includes built-in integration with RDS, DocumentDB, and Redshift for automated credential rotation. AWS Systems Manager Parameter Store (option a) can store parameters but does not include automatic rotation capabilities. AWS KMS (option b) manages encryption keys, not the credentials. AWS Certificate Manager (option d) manages SSL/TLS certificates, not the database credentials.

Question 38: a

Explanation: The aws: SecureTransport condition key in an S3 bucket policy can be used to deny access when the request is not using HTTPS. This enforces encrypted data transmission for all requests to the bucket. `aws: SourceIp` (option b) checks the requester's IP address. The `aws: PrincipalArn` (option c) checks the ARN of the requesting IAM principal. The `aws: RequestMethod` (option d) checks the HTTP method used (GET, PUT, and so on), but does not enforce HTTPS.

Question 39: b

Explanation: Amazon Macie is specifically designed for data loss prevention in S3 buckets. It automatically discovers, classifies, and protects sensitive data using machine learning. Amazon GuardDuty (option a) detects threats, not data loss. AWS CloudTrail (option c) logs API activity but does not detect the sensitive data. AWS Config (option d) tracks resource configurations but does not focus on data protection.

Question 40: b

Explanation: AWS CloudHSM provides Hardware Security Modules (HSMs) that are validated under FIPS 140-2 Level 3, offering the highest level of security for cryptographic operations. AWS KMS (option a) is validated under FIPS 140-2 Level 2, and for many use cases. Amazon S3 (option c) is a storage service, not a key management service. AWS Certificate Manager (option d) manages SSL/TLS certificates, not a general key management service with FIPS validation.

Question 41: a

Explanation: CloudTrail logs capture all API calls made to AWS KMS, providing a comprehensive audit trail of key usage. This allows you to track who used which key, when, and for what purpose. KMS key aliases (option b) provide friendly names for keys, but do not track usage. KMS key tags (option c) help organize keys, but do not track usage. KMS grants (option d) delegate permissions to use keys, but do not track usage history.

Question 42: c

Explanation: AWS KMS is used in conjunction with CloudFront to implement field-level encryption, which encrypts specific data fields, before they reach your origin. This provides an additional layer of security for sensitive data. AWS Certificate Manager (option a) manages SSL/TLS certificates for HTTPS connections but does not handle field-level encryption. AWS WAF (option B) protects against web attacks but does not perform encryption. AWS Secrets Manager (option d) stores secrets but does not handle field-level encryption.

Question 43: c

Explanation: Amazon CodeGuru analyzes code for vulnerabilities, providing recommendations to improve code quality and security. It uses machine learning to identify security issues in your Lambda function code. Amazon Inspector (option a) focuses on EC2 instance assessment, not on Lambda code. Lambda@Edge (option b) extends CloudFront with Lambda functions but does not analyze code security. AWS Config (option d) tracks resource configurations, not the code vulnerabilities.

Question 44: a

Explanation: Amazon Inspector is specifically designed to run security assessments against EC2 instances, identifying vulnerabilities and deviations from security best practices. AWS Config (option b) tracks resource configurations but does not perform vulnerability assessments. AWS Systems Manager (option c) can help manage instances but does not perform security assessments. AWS Security Hub (option d) aggregates security findings but does not perform assessments.

Question 45: b

Explanation: AWS Organizations with Service Control Policies (SCPs) allows you to implement security controls that apply to all AWS accounts in your organization. SCPs act as permission guardrails, restricting what actions users and roles in member accounts can perform. AWS IAM (option a) manages permissions within a single account. AWS Config (option c) tracks resource configurations across accounts, but does not enforce controls. AWS Firewall Manager (option d) centralizes firewall rules, but not all security controls.

Question 46: a

Explanation: AWS Shield Advanced provides comprehensive protection against DDoS attacks at both the network layer (Layer 3/4) and application layer (Layer 7). It includes 24/7 access to the AWS DDoS Response Team and cost protection against usage spikes due to DDoS attacks. AWS WAF (option b) protects against application layer attacks but not network layer attacks. Amazon GuardDuty (option c) detects threats but doesn't actively protect against DDoS. AWS Security Hub (option d) aggregates security findings but doesn't provide DDoS protection.

Question 47: a

Explanation: AWS Audit Manager is specifically designed to provide a comprehensive security assessment solution, helping you assess your AWS resources' compliance with industry standards and regulations. It automates evidence collection and simplifies assessment reporting. AWS Systems Manager (option b) focuses on operational management. AWS Security Hub (option c) aggregates security findings but does not automate assessments. AWS Config (option d) tracks resource configurations, but does not provide comprehensive assessment capabilities.

Question 48: a

Explanation: AWS Config is designed to validate resource configurations against compliance rules. It continuously monitors, and records AWS resource configurations, allowing you to evaluate them against desired configurations and compliance rules. AWS Trusted Advisor (option b) provides general best practice recommendations. AWS CloudTrail (option c) logs API activity, but does not validate compliance. Amazon Inspector (option d) assesses EC2 instances for vulnerabilities, but does not validate overall resource compliance.

Question 49: b

Explanation: Using TLS/SSL for all API connections ensures that data in transit between AWS services is encrypted. This approach provides comprehensive protection regardless of network path. VPC endpoints (option a) secure connections to some AWS services but not all service-to-service communications. Client-side encryption (option c) protects data before it's sent but adds implementation complexity. Configuring HTTPS endpoints (option d) is part of implementing TLS/SSL but isn't as comprehensive as option b.

Question 50: c

Explanation: AWS Service Control Policies (SCPs) provide the most effective way to implement proactive security controls because they limit permissions across all accounts in an AWS Organization, preventing the deployment of non-compliant resources. AWS Config Rules (option a) can detect non-compliance but typically operate reactively. AWS CloudFormation Guard (option b) validates CloudFormation templates but doesn't prevent resource deployment outside of CloudFormation. AWS IAM Policies (option d) control permissions but are limited to a single account.

Question 51: b

Explanation: AWS Audit Manager is specifically designed to create security assessment reports for regulatory compliance. It helps you continuously audit your AWS usage, collecting evidence automatically and organizing it by compliance requirement. AWS Artifact (option a) provides access to AWS compliance reports, not your own assessment reports. AWS Security Hub (option c) aggregates security findings, but does not generate compliance reports. AWS Trusted Advisor (option d) provides best practice recommendations, not compliance reports.

Question 52: c

Explanation: AWS Certificate Manager provides the most secure method for storing and managing TLS certificates because it handles secure certificate deployment, automatic renewal, and integration with AWS services such as CloudFront and ELB. The private keys for certificates are protected, and never exposed to users. Amazon S3 with server-side encryption (option a) does not provide certificate lifecycle management. Systems Manager Parameter Store (option b) and Secrets Manager (option d) could store certificates, but do not provide the specialized certificate management features of ACM.

Question 53: a, b

Explanation: AWS Config combined with AWS Lambda provides the most effective solution for automatically remediating non-compliant resources. AWS Config detects non-compliant resources based on rules, and Lambda functions can be triggered to remediate the issues automatically. AWS Systems Manager (option c) can be used for remediation, but requires additional configuration compared to Lambda. AWS CloudTrail (option d) logs API activity, but does not remediate issues. AWS Trusted Advisor (option e) provides recommendations, but does not implement remediation.

Question 54: b

Explanation: Amazon GuardDuty is specifically designed to detect anomalous API calls by analyzing CloudTrail logs, VPC Flow Logs, and DNS logs using machine learning and threat intelligence. AWS CloudTrail (option a) logs API activity, but does not analyze it for anomalies. AWS Config (option c) tracks resource configurations, not API call patterns. Amazon Detective (option d) helps to investigate security findings, but does not provide real-time detection of anomalous API calls.

Question 55: c

Explanation: VPC Endpoints with endpoint policies provide the most effective control for outbound traffic to specific AWS services because they allow you to create private connections to AWS services with policies that restrict which operations can be performed. Network ACLs (option a) and Security Groups (option b) can restrict traffic, but lack the service-specific control of endpoint policies. Internet Gateway with route tables (option d) controls all outbound traffic, not specific service traffic.

Question 56: c

Explanation: Customer-managed keys in AWS CloudHSM provide the strongest security control for EBS volume encryption because CloudHSM uses dedicated Hardware Security Modules (HSMs) that are validated under FIPS 140-2 Level 3, ensuring that you have exclusive control over the key material. AWS-managed keys (option a) are convenient but managed by AWS. Customer-managed keys in AWS KMS (option b) offer strong security, but are validated under FIPS 140-2 Level 2. Customer-provided encryption keys (option d) might introduce key management challenges.

Question 57: c

Explanation: Amazon ECR Scan provides a comprehensive vulnerability management solution for containerized applications running on Amazon ECS. It automatically scans container images for software vulnerabilities, when they are pushed to ECR repositories. Amazon Inspector (option a) focuses on EC2 instances, not containers. AWS Systems Manager (option b) manages operational tasks, but does not provide container vulnerability scanning. AWS Config (option d) tracks resource configurations. but does not scan for vulnerabilities.

Question 58: b

Explanation: Amazon Athena is the most effective service for analyzing CloudTrail logs because it allows you to run SQL queries directly against log files stored in S3. This provides the flexibility to identify potential security issues and policy violations through custom queries. CloudWatch Logs Insights (option a) is powerful, but more limited in complex analysis capabilities. Amazon QuickSight (option c) is for visualization after analysis. Amazon Redshift (option d) would require loading the data first.

Question 59: a

Explanation: AWS Config Rules with AWS Systems Manager Automation provides the most effective solution for automatically remediating security misconfigurations. Config Rules detect non-compliant resources, and Systems Manager Automation runbooks can be triggered to remediate the issues. Security Hub and Lambda (option b) can work together, but are not as specialized for resource remediation. GuardDuty and Lambda (option c) focus on threat detection, rather than misconfigurations. Trusted Advisor and CloudFormation (option d) are not designed for automated remediation.

Question 60: a

Explanation: AWS Control Tower provides the most comprehensive solution for enforcing infrastructure compliance at scale across multiple AWS accounts. It sets up and governs a secure, compliant multi-account environment, based on blueprints and guardrails that implement prescriptive best practices. AWS Config (option b) tracks compliance, but does not provide comprehensive governance. AWS Organizations (option c) enables policy-based management, but lacks the compliance blueprints of Control Tower. AWS Systems Manager (option d) manages operational tasks, but does not focus on compliance governance.

Question 61: c, d

Explanation: Amazon API Gateway with AWS WAF and AWS IAM with VPC endpoints provide the most comprehensive solution for securing API access. API Gateway with WAF protects APIs from common web exploits and application-layer attacks. IAM with VPC endpoints ensures that API access is limited to authorized users within your VPC, without exposing APIs to the internet. API Gateway with usage plans (option a) controls throttling and quotas, but does not add security. Lambda with resource-based policies (option b) secures Lambda function access, but not the API itself. Shield with Route 53 (option c) protects against DDoS attacks, but not unauthorized API access.

Question 62: a

Explanation: Amazon Detective is specifically designed to help investigate identity and access management anomalies by analyzing and visualizing patterns of activities, behaviors, and interactions across multiple data sources. It helps you identify the root cause of security findings and unusual activities. Amazon GuardDuty (option b) detects threats, but does not provide detailed investigation capabilities. AWS CloudTrail (option c) logs API activity, but does not analyze it for anomalies. AWS IAM Access Analyzer (option d) identifies resources shared with external entities, but does not investigate IAM anomalies.

Question 63: b

Explanation: AWS Security Hub is specifically designed to provide a centralized solution for managing security findings across multiple AWS accounts and services. It aggregates, organizes, and prioritizes security findings from services such as GuardDuty, Inspector, Macie, and third-party tools. AWS Control Tower (option a) sets up, and governs multi-account environments. However, it does not focus on security findings. AWS Organizations (option c) manages multiple accounts, but does not aggregate security findings. AWS IAM (option d) manages access, but does not handle security findings.

Question 64: b

Explanation: AWS Direct Connect provides the most secure and reliable network connectivity between on-premises systems and AWS because it establishes a dedicated network connection, bypassing the public internet entirely. This ensures consistent, low-latency performance, and enhanced security. AWS Site-to-Site VPN (option a) encrypts traffic, but still uses the public internet. VPC Peering (option c) connects VPCs, not on-premises systems. AWS Transit Gateway (option d) facilitates connectivity between VPCs and on-premises networks, but requires Direct Connect or VPN for the on-premises connection.

Question 65: b

Explanation: AWS Security Hub provides the most comprehensive visibility into the overall security posture of your AWS resources by aggregating, organizing, and prioritizing security findings from multiple sources, including other AWS security services, and integrated third-party products. AWS Trusted Advisor (option a) provides the best practice recommendations, but lacks comprehensive security coverage. AWS Config (option c) tracks resource configurations, but does not provide security posture visibility. AWS CloudTrail (option d) logs API activity, but does not provide security posture assessment.

Applying AWS Security Knowledge in Real-World Scenarios

Now that you have tested your knowledge with our comprehensive practice exam, let us explore how these concepts apply in real-world scenarios. Understanding the practical applications of AWS security principles will not only help you pass the certification exam, but also excel in your professional role.

Healthcare: Securing Patient Data in the Cloud

Healthcare organizations face strict regulatory requirements like HIPAA, when moving the patient data to the cloud. Here is how AWS security services can be applied:

Challenge: A healthcare provider needs to store and process Protected Health Information (PHI) in AWS, while maintaining HIPAA compliance.

Solution:

- Implement encryption at rest with AWS KMS for all patient data stored in S3 and RDS.
- Configure CloudTrail to log all access to the PHI data, and store logs in a dedicated, encrypted S3 bucket.
- Use IAM roles and policies with least privilege principles to restrict access to PHI data.
- Implement AWS Shield Advanced and AWS WAF to protect web applications that handle patient information.
- Set up Amazon Macie to scan for unintentional PHI exposure in documents and data stores.
- Use AWS Config Rules to continuously monitor and enforce compliance with security policies.
- Implement AWS Security Hub to centralize security findings, and maintain a comprehensive compliance dashboard.

Real-World Impact: By implementing this security architecture, the healthcare provider can confidently leverage cloud capabilities, while demonstrating HIPAA compliance to auditors, and maintaining patient trust.

Financial Services: Protecting Payment Processing Systems

Financial institutions have stringent security requirements for payment processing systems, including PCI DSS compliance.

Challenge: A financial services company wants to build a secure payment processing system on AWS that meets PCI DSS requirements.

Solution:

- Implement network segmentation using VPCs with strict security groups and network ACLs to isolate Cardholder Data Environment (CDE).
- Deploy AWS WAF with specific rules to protect against common web application vulnerabilities like SQL injection and XSS.
- Use AWS CloudHSM for secure cryptographic operations, and key management.
- Implement GuardDuty and Detective for continuous monitoring, and threat detection.
- Set up AWS Config Rules to automatically enforce compliance with PCI DSS requirements.
- Deploy AWS Systems Manager Session Manager for secure, audited administrative access without SSH keys.
- Implement AWS Lambda to automate security responses for specific events.
- Use AWS Secrets Manager to securely store, and automatically rotate database credentials.

Real-World Impact: This implementation allows the financial institution to process payments securely, while maintaining compliance with PCI DSS, building customer trust, and avoiding potential fines for non-compliance.

E-Commerce: Scaling Securely during Peak Seasons

E-commerce platforms face unique challenges, particularly during high-traffic periods like holiday shopping seasons.

Challenge: An e-commerce company needs to scale securely during Black , while protecting against increased DDoS threats and maintaining performance.

Solution:

- Implement AWS Shield Advanced for comprehensive DDoS protection.
- Deploy AWS WAF with rate-limiting rules to prevent credential stuffing, and brutal force attacks.
- Use Auto Scaling groups with security-hardened AMIs to handle traffic spikes.
- Configure Amazon GuardDuty to detect unusual patterns that might indicate compromised accounts.
- Implement AWS Systems Manager Patch Manager to ensure all instances are patched, even during rapid scaling.

- Set up AWS Config Rules to ensure that all new resources adhere to security standards.
- Use AWS CloudFront with Origin Shield to cache content, and absorb traffic spikes, while maintaining security
- Implement just-in-time access using IAM roles for emergency management access.

Real-World Impact: The e-commerce platform successfully handles peak traffic periods without security compromises, maintaining customer trust and maximizing revenue during critical business periods.

Government: Secure Multi-Account Architecture

Government agencies often require strict isolation between different departments, while maintaining centralized security oversight.

Challenge: A government agency needs to implement a secure, compliant multi-account structure with appropriate separation of duties, and centralized security monitoring.

Solution:

- Implement AWS Organizations with Service Control Policies to enforce security guardrails across all accounts.
- Deploy AWS Control Tower to set up and govern a secure, compliant multi-account environment.
- Use AWS IAM Identity Center for centralized access management across accounts.
- Implement AWS Security Hub with security standards enabled for continuous compliance monitoring
- Configure AWS Config with organization-wide rules to enforce security policies.
- Deploy centralized logging using CloudTrail Organization Trails, and centralized log analysis
- Implement AWS KMS with centralized key management and strict key policies.
- Use AWS Network Firewall for east-west traffic inspection between accounts.

Real-World Impact: The government agency achieves appropriate separation between departments while maintaining comprehensive security visibility, ensuring that the sensitive data remains protected, while still enabling collaboration where appropriate.

Career Advancement with AWS Security Expertise

Earning the AWS Security Specialty certification positions you for several career opportunities. Here is how, you can leverage your expertise for professional growth:

In-Demand Roles for AWS Security Professionals:

- **Cloud Security Architect**
  - Design and implement secure cloud environments using AWS services.
  - Develop security frameworks and governance models.
  - Salary range: $130,000-$180,000.
- **Security Operations Engineer**
  - Implement monitoring and detection systems using GuardDuty, Security Hub, and Detective.
  - Develop automated response workflows for security incidents.
  - Salary range: $110,000-$150,000.
- **Cloud Security Consultant**
  - Help organizations assess their AWS security posture.
  - Provide recommendations for security improvements.
  - Salary range: $120,000-$170,000.
- **Compliance Specialist**
  - Ensure that AWS environments meet the regulatory requirements.
  - Implement automated compliance monitoring.
  - Salary range: $100,000-$140,000.
- **DevSecOps Engineer**
  - Integrate security into CI/CD pipelines.
  - Automate security testing and compliance validation.
  - Salary range: $120,000-$160,000

Building Your Security Portfolio

To stand out in the competitive job market, consider these steps beyond certification:

- **Contribute to Open Source Security Projects**
  - Develop AWS security tools, or contribute to the existing ones.

   - Share automation scripts for common security tasks.
- **Build a Security Blog or Technical Portfolio**
   - Document real-world security implementations.
   - Share your approach to solving complex security challenges.
- **Participate in Security Communities**
   - Join AWS security-focused forums and discussion groups.
   - Contribute to AWS security discussions on platforms such as GitHub and Stack Overflow
- **Continue Learning and Certification**
   - Consider complementary certifications such as CISSP, CCSP, or other AWS certifications.
   - Stay current with AWS security services and features through continuous learning

Next Steps after Certification

Congratulations on coming this far in your AWS Security Specialty certification journey! After passing the exam, consider these next steps to continue growing your expertise:

Immediate Actions After Certification:

- **Update Your Professional Profiles**
   - Add your certification to LinkedIn, and other professional platforms.
   - Update your resume to highlight your new credential.
- **Share Your Achievement**
   - Announce your certification on professional networks.
   - Connect with other AWS security professionals.
- **Apply for AWS Community Programs**
   - Consider the AWS Community Builders program.
   - Explore AWS Hero nomination opportunities as you build expertise.

Long-Term Growth Strategies:

- **Specialize in a Security Domain**
   - Focus on a specific area such as container security, serverless security, or compliance.
   - Develop deep expertise that sets you apart from other security professionals.

- **Mentor Others**
  - Help colleagues prepare for their AWS Security Specialty certification.
  - Share your knowledge through mentoring programs.
- **Pursue Advanced Certifications**
  - Consider the AWS Certified Advanced Networking Specialty.
  - Explore non-AWS security certifications that complement your AWS expertise.
- **Stay Current with AWS Security Innovations**
  - Regularly review AWS security blog posts and whitepapers.
  - Participate in AWS reinvent, and other security-focused events.

Conclusion

The AWS Security Specialty certification validates your ability to secure AWS environments effectively. By mastering the exam material, and understanding how to apply these principles to real-world scenarios, you are well-positioned to advance your career in cloud security.

Remember that security is not a one-time achievement but a continuous journey. AWS regularly introduces new security features and services, requiring ongoing learning and adaptation. By staying current with AWS security developments, and applying best practices consistently, you will continue to grow as a security professional long after earning your certification.

The next and final chapter, *Advanced Topics in AWS Security*, will delve into deeper security practices, including advanced threat detection, automated governance, and secure multi-account strategies on AWS.

CHAPTER 9
Advanced Topics in AWS Security

Introduction

Welcome to the final chapter of our AWS Security Specialty certification journey. As organizations increasingly adopt cloud technologies, security practitioners must stay aware of evolving threats and advanced security challenges. This chapter explores cutting-edge AWS security topics that go beyond the fundamentals and help you develop expertise in specialized areas like serverless security, threat detection, machine learning integration, and advanced compliance strategies.

The security landscape is evolving constantly, with attackers developing highly sophisticated techniques to breach defences. AWS responds to these threats by enhancing its security services with advanced capabilities like machine learning-based anomaly detection, automated remediation, and threat intelligence integration. By mastering these advanced topics, you will not only be well-prepared for the AWS Security Specialty exam, but also equipped to implement robust security solutions for complex enterprise environments.

In this chapter, we will explore how to secure serverless architectures that present unique security challenges compared to traditional infrastructure. We will also dive into Amazon GuardDuty's capabilities for threat detection and response, examine how machine learning can automate and enhance security operations, and investigate advanced compliance strategies for regulated industries. By the end of this chapter, you will have a comprehensive understanding of advanced AWS security concepts and be ready to tackle the certification exam with confidence.

Structure

This chapter will cover the following topics:

- Securing Serverless Architectures
    - Security challenges in serverless computing

  - Best practices for Lambda security
  - API Gateway security
  - Event source security
- Threat Detection with Amazon GuardDuty
  - Understanding GuardDuty's architecture
  - Integration with other AWS security services
  - Customizing GuardDuty for enterprise environments
  - Responding to GuardDuty findings
- Machine Learning for Security Automation
  - AWS security services with ML capabilities
  - Building custom ML security solutions
  - Security automation using ML insights
  - Ethical considerations in ML-based security
- Advanced Compliance Strategies
  - Meeting complex regulatory requirements
  - Continuous compliance monitoring
  - Automating compliance reporting
  - Global compliance challenges in multi-region deployments

Securing Serverless Architectures

Serverless computing has revolutionized application development by abstracting infrastructure management and allowing developers to focus on the code. While AWS handles many infrastructure security concerns in serverless architectures, security practitioners must understand the unique challenges and best practices specific to this sphere.

Security Challenges in Serverless Computing

Serverless architectures introduce several distinct security challenges compared to traditional infrastructure:

- **Attack Surface Transformation**: In serverless environments, the attack surface shifts from infrastructure to application-level vulnerabilities. Without traditional servers to secure, security teams must focus on securing code, dependencies, and event triggers
- **Shared Responsibility Model Changes**: In serverless computing, AWS

manages more of the infrastructure stack, but this does not eliminate security responsibilities for customers. Instead, it shifts the focus to areas like code security, authentication, and data protection

- **Ephemeral Execution Environment**: Serverless functions typically run in short-lived containers that are created on demand and destroyed after execution. This complicates traditional security approaches like network monitoring and host-based security
- **Event-Driven Security**: Serverless applications are triggered by various events from multiple sources like HTTP requests, database changes, and message queues, with each having its own security considerations
- **Dependencies Management**: Serverless functions often rely on numerous third-party dependencies, thereby increasing the risk of supply chain attacks and vulnerability exploitation

Example: Vulnerable Dependencies

A common serverless security issue occurs when developers include vulnerable libraries in their function packages. Consider the following scenario:

A Lambda function for processing payment information uses an outdated version of a JSON parsing library with a known vulnerability. An attacker crafts a specially formatted JSON payload that exploits this vulnerability, potentially leading to code execution within the Lambda environment.

To address this risk, implement automated dependency scanning in your CI/CD pipeline to identify and remediate vulnerable dependencies before deployment.

Best Practices for Lambda Security

AWS Lambda functions form the backbone of many serverless architectures. Implementing the following best practices will help in making Lambda-based applications more secure:

- **Principle of Least Privilege**: Create fine-grained IAM roles specific to each Lambda function's needs. Avoid using overly permissive policies
- **Resource-Based Policies**: Use resource-based policies to control which services can invoke your Lambda functions. Following this step will provide an additional layer of access control for applications
- **Environment Variable Encryption**: Encrypt sensitive configuration information stored in Lambda environment variables using KMS
- **Runtime Environment Security**: Keep Lambda runtimes updated to benefit from security patches, and consider implementing custom runtimes for specialized security requirements

- **Execution Timeout and Memory Limits**: Set appropriate timeout and memory allocation to prevent resource exhaustion attacks and reduce the impact of potential breaches
- **Code Scanning and Vulnerability Management**: Implement static code analysis to identify vulnerabilities before deployment and establish a process for updating functions when new vulnerabilities are discovered
- **Securing Lambda Layers**: When using Lambda Layers for shared code, ensure they undergo the same security scrutiny as function code, including vulnerability scanning and access control
- **Function Concurrency Controls**: Set concurrency limits to prevent denial-of-service attacks, or unexpected scaling that could impact other services or lead to excessive costs

API Gateway Security

API Gateway often serves as the front door to serverless applications, making its security critical to the overall architecture.

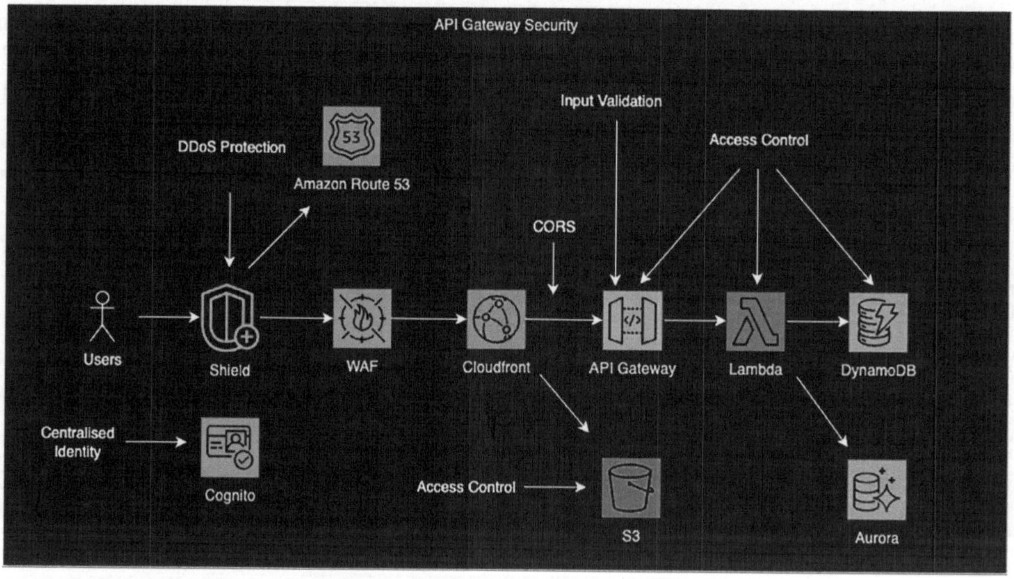

Figure 9.1: *API Gateway Security*

- **Authentication Methods**: API Gateway offers multiple authentication options:
    - **IAM Authorization**: Users must sign requests using AWS SigV4 signatures
    - **Cognito User Pools**: Managed user directory service for web and mobile authentication

    - **Lambda Authorizers**: Custom authorization logic implemented in Lambda functions
    - **JWT Authorizers**: Validation of JSON Web Tokens from OpenID Connect or OAuth 2.0 providers
- **Request Validation**: API Gateway can validate request parameters, headers, and body to prevent malformed requests from reaching your Lambda functions
- **Request Throttling**: Configure throttling limits to protect backend services from traffic spikes, whether intentional (DDoS) or unintentional
- **Response Headers**: Set security-related HTTP headers like Content-Security-Policy, Strict-Transport-Security, and X-XSS-Protection to protect clients consuming your API
- **WAF Integration**: Integrate API Gateway with AWS WAF to add protection against common web exploits like SQL injection and cross-site scripting
- **API Keys and Usage Plans**: Manage and monitor third-party access to your APIs using API keys combined with usage plans
- **Private APIs**: For internal services, consider making your API private so it's only accessible from within your VPC or through VPC endpoints

Event Source Security

Serverless applications are triggered by various event sources, each with unique security considerations:

- **Amazon S3**: Secure S3 buckets that trigger Lambda functions with appropriate bucket policies, encryption, and access logging
- **DynamoDB Streams**: Ensure stream-enabled tables have encryption enabled and restrict Lambda function roles to only the necessary stream actions
- **SQS/SNS**: Implement message encryption, access policies, and consider using FIFO queues for sensitive operations where processing order matters
- **EventBridge**: Create fine-grained event patterns and limit which targets can be triggered by specific events
- **Kinesis**: Enable server-side encryption for sensitive data streams and implement proper shard-level access controls

Event Injection Prevention

Event Injection occurs when untrusted data in an event triggers unexpected behavior in a serverless function. To prevent this, remember to follow the steps mentioned here:

1. Validate event data against expected schemas
2. Use parameterized queries when interacting with databases
3. Escape output to prevent cross-site scripting when rendering HTML
4. Implement context-aware input sanitization

Threat Detection with Amazon GuardDuty

Amazon GuardDuty is a threat detection service that monitors your AWS accounts and workloads for malicious activity and unauthorized behavior. This section explores GuardDuty's architecture, integration capabilities, customization options, and response strategies.

Understanding GuardDuty's Architecture

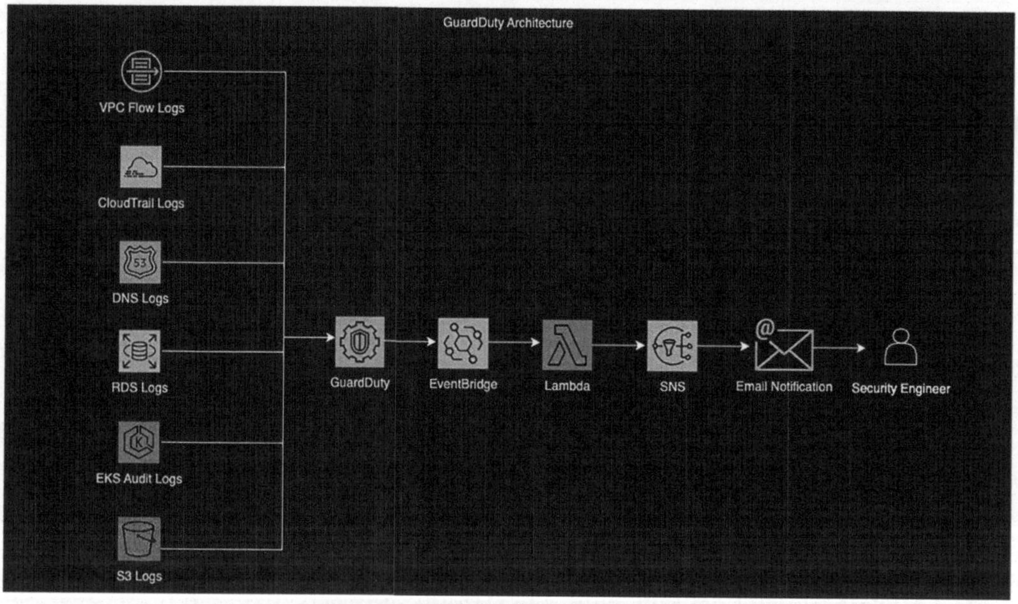

***Figure 9.2**: GuardDuty Architecture*

GuardDuty operates as a fully managed service that analyzes multiple data sources to detect potential security threats:

- **Data Sources**
  - **AWS CloudTrail Event Logs**: Management and data events showing API calls to AWS services

   - **VPC Flow Logs**: Network traffic data showing IP connections
   - **DNS Logs**: Domain lookup information from VPC DNS resolvers
   - **Amazon EKS Audit Logs**: Kubernetes control plane audit logs
   - **Amazon S3 Data Events**: Information about object-level operations in S3 buckets
   - **RDS Login Activity**: Information about login attempts to your RDS databases
- **Detection Methods**
   - **Threat Intelligence Feeds**: GuardDuty compares activity against known malicious IP addresses and domains
   - **Machine Learning**: Algorithms establish baselines and detect anomalies in account and resource behavior
   - **Behavioral Analytics**: Identifies suspicious patterns that deviate from normal usage
- **Architecture Components**
   - **GuardDuty Detector**: This is the core component of GuardDuty, created per AWS region
   - **Findings**: These are security detections that are generated whenever potential threats are identified
   - **Trust IP Lists**: These IP addresses are designated as trusted and GuardDuty will not generate findings for them
   - **Threat Lists**: These are custom lists of known malicious IP addresses that supplement GuardDuty's built-in threat intelligence

How GuardDuty Works

To understand GuardDuty's role in AWS threat detection, it's important to know how the service operates behind the scenes and processes data to identify potential security threats:

- GuardDuty ingests log data directly from its supported data sources without requiring you to enable or configure logging
- It processes this data using threat intelligence, machine learning, and behavior modeling
- When suspicious activity is detected, GuardDuty generates a finding with details about the potential threat
- Findings are delivered to the GuardDuty console, Amazon EventBridge, and optionally to Security Hub

- You can configure automated responses or investigate findings manually

Integration with Other AWS Security Services

GuardDuty is the most powerful tool, when it is integrated with other AWS security services to create a comprehensive security posture:

- **AWS Security Hub Integration**: GuardDuty sends findings to Security Hub, which consolidates and prioritizes security alerts from multiple AWS services and partner products
- **Amazon EventBridge Integration**: EventBridge receives GuardDuty findings and can trigger automated responses based on finding types or severity
- **AWS Lambda Integration**: Lambda functions can be triggered by EventBridge rules to automatically remediate specific types of findings
- **Amazon SNS Integration**: SNS can be used to send notifications about critical GuardDuty findings to security teams
- **AWS Organizations Integration**: In organization-wide deployments, delegated administrator accounts can centrally manage GuardDuty across all member accounts

Customizing GuardDuty for Enterprise Environments

Large enterprise environments often require customization to optimize GuardDuty's detection capabilities:

- **Multi-Account Configuration**: Use AWS Organizations to implement a centralized GuardDuty deployment with the following features:
  - A delegated administrator account that manages GuardDuty across the organization
  - Automatic enablement of GuardDuty for new accounts
  - A centralized configuration of protection plans and features
- **Protection Plans**: Select appropriate protection plans based on your environment:
  - **Core Findings (S3, EC2, IAM)**: Always recommend enabling this foundational protection
  - **S3 Protection**: Enable for environments with sensitive S3 data
  - **EKS Protection**: Enable for environments running Kubernetes on Amazon EKS

- **RDS Protection**: Enable for environments with RDS databases to detect unusual login behavior
- **Lambda Protection**: Enable for serverless environments to detect anomalous Lambda invocations
- **Malware Protection**: Enable for scanning EC2 and container workloads for malware

- **Custom Threat Lists**: Integrate organizational threat intelligence by creating custom lists of known malicious IP addresses
- **Trusted IP Lists**: Reduce false positives by creating lists of IP addresses that should not generate findings like trusted security testing IPs, known partners, and so on
- **Finding Filters**: Create filters to suppress specific finding types in environments where they represent expected behavior
- **Custom Event Sources**: For organizations with hybrid cloud environments, integrate CloudTrail logs from on-premises resources through CloudTrail Lake

Responding to GuardDuty Findings

Effectively responding to GuardDuty findings requires following a structured approach as mentioned here in this section:

- **Finding Triage and Prioritization**: Develop a process to prioritize findings based on:
    - Severity (High, Medium, Low)
    - Resource criticality
    - Finding type and potential impact
    - Context from other security tools
- **Investigation Workflows**: Make sure to establish the following procedures clearly for investigating different types of findings:
    - **Unauthorized Access Attempts**: Check IAM credential usage, CloudTrail logs, and VPC Flow Logs
    - **Compromised Resources**: Isolate instances, analyze logs, and check for persistence mechanisms
    - **Data Exfiltration**: Review VPC Flow Logs, CloudTrail S3 data events, and resource configurations
    - **Cryptocurrency Mining**: Examine processes running on instances and network connections

- **Automated Remediation**: Implement automated remediation for common findings when appropriate:
    - Revoking exposed IAM credentials
    - Isolating compromised instances
    - Blocking suspicious IP addresses with Network ACLs
    - Restoring modified security group rules
    - Removing unauthorized IAM roles
- **Tracking and Metrics**: Maintain metrics to measure security posture and response effectiveness:
    - Mean time to remediation
    - False positive rate
    - Finding trends over time
    - Recurring findings by resource or account

Example: GuardDuty Response Playbook

Here is a sample response playbook for a "Backdoor /C&CActivity.B" finding:

- **Initial Assessment**
    - Verify finding details in GuardDuty console
    - Check if affected instance is business-critical
    - Review recent changes to the instance
- **Containment**
    - Isolate the instance by applying a restrictive security group
    - Create EBS snapshots for forensic analysis
    - Block the C&C IP address at the VPC NACL level
- **Investigation**
    - Analyze OS logs for signs of compromise such as login attempts and process creation
    - Review VPC Flow Logs for other communication patterns
    - Check for persistence mechanisms like cron jobs and startup scripts
    - Identify initial access vector by reviewing CloudTrail logs
- **Remediation**
    - Terminate the compromised instance
    - Build a new instance from a verified AMI

  - Review and strengthen security controls such as patches and configurations
  - Update threat detection rules based on findings
- **Documentation**
  - Document the incident timeline
  - Record all remediation actions
  - Update security policies if needed
  - Share lessons learned with security team

Machine Learning for Security Automation

Machine Learning is transforming security operations by enhancing detection capabilities, automating routine tasks, and helping security teams process the vast amount of data generated in cloud environments. This section explores how AWS leverages ML for security and how you can build custom ML-based security solutions.

AWS Security Services with ML Capabilities

AWS integrates machine learning into its security services to improve threat detection, anomaly identification, and automated response. These services are as follows:

- **Amazon GuardDuty**: Uses supervised and unsupervised ML to establish baseline behavior for accounts and resources, allowing it to detect anomalies that might indicate compromise
- **Amazon Macie**: Employs ML to automatically discover, classify, and protect sensitive data like Personally Identifiable Information (PII), financial data, and intellectual property
- **Amazon Detective**: Utilizes ML to analyze relationships between AWS resources, IP addresses, and AWS accounts to identify suspicious patterns and help investigate security issues
- **AWS Security Hub**: Incorporates ML to aggregate and prioritize security findings from multiple sources based on severity and context
- **Amazon Fraud Detector**: Uses ML to identify potentially fraudulent online activities, such as account creation fraud or payment fraud
- **Amazon CodeGuru Security**: Applies ML-based code analysis to identify security vulnerabilities and suggest fixes during application development

- **Amazon Inspector**: Integrates ML to prioritize vulnerabilities based on their exploitability and potential impact

Building Custom ML Security Solutions

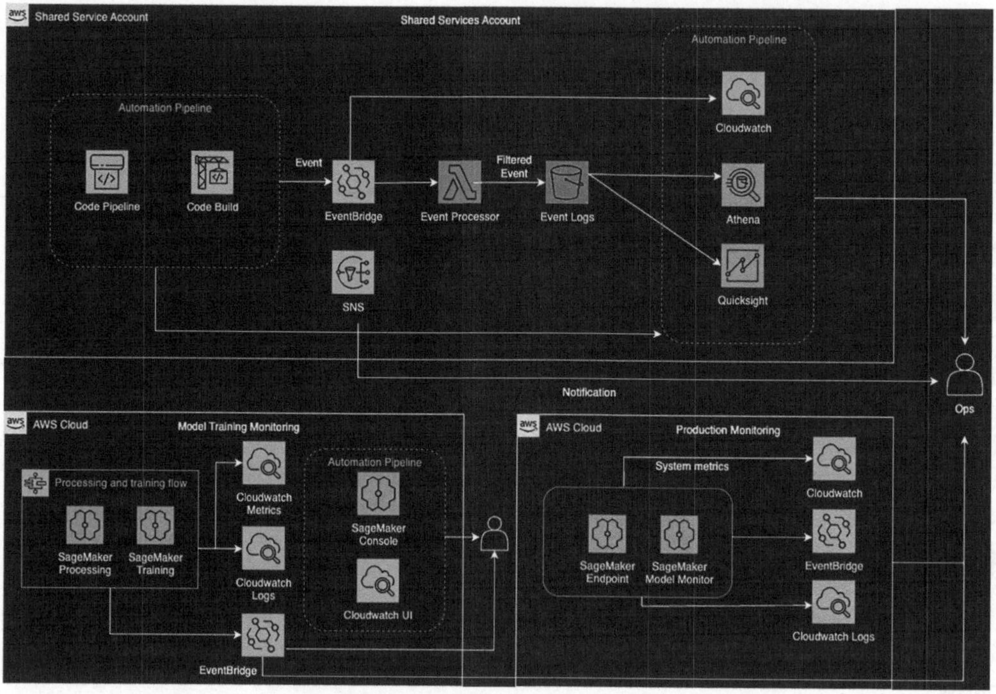

Figure 9.3: *Sample ML Architecture*

While AWS provides managed ML-based security services, organizations with specific requirements can build custom ML security solutions using Amazon SageMaker:

- **Data Collection and Preparation**
    - Gather security-relevant data from CloudTrail, VPC Flow Logs, and application logs
    - Store data in S3 for processing
    - Use AWS Glue for ETL operations to prepare data for ML models
    - Label data for supervised learning like marking known security incidents
- **Feature Engineering**
    - Extract meaningful features from raw log data
    - Create temporal features to capture behavior over time
    - Normalize data to improve model performance
    - Use dimensionality reduction techniques for complex datasets

- **Model Selection and Training**
    - **Anomaly Detection**: Use algorithms like Random Cut Forest to identify unusual patterns
    - **Classification**: Apply algorithms like XGBoost to classify events as malicious or benign
    - **Clustering**: Employ algorithms like K-means to group similar security events
    - **Deep Learning**: Use neural networks for complex pattern recognition in security data
- **Model Deployment and Monitoring**
    - Deploy models using SageMaker endpoints for real-time inference
    - Implement A/B testing to compare model effectiveness
    - Monitor model performance and drift
    - Retrain models regularly with new data

Security Automation Using ML Insights

Here are the key steps and options to follow when leveraging machine learning insights to automate security operations and streamline incident response:

- **Automated Investigation**
    - Trigger detailed log analysis when anomalies are detected
    - Automatically correlate events across multiple data sources
    - Generate context-rich incident reports for security teams
- **Automated Remediation**
    - Implement graduated responses based on ML confidence scores
    - Apply least-disruptive remediation first such as additional authentication
    - Escalate to more restrictive measures for high-confidence threats
- **Continuous Learning**
    - Incorporate feedback from security analysts to improve models
    - Track false positives and false negatives
    - Retrain models with confirmed incidents
- **Intelligent Alerting**
    - Use ML to reduce alert fatigue through prioritization
    - Group related alerts into meaningful incidents
    - Suppress alerts for known benign anomalies

Ethical Considerations in ML-Based Security

As you implement ML-based security solutions, consider these ethical implications:

- **Bias and Fairness**
  - Ensure training data represents diverse patterns of legitimate use
  - Regularly audit ML models for bias against specific user groups
  - Test models against different scenarios to ensure consistent performance
- **Privacy Concerns**
  - Minimize collection of personally identifiable information
  - Implement data minimization and anonymization techniques
  - Be transparent about what data is used for security ML models
- **Explainability**
  - Ensure security decisions based on ML can be explained to stakeholders
  - Implement tools for understanding why a model flagged an activity as suspicious
  - Document the reasoning behind automated security actions
- **Human Oversight**
  - Maintain human review of high-impact security decisions
  - Implement escalation paths for questionable ML determinations
  - Create feedback loops for continuous model improvement

Advanced Compliance Strategies

As organizations move sensitive workloads to the cloud, meeting regulatory compliance requirements becomes a complex exercise. This section explores advanced strategies for maintaining compliance in AWS environments, while focussing on automation, continuous monitoring, and global compliance challenges.

Meeting Complex Regulatory Requirements

Different industries face unique regulatory requirements for data security and privacy. Here are some ways to address these requirements in AWS:

- **Healthcare (HIPAA/HITECH)**
  - Implement end-to-end encryption for Protected Health Information (PHI)
  - Configure AWS CloudTrail to maintain detailed access logs for PHI
  - Use AWS Config to enforce security configurations for HIPAA-compliant resources

- Implement network segmentation to isolate systems containing PHI
- **Financial Services (PCI DSS, SOX, GLBA)**
  - Deploy AWS WAF with rules specifically designed for PCI DSS compliance
  - Implement strict IAM controls with regular access reviews
  - Configure AWS Config rules to validate PCI DSS requirements
  - Use AWS KMS with CMKs (Customer Managed Keys) for financial data
- **Government (FedRAMP, CJIS, ITAR)**
  - Deploy workloads in AWS GovCloud for regulated government workloads
  - Implement additional data sovereignty controls
  - Configure VPC endpoints to ensure data stays within approved boundaries
  - Enable AWS CloudTrail in all regions and integrate with centralized logging
- **Global Data Privacy (GDPR, CCPA, LGPD)**
  - Implement data classification and tagging for personal data
  - Configure geographic restrictions for data storage and processing
  - Deploy pattern-matching rules using Amazon Macie to identify personal data
  - Implement data subject access request (DSAR) workflows

Example: PCI DSS Compliance Architecture

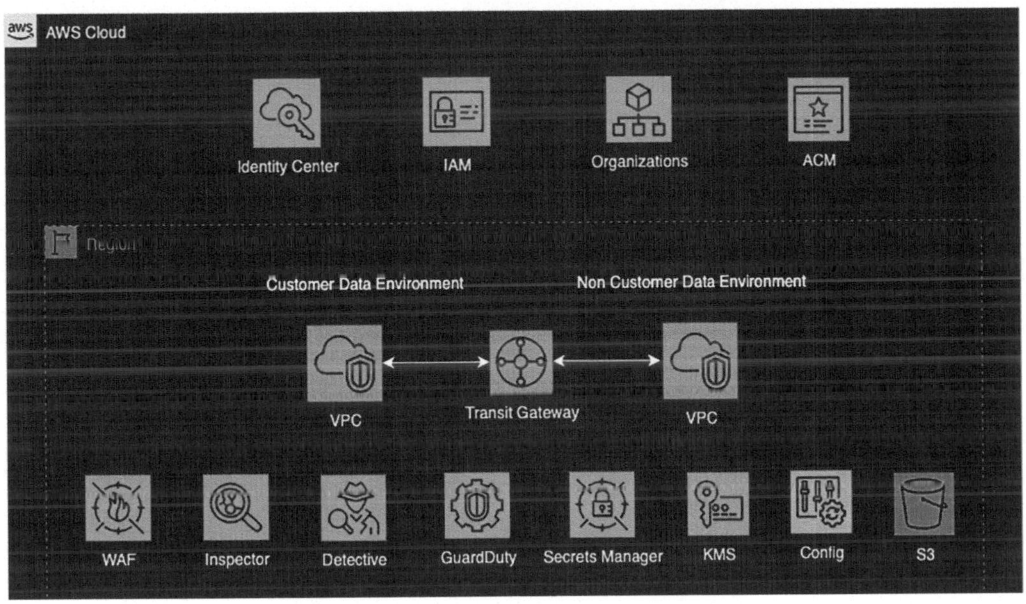

Figure 9.4: *Indicative PCI DSS Architecture*

Let us examine a reference architecture for a PCI DSS compliant payment processing system on AWS:

- **Network Segmentation**
  - Create separate VPCs for cardholder data environment (CDE) and non-CDE systems
  - Implement Transit Gateway with strict routing controls between VPCs
  - Configure Network ACLs and Security Groups with default deny rules
  - Use VPC Endpoints for AWS services to avoid traversing the public internet
- **Access Controls**
  - Implement bastion hosts with MFA for administrative access
  - Require encryption and MFA for all management connections
  - Configure IAM policies using the principle of least privilege
  - Rotate credentials automatically using AWS Secrets Manager
- **Data Protection**
  - Encrypt cardholder data using AWS KMS with CMKs
  - Implement point-to-point encryption for payment transactions
  - Configure S3 buckets with object-level encryption and versioning
  - Use DynamoDB encryption at rest for all tables containing cardholder data
- **Monitoring and Logging**
  - Enable AWS CloudTrail with log file validation
  - Configure VPC Flow Logs with retention aligned to PCI requirements
  - Implement centralized logging with encrypted transport and storage
  - Configure AWS Config rules to detect drift from PCI-compliant configurations

Continuous Compliance Monitoring

Maintaining continuous compliance requires automated monitoring systems that can detect and alert on compliance drift in real-time:

- **AWS Config for Compliance**
  - Create custom AWS Config rules aligned with specific compliance requirements
  - Implement Config Conformance Packs for comprehensive compliance management
  - Set up automated remediation actions for non-compliant resources

- Generate compliance reports for auditors
- **Security Hub Compliance Standards**
  - Enable relevant compliance standards (CIS AWS Foundations, PCI DSS, and so on.)
  - Configure automated workflows for addressing compliance findings
  - Integrate with ticketing systems for compliance issue remediation
  - Establish compliance score tracking over time
- **Compliance as Code**
  - Define compliance requirements as code through Infrastructure as Code (IaC) tools
  - Implement Guard Rules with AWS CloudFormation Guard or Open Policy Agent
  - Validate infrastructure templates before deployment
  - Integrate compliance checks into CI/CD pipelines
- **Third-Party Compliance Tools**
  - Integrate specialized compliance tools available in AWS Marketplace
  - Implement tools for specific regulations (HIPAA, GDPR, and so on)
  - Deploy agents for enhanced compliance visibility
  - Leverage SaaS solutions for compliance reporting

Automating Compliance Reporting

Automated compliance reporting is essential to maintain an efficient security program and satisfy auditor requirements:

- **Scheduled Compliance Reporting**
  - Configure scheduled AWS Config compliance snapshots
  - Generate automated compliance dashboards using QuickSight
  - Implement regular Security Hub compliance exports
  - Establish automated report delivery to stakeholders
- **Custom Compliance Dashboards**
  - Create CloudWatch dashboards for compliance metrics
  - Develop custom compliance visualizations using Kibana
  - Implement executive-level compliance scorecards
  - Configure real-time compliance status views

- **Compliance Evidence Collection**
  - Automate collection of compliance artifacts and evidence
  - Create structured repositories for compliance documentation
  - Implement version control for compliance evidence
  - Generate audit-ready documentation packages
- **Stakeholder-Specific Reporting**
  - Create role-based compliance reports for different audiences
  - Configure business unit-specific compliance views
  - Develop technical and executive compliance summaries
  - Implement trend analysis for compliance posture

Global Compliance Challenges in Multi-Region Deployments

Global organizations face unique compliance challenges due to varying regional requirements. Here are some strategies to maintain compliance across multiple AWS regions:

- **Data Sovereignty Requirements**
  - Deploy region-specific resources to comply with data residency laws
  - Implement controls to prevent cross-region data transfers
  - Configure resource policies to enforce geographic boundaries
  - Use AWS Organizations SCPs to limit region usage
- **Regional Compliance Variations**
  - Develop region-specific compliance profiles
  - Implement varying controls based on local regulations
  - Maintain documentation of regional compliance requirements
  - Deploy custom Config rules for region-specific compliance
- **Centralized Compliance Management**
  - Use AWS Organizations for multi-account, multi-region governance
  - Implement centralized logging across regions
  - Deploy consistent baselines with region-specific customizations
  - Create unified compliance dashboards for global visibility
- **Cross-Region Disaster Recovery**
  - Design compliant DR strategies that respect data sovereignty
  - Implement region-specific backup and recovery procedures

- Create compliant data replication patterns
- Document approval processes for cross-region data movement

Conclusion

In this final chapter, we have explored advanced topics in AWS security that extend beyond the fundamentals covered earlier. We have also examined securing serverless architectures, where the traditional security boundaries have shifted, thus requiring new approaches to protect Lambda functions, API Gateway endpoints, and event sources. Additionally, we have delved into Amazon GuardDuty's threat detection capabilities, while learning how to customize it for enterprise environments and implement effective response strategies.

The integration of machine learning into security operations represents a significant advancement in cloud security. We have explored both AWS's native ML-enabled security services and approaches for building custom ML security solutions using Amazon SageMaker. These capabilities enable more proactive security postures through anomaly detection, automated investigations, and intelligent alerting.

Finally, we have addressed the complex challenges of maintaining compliance in AWS environments, with strategies for meeting regulatory requirements, implementing continuous compliance monitoring, automating compliance reporting, and addressing global compliance challenges in multi-region deployments.

As you prepare for the AWS Security Specialty exam, remember that these advanced topics build upon the foundational security concepts and services covered throughout this book. Implementing robust AWS security successfully requires both breadth (understanding the full range of AWS security services) and depth (knowing how to apply these services to solve specific security challenges).

In the upcoming years, cloud security will continue to evolve. New threats will emerge and AWS will introduce new security capabilities to tackle them. By mastering the concepts and practices covered in this book, you will be well-poised to adapt to these changes and maintain strong security postures for your AWS workloads.

Good luck with your certification exam and your ongoing journey in AWS security!

Points to Remember

- Serverless security focuses on code-level vulnerabilities, event source security, and API Gateway protection rather than traditional infrastructure security
- Amazon GuardDuty combines threat intelligence and machine learning to detect suspicious activities across multiple data sources, including CloudTrail, VPC Flow Logs, and DNS logs

- Machine learning enhances security through automated anomaly detection, behavioral analytics, and intelligent prioritization of security findings
- Advanced compliance requires continuous monitoring, automated evidence collection, and region-specific controls to address data sovereignty requirements
- Customizing security services for enterprise environments often involves multi-account architectures, central management, and integration with existing security tools
- Automated remediation workflows can significantly reduce the time from detection to resolution for security incidents
- Security in multi-region deployments requires careful consideration of data sovereignty, cross-region access, and region-specific compliance requirements

Multiple Choice Questions

1. Which AWS service uses machine learning to automatically discover and classify sensitive data?
    a. Amazon Detective
    b. Amazon GuardDuty
    c. Amazon Macie
    d. AWS Security Hub
2. When securing serverless architectures, which of the following is NOT a best practice?
    a. Implementing function-level authorization
    b. Setting appropriate IAM roles with least privilege
    c. Installing host-based intrusion detection
    d. Validating input from event sources
3. How does GuardDuty detect threats in your AWS environment?
    a. By requiring you to install agents on EC2 instances
    b. By analyzing CloudTrail, VPC Flow Logs, and DNS logs
    c. By scanning your code repositories for vulnerabilities
    d. By monitoring network traffic using packet capture

4. Which AWS service would you use to evaluate your resources against multiple compliance standards?
    a. AWS Config
    b. AWS Security Hub
    c. Amazon Inspector
    d. AWS CloudTrail
5. Which of the following is a key consideration when implementing machine learning for security automation?
    a. Training models only on normal behavior patterns
    b. Eliminating human review for all security decisions
    c. Ensuring models can explain their security decisions
    d. Deploying models only in production environments
6. What is the primary purpose of AWS Organizations Service Control Policies (SCPs) in a compliance context?
    a. To authenticate users across multiple accounts
    b. To implement preventative guardrails and boundaries
    c. To detect compliance violations after they occur
    d. To encrypt data transferred between regions
7. Which feature of API Gateway helps protect your backend services from excessive traffic?
    a. Lambda authorizers
    b. Request validation
    c. Usage plans and throttling
    d. Resource policies
8. When implementing a custom machine learning model for security monitoring, which AWS service would you use?
    a. AWS Glue
    b. Amazon SageMaker
    c. Amazon Comprehend
    d. AWS Lambda

Answers

1. c
2. c
3. b
4. b
5. c
6. b
7. c
8. b

References

- AWS Security Best Practices: https://docs.aws.amazon.com/wellarchitected/latest/security-pillar/welcome.html
- AWS Serverless Security Workshop: https://catalog.workshops.aws/serverless-security/en-US
- Amazon GuardDuty Documentation: https://docs.aws.amazon.com/guardduty/latest/ug/what-is-guardduty.html
- AWS Compliance Programs: https://aws.amazon.com/compliance/programs/
- AWS Security Hub Documentation: https://docs.aws.amazon.com/securityhub/latest/userguide/what-is-securityhub.html
- Amazon SageMaker Documentation: https://docs.aws.amazon.com/sagemaker/latest/dg/whatis.html
- AWS Lambda Security Overview: https://docs.aws.amazon.com/lambda/latest/dg/lambda-security.html
- AWS Organizations SCPs: https://docs.aws.amazon.com/organizations/latest/userguide/orgs_manage_policies_scps.html

Index

A

D

N

O

P

T

V

W